CRUSADING THROUGH TURKEY

by the same author

MINI RACING

SEVEN COUNTRIES OF SOUTH AMERICA

CRUSADING THROUGH TURKEY

CHRISTABEL WATSON

K.A.F. BREWIN BOOKS

First published in 1986 by
K.A.F. Brewin — Books
Studley, Warwickshire. B80 7LX

ISBN 0 947731 16 4

Typeset in Baskerville and
printed by Supaprint (Redditch) Limited.
Made and printed in Great Britain.

CONTENTS

ILLUSTRATIONS

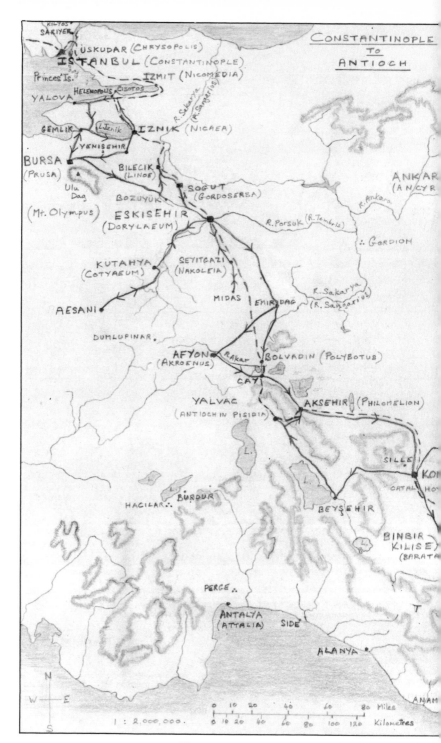

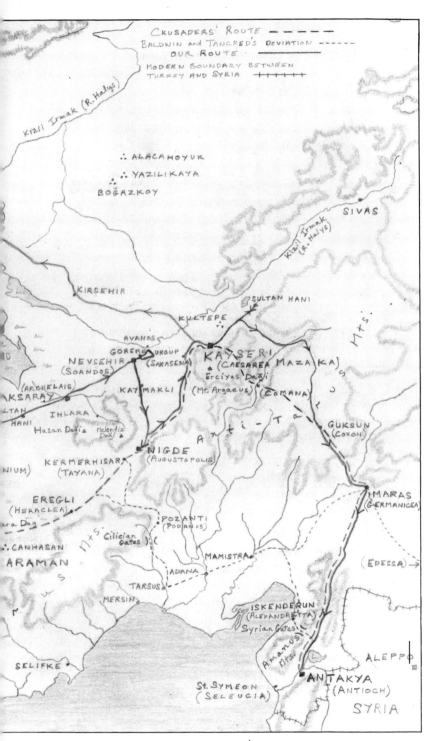

CRUSADERS' ROUTE ———————
BALDWIN and TANCRED'S DEVIATION —————
OUR ROUTE · · · · ·
MODERN BOUNDARY BETWEEN
TURKEY AND SYRIA ┼┼┼┼┼

Kizil Irmak (R. Halys)

∴ ALACAHOYUK
∴ YAZILIKAYA
∴ BOĞAZKOY

SIVAS

Kizil Irmak
(R. Halys)

KIRSEHIR

SULTAN HANI

KULTEPE

AVANOS

GOREME URGUP
(SAKASENA)

KAYSERI
(CAESAREA MAZAKA)

NEVSEHIR
(SOANDOS)

Erciyas Dagi
(Mt. Argaeus)

(COMANA)

(ARCHELAIS)

KAYMAKLI

AKSARAY

ULTAN
HANI

IHLARA

Hasan Dagi

Melendiz
Dagi

A n t i - T a u r u s

GUKSUN
(COXON)

NIGDE
(AUGUSTOPOLIS)

KERMERHISAR
(TAYANA)

NIUM)

EREGLI
(HERACLEA)

ara Dag

MARAS
(GERMANICEA)

POZANTI
(PODANDUS)

∴ CANHASAN

ARAMAN

M t s. Cilician
Gates

MAMISTRA

(EDESSA) →

ADANA

TARSUS

MERSIN

ISKENDERUN
(ALEXANDRETTA)
Syrian Gates

ALEPPO

SELIFKE

Amanus Mts.

St. SYMEON
(SELEUCIA)

ANTAKYA
(ANTIOCH)

SYRIA

INTRODUCTION

The decision to follow the path of the First Crusade (1096–1099) came from Martin Dunne. Though fascinated by the organisation of the army and the motives of the Crusaders, he found the actual route they took more intriguing, and decided to ride and discover for himself the difficulties they had to face. In October Martin asked my husband, Andrew, if he would like to accompany him.

I became increasingly jealous of this 'Turkey talk'. It was not that I had been refused permission to accompany the men, simply that I had not been considered at all — for Turkey is a Muslim country where women tend to be overlooked. By the following March I could restrain myself no longer and asked if I could join the party. Andrew was delighted. Martin, though now a farmer, had once been a diplomat and knew how to cope with unexpected requests. He suggested that a visit to the Turkish Embassy for advice might be helpful and pointed out that the going would be tough; we were bound to suffer from saddle sores, gippy tummies and might have to camp if we were unable to reach habitation. When we arrived in some remote village, he and Andrew would approach the headman and would be ushered into his house for a discussion and tea, while I would be entertained by the women. Immediately I translated house for bedouin tent and the women for the harem, and was therefore excited by the prospect of seeing genuine Turkish life and longed, if possible, to sleep under the stars.

My visit to the Turkish Embassy proved most rewarding. I handed our application forms, which had to be completed in sextuplicate, to the second secretary — a woman. I asked advice about clothes and whether she thought it wise for me to accompany the men on this expedition. She replied in almost perfect English, "I am sure that the reception you receive in the villages will be greatly helped by the fact that there is a woman in your party." I was not quite sure how to interpret this statement but took it to be reassuring.

Somewhat encouraged I dashed to the second-hand markets in Kensington and Chelsea, to try to find old fashioned baggy jodphurs or breeches which I felt would be comfortable and suitable. From a camping shop I purchased a water bottle and a knapsack which, besides taking everything I needed for the day, would also carry my camera and special lenses, for Martin had put me in charge of flora and fauna. I even had riding lessons because I could not remember having sat upon a horse for twenty years, and duly ached in all the right places. Andrew acquired gaiters to protect his legs from rabid dogs and a sheepskin in the hope of avoiding saddle sores. Martin spent hours comparing Steven Runciman's 'The First Crusade' and Professor Ramsay's 'The Historical Geography of Asia Minor', and transposing the route followed by the Crusaders on to modern maps. We all had the recommended inoculations, including rabies, considered essential for those travelling by strange methods in the remoter areas of Anatolia.

Martin was anxious to gain official recognition with some sort of document that he could flourish in case of emergency. That was the reason we had filled in numerous forms, though the normal tourist has no such problem. Having received confirmation from the Turkish Embassy in London that everything was in order, Martin flew to Ankara at the end of March to conclude the arrangements, and also to see his Turkish friend who lived not far from Istanbul about the hiring of horses. He returned a week later in the depths of despair. He had called repeatedly at the Ministry of the Interior, had endless interviews, and finally was told that permission had been withdrawn. After all the preparation, the anticipation, and having told friends that we were going to ride the route of the First Crusade, the disappointment was considerable.

We took about a fortnight to recover from the blow, but then the planning started anew. To follow the tramping feet by landrover was out of the question, the cost being prohibitive, and hiring a car in Turkey was also expensive. It was possible to 'fly-drive', but for anything except a short stay the price rises rapidly. There was only one solution left — to travel by bus. We would begin our Crusade on the first of May.

In the event we were grateful for the Turkish government's decision to ban our ride, for we would never have seen even half the glorious treasures that Turkey has to offer from the back of a horse. We would never have visited Bursa once capital of the Ottoman empire; the beautiful Roman temple at Aesani would have been too far from our path; we would have bypassed the Cappadocian rock churches, and how could we have tethered our horses in Konya and been free to discover its Seljuk mosques? The way we journeyed through Turkey was perfect for we had a theme and a reason for travelling in a certain direction. The further we penetrated the interior, the more fascinating the expedition became. There were fewer tourists and frequently we were the only people exploring amazing ruins.

We managed to follow most of the route taken by the First Crusade, and I have related the method and means of transport whereby we achieved this ambition. I have also described places of interest we visited during our journey. There was so much to explore and our sightseeing ranged from mosques and churches to museums and citadels; from temples and underground villages to prehistoric sites and bazaars, some of these entailing considerable diversions from the Crusaders' path.

We spent some time at the beginning and the end of our holiday in Istanbul. As Constantinople, it had been the most important political and cultural centre of the western world for over one thousand years and therefore could not be left out of our itinerary — besides which the Crusaders passed the city before crossing into Asia. Nor could I leave out references to the most traumatic episode in its history, the collapse of the Byzantine Empire.

The journey we made was one that any traveller could tackle, and I hope that this book will encourage the reader to visit places that otherwise he might not have considered, and perhaps follow us in our modern Crusade through Turkey.

to ANDREW and MARTIN

DAY I : ISTANBUL 1

As dawn broke the wail of the muezzin summoning his followers to prayer woke me from a deep sleep.   A loud-speaker amplified the intonation so no one could escape the call to prayer.   Soon the noises on the water took over, sirens and blasts from tugs rising to a crescendo.   Heavy lorries rumbled past on the dual carriageway that ran between the sea and our hotel.   These were modern sounds for twentieth century travellers. The sounds that woke the Crusaders would have been different but equally disturbing.

In 1097 A.D. the crusading armies camped outside Constantinople, resting from their arduous marches across Europe and waiting for their companions to join them.   They were allowed to enter the city in small groups to view its splendour.   Through one of the gateways guarded by the Emperor's soldiers, they would have wended their way up the hill and worshipped at the greatest monument in western Christendom, the Church of the Holy Wisdom.*   The Imperial Palace of Byzantium overlooked the Sea of Marmara, the Roman Hippodrome displayed a wealth of statues, and numerous Byzantine Churches contained such riches and beauty unknown to the common soldier.

We were staying two days in Istanbul — the twentieth century name for Constantinople — and had a great deal to see before setting foot in Asia to follow the path of the First Crusade.   Behind our hotel an archway enabled us to pass under the ancient wall which took us away from the coastal traffic and led us into the old part of the city.   The wooden houses were extraordinary.   They were squashed together in various stages of dilapidation, flues sticking out from improbable places and washing drying on a complex system of lines.   If possible they backed on to the original walls whose lasting strength and sturdiness provided warmth and comfort.   The clatter of wheels on cobbles warned of the approach of carts delivering fruit and vegetables; they were drawn however by silent ponies, due to their hooves being shod with off-cuts from rubber tyres.   A single rail barred a street with a soldier standing at ease, a gun slung nonchalantly over his shoulder.   On landing at Istanbul airport the day before, we had been greeted by an Armoured Personnel Carrier which approached menacingly and followed our walk to the terminal.   Soldiers guarded the aeroplane and were much in evidence elsewhere.   This area looked perfectly harmless, pedestrians strolled by and children played football outside their houses.   Higher up the hill we passed a dusty military parade ground surrounded by barbed wire each strand painted white, and also every tree trunk to the height of a metre and a half.   A company of soldiers was being drilled, while others lolled around smoking and looking extremely bored.

---

* In Greek, Haghia Sophia, Aya Sofya to the Turks, and St. Sophia in English.

1

A folly across the road invited inspection. Five cupolas crowned the roof and marble reliefs decorated the walls of what turned out to be an ornate watering place. At each side a fountain was set into a niche framed in a decorative ogive, while through grilled openings at the corners attendants used to hand cups of water to anyone in need of sustenance. Now restored it is purely a monument, but when originally built by Sultan Ahmet III in 1728, water flowed for the citizens of Istanbul.

St. Sophia was not yet open so we walked across colourful gardens to the Blue Mosque. The morning sun was ideal for taking photographs, the perfectly proportioned mosque and its six minarets shining in splendour. Sultan Ahmet I was so enthusiastic and eager to see the building finished, that he often worked on the site himself. He commanded six minarets equalling in number the mosque at Mecca, but later was compelled to donate a seventh to the eastern shrine in order to preserve its superior status.

The outer courtyard was the same size as the mosque. To try to convey the enormous size of both, we were told that ten thousand men filled the complex for the main celebration during Ramadan. A charming hexagonal sadirvan — fountain for ritual washing — stood in the centre of the cobbled courtyard, the entire area surrounded by colonnades of granite pillars supporting cupolas. We thought that it would make an excellent stage set for the race against the chimes of midday in 'Chariots of Fire'. Might the race be improved if timed against the wails of the muezzin? Or if the muezzin ran from minaret to minaret, how many circuits of the courtyard would the challenger have to complete to be fair? A Turk with no legs selling postcards brought us sharply back to reality. The whole setting, the courtyard and the porticos reminded me of cloisters adjoining Christian churches. Even the basic structure was similar to St. Sophia, confirming that St. Sophia was much admired and its plan adapted for every imperial mosque in Istanbul.

The mosque completed after eight years in 1617, was known by the name of its patron, Sultan Ahmet I. Europeans have called it the Blue Mosque on account of the brilliance of the interior tiles and decoration. I took off my shoes and tiptoed inside, anticipating that I would be dazzled by the spectacle. What a disappointment. Nothing reflected from the domes. They had been painted a light fawn with arabesques in pastel shades. Below, coarse imitation Iznik tiles covered the walls, and only on the lower level were there the originals. So I concentrated on them, searching for the carnation, tulip, lily and rose motifs, the intricate patterns and subtle greens and blues. Iznik, which we were to visit later, produced tiles for the Ottoman Turks who used them to adorn their palaces and mosques during the fifteenth to eighteenth centuries.

A Turk commiserated, expressing dissatisfaction at the restoration but, on the other hand, no one could deny the grandeur of the building. The great open space beneath the central dome — supported by four huge columns — and the wide aisle with semi domes gave a feeling of space. From virtually anywhere in the mosque the whole of the interior could be

seen, helped by the light thrown from two hundred and sixty windows.
All mosques have similar features. The mihrab is a niche set into the centre of the front wall indicating the direction of Mecca, towards which the faithful must face when saying their prayers. To the right is a pulpit or mimber, and the Koran Kurser is where the imam sits when reading the Koran to the congregation; a section is reserved for the choir. Depending on the importance of the mosque, a royal loggia is incorporated in the building for the Sultan and his party. Carpets are often donated and vary in quality according to the wealth of the local Muslims. Large carpets covered the floor of the Blue Mosque upon which were scattered beautiful old prayer-rugs. Women are not allowed to worship near the men. They rarely venture inside mosques and often I never realised their presence, suddenly being surprised by those black shrouded figures sitting cross-legged in alcoves at the back or sides.

From the steps of the Blue Mosque the view of St. Sophia was striking. Judas (Cercis siliquastrum) and chestnut trees were in full blossom, their red and white flowers contrasting superbly. I went back to photograph this scene in the late afternoon when the sun was in the correct position, throwing a gentle light and picking out the softer tones and recesses in the stonework.

A formal garden filled the space between the two buildings. The flower beds were rather weedy, but as the tourist season was beginning gangs of workers tackled the soil. A row of men skilfully wielded scythes giving a close cut finish to the grass. We were besieged by small boys and young men trying to sell us postcards, transparencies, guide books and kebab sticks. I ignored them and remained relatively unmolested. Andrew and Martin were more polite finding it difficult to say no which at once encouraged a growing horde. The pedlars could become extremely annoying if not treated firmly from the start.

We were diverted to a pink stuccoed building on our right. Scaffolding covered the entrance but I tiptoed gingerly over planks to the door. I beckoned to Andrew and Martin to come quickly and we explored an enchanting building housing the public baths. This Hamam of Haseki Hurrem was built by Suleyman the Magnificent for his wife Roxelana in 1556. The architect was the famous Sinan who designed so many mosques in Istanbul. Each end mirrored the other, therefore the women's and men's sides were identical. We clambered up and down ramps, under perilous looking wooden scaffolding, amidst concrete laying and incongruous modern cisterns. Ornamental carvings adorned the basins, and the old heating ducts that ran around the edges of the pool were clearly visible at this stage of restoration. We thanked the workmen as we left. I think they were astonished that we had wanted to enter in the first place, but the chance visit can often reveal a pleasant surprise.

By now St. Sophia was open. This was the third church to be constructed on the site, the first two having been destroyed by fire. Emperor Justinian was determined that it was to exceed the Temple of Solomon in beauty and size. Taking only five years he employed ten

3

thousand workers under his personal surveillance, and one hundred masters from all over the Empire. He appointed Anthemius of Tralles as his chief architect, the most distinguished mathematician and physicist of his age and, as his assistant, Isidorus of Miletos the great geometer and former head of the Platonic Academy in Athens. Inflammable material such as timber was forbidden and no mortar was used; blocks of stone were fixed with molten lead and special light bricks were used for the cupolas. It has long been rumoured that the green marble columns on both sides of the central nave came from Ephesus and the eight porphyry columns from Baalbek, while yet more ancient pillars and stones were scoured from Heliopolis and Delphi. Other sources say that the marble was expressly hewn from quarries within the Empire. The latter theory has more factual support, due to a description left by Paul of Silentium one of Justinian's court officials. A clever design was achieved by covering the interior walls with marble and porphyry. The mosaics must have been spectacular. Light came from forty windows surrounding the base of the dome and twelve on each of the tympanum walls. The Emperor was surely justified when he called out at the inauguration in 537 "Oh, Solomon, I have surpassed thee!"

Visitors to Constantinople during subsequent decades were stunned by this building. Even the Crusaders would never have seen anything remotely resembling its magnificence in their native lands. Mehmet the Conqueror had obviously been prepared for its splendour for, when entering the city at the end of May 1453, he rode straight to the Cathedral. He stopped a soldier hacking at the marble and ordered its conversion to a mosque: three days later he participated in Friday prayers. He built a wooden minaret later to be replaced by one in brick, his successors adding three more in stone. Sinan carried out restorations and, when the walls were in danger of collapsing due to weakening by earthquakes, large buttresses were constructed to support them. In accordance with Islamic dogma no figurative representations were allowed and the mosaics were eventually covered with layers of plaster; not until Ataturk's rule was St. Sophia named a museum and a thorough restoration carried out.

We entered St. Sophia through a long vestibule. Above the doorway into the narthex we saw our first mosaic; Mary with Jesus, on her left Emperor Constantine* with a model of the city and on her right Emperor Justinian with a model of St. Sophia. The walls of the long narthex were covered with marble and porphyry and the vaults with the original plain gold mosaics. A door in each bay led to the nave but only the Emperor was permitted to use the Imperial Gate; the flag stones at each side had become worn with the constant stamping to attention by the guards. Above the Imperial Gate another mosaic represented Christ on the throne, flanked by two medallions of the Virgin and Archangel Gabriel, and a kneeling Emperor thought to be Leo VI who ruled from 886—912.

---

* Constantine the Great, founder of Constantinople.

A guided tour swept us into St. Sophia, but we soon lost them so vast was the interior. St. Sophia was the fourth greatest cathedral in the world after St. Peter's and those of Seville and Milan. To give some idea of its size, the nave was 82 metres long and 38 metres wide, with two side aisles adding a further 18 metres each; the dome rose to a height of 56 metres. Four large discs attached to the tops of the pillars with texts of the Koran in Islamic script and the mimber intruding into the central nave, reminded the visitor of the Muslim faith. The mihrab was placed off centre in order to face Mecca which is not due east but south-south-east of Istanbul. This spoilt the symmetry, but nevertheless lent a certain character to the apse.

The most striking mosaic was in the couch of the apse, the only fragments remaining were the Virgin holding Jesus on her lap and the Archangel Gabriel. Martin, who had been here before, told us the best mosaics were in the gallery, but the large door leading to it was locked. "Restoration", was the mumbled answer of a passing official. Walking dejectedly into the bright sunlight, passing the old baptistry and the tombs of the Sultans, we saw a notice saying 'Director'. Martin, the best dressed of us three always wearing a tweed jacket, grey flannel trousers and leather shoes, now adopted our nickname of Herr Professor. He certainly looked the part with receding hair and an erudite expression, so was therefore detailed to approach the office. No problem! Out he came with a guide carrying a large key.

Instead of a narrow stairway, a graded curving path led to the gallery. The mosaics were glorious. The most famous was the fourteenth century Deesis described as one of the greatest works of art produced in Byzantium. Although much was destroyed the faces of Christ, John the Baptist and the Virgin Mary were complete and revealing portraits. Christ gave the blessing with his right hand and gazed straight ahead with an air of infinite sadness, John the Baptist bore a grief-stricken expression both moving and haunting, while Mary, with lowered eyes, inclined her head towards the other two.

In a room reserved for the Emperor two mosaics flanked a window. They were of an earlier date therefore the figures and clothes were stiffer and more stylised. One, eleventh century, depicted Christ between Empress Zoe and her third husband, the new Emperor's head replacing the portraits of Zoe's former husbands. The other, early twelfth century, showed the figure of John II Comnenus, his son and his wife Irene who, having been noted for her piety and charity, was venerated as a saint in the Greek Orthodox Church. There was one other full length portrait in the north gallery, of Emperor Alexander. He succeeded his brother Leo VI in 912, who on his deathbed hailed Alexander saying, "Here comes the man of thirteen months." Surely enough, the following June and thirteen months later, Alexander died of apoplexy during a drunken game of polo.

A cracked sarcophagus lid inscribed with the name of Dandolo was set in the paving opposite the Deesis. Dandolo, Doge of Venice, was one of the leaders of the Fourth Crusade (1202–04). This Crusade originally intended to go beyond Jerusalem to Egypt which had become the centre of Mohammedan power, but the personal vendetta waged by the Venetians, plus greed, commercialism and above all political motives, swayed their allies and they wrought vengeance on Constantinople instead. More damage was done to the city between Christian peoples than at practically any other time in history. Constantinople was plundered, irreplaceable works of art destroyed and St. Sophia suffered its worst desecration. The Doge thrilled at the victory for his Empire, added the title of Despot to his name. The Latin Empire lasted for fifty-seven years before Constantinople was retaken and restored to the Byzantines. Dandolo's tomb was discovered in the gallery of St. Sophia and broken into, his bones scattered to the dogs.

A throne had stood in the centre of the western gallery flanked by green marble pillars. From a disc of Thessalian marble which marked the spot I took a last look at the nave. The groups of sightseers were a long way below; the glittering mosaic in the apse, the marble and the imposing dome could not fail to leave an impression on any visitor.

We now felt the need for a rest and a change. What about going to see Agatha Christie's room at the Pera Palace Hotel? We guiltily climbed into a taxi feeling that we ought to have taken a bus, but at this stage unable to cope with the new complexities of that kind of transport. We were quickly clambering out as the driver demanded too high a price for the journey. From the airport we had paid for our taxi at a ticket office where the sum fixed for the journey was calculated on distance. Now, though, we had to bargain. Due to Andrew and Martin's skill we were soon back in the taxi as the driver agreed to their offer.

The Hotel, commanding a superb position, had been built at the end of the last century on the heights of Pera, the narrow wedge-shaped plateau of New Istanbul. During its heyday everyone of note stayed at this famous hotel which became a natural meeting place and the centre for gossip and intrigue. The preponderance of marble, plush carpets, leather chairs and ferns in tubs served as a reminder of its past, but the freshly squeezed orange juice related to modern and grossly inflated prices. Had we arrived four hours later, I would have expected to have heard a band playing from the raised platform in the dining room with a thé dansant in full progess. The open lift was operated by uniformed bell boys. A framed notice inside gave the impression that when Agatha Christie disappeared she had spent the weeks at the Pera Palace Hotel writing 'Murder on the Orient Express'.* The notice mentioned that her room was on view to those enquiring at the desk. We followed those instructions to be told that the key had been mislaid.

---

* Agatha Christie suffered from loss of memory in 1926 and spent her missing days at the Hydropathic Hotel in Harrogate. She wrote 'Murder on the Orient Express' in 1933 inspired by two journeys she made on this celebrated railway, one in 1928 — the first time she visited Istanbul — and the second in 1931 when her train was halted during a thunderstorm.

We had arrived in the new town crossing the Golden Horn by Ataturk Bridge. I hardly noticed the way we had come, our taxi being driven so fast and furiously that I had shut my eyes at converging cars, and heard only the sound of screeching brakes and blaring horns. Every Turkish driver wanted to demonstrate his prowess behind the wheel determined to reach his destination in record time. This district, Beyoglu, contained the most important shops, hotels and embassies. We had no desire to linger here and decided to have a late lunch in a restaurant at the top of Galata Tower. No sooner had we turned off the main road, thinking to take a short cut down the narrow cobbled streets, than we were lost. This seemed curious for our objective was a 70 metre tower, but the tall houses on either side prevented us from seeing anything except a narrow strip of sky. These old streets proved fascinating as well as frustrating, twisting and turning often with steps denying the entry of cars. Through barred cellar windows the inhabitants revealed their trades, most of them working in metal or wood. When glancing upwards I would often catch sight of a veiled face peering at us through an array of flower pots. We felt rather foolish having to ask the way, but gathered later that Galata Tower enjoyed the reputation of being elusive. The strong solid mass seemed to mock at our bewilderment when we suddenly came across it at the junction of many streets — we had reached the centre of the maze.

Erected by the Genoese in 1349 as part of their defence system, the tower suffered from the usual earthquakes; it had been rebuilt several times and used in turn as a prison and a look-out for fires. Recently converted, there was a lift to whisk diners to the restaurant saving them the one hundred and forty three original steps. To reach the top of the tower we climbed one floor higher up a circular staircase to be rewarded with a panoramic view of Istanbul. Topkapi Palace stood out well and countless minarets littered the skyline. Hopefully skyscrapers will never be allowed in Old Stamboul — the colloquial name given by the citizens to their ancient city. The roofs immediately below us were in an appalling state with great chunks of tiles missing; crude repairs had been carried out using pieces of corrugated iron and black polythene.

The restaurant, despite its view, looked uninviting and smelled of stale smoke. I expect it came to life at night, the prices on the menu indicating its type of clientele. By now we were very hungry but were unable to discover anywhere to eat. We asked and, as always, I was pleasantly surprised by the way the Turks tried hard to help. This man took us to his friends at the far end of the street, even though it meant retracing his steps, and they in turn showed us the way to a grotty looking self-service restaurant in an underpass. The stacked objects shaped like pancakes appeared edible, and indeed were delicious, turning out to be unleavened bread with a sprinkling of mince meat. There was lemonade to drink, and afterwards we bought sesame rings from a barrow to nibble as we wandered over Galata Bridge. This had been built by the Germans in 1913 to replace an older wooden structure. At night it swings open to allow ships to reach the docks beyond, in the same way as the great boom operated during the Siege of Constantinople allowing the lofty sailing ships manned by Christians to pass into the safety of the Golden Horn.

On the day in 1453 that the Turkish troops appeared over the horizon, Constantine XI, Emperor of Byzantium, ordered a boom to be stretched across the entrance to the harbour; one end of the chain was fixed to the Tower of Eugenius under the acropolis and the other to a tower on the sea walls of Pera. It was supported on wooden floats and proved an effective barrier against the Turkish fleet. The Christian fleet lined up outside the boom and easily repulsed the first attack, for the Turks' cannon-balls could not achieve sufficient elevation to do any harm to the tall ships. Pails of water carried by relays of men put out fires, and the Christians' arrows and javelins did far more harm fired from the greater height of their decks and crows nests. The Turks then brought a cannon to Galata Point and managed to hit and sink a galley, so from then on the Christian fleet sought shelter behind the boom.

An exciting naval battle took place a week later. The wind at last changed to the south and three Genoese galleys which were becalmed in the Aegean, entered the Sea of Marmara. They had been sent by Pope Urban II crammed with arms and provisions, and were joined by a large Imperial transport laden with corn brought by the Emperor's ambassador in Sicily. The Turkish fleet, with drums beating and trumpets sounding, met them off the south-eastern corner of the city. For nearly an hour the tall Christian ships were able to shake them off but suddenly, rounding the acropolis, the wind dropped and their sails flapped idly. For those watching it must have been agonising. The ships caught by the current were slowly drawn towards the Pera shore where Sultan Mehmet II, in his enthusiasm, kept urging his horse into the water. The discipline on the galleys was superb. The Genoese wore effective armour and had ample supplies of water with which to put out fires, stones to drop and break the oars of the Turkish vessels, axes to chop off heads and hands of those trying to board and inflammable liquid known as Greek Fire.*

Evening approached and it seemed impossible for the Christian ships to last much longer. They had inflicted a great deal of damage but the size of the Turkish fleet was too great, the enemy possessing a never ending supply of ships to launch fresh attacks. Then, miraculously, as the sun set the wind rose in great gusts. The sails filled and the powerful ships shook off their adversaries as they glided towards the boom. Darkness fell, the boom was opened and three Venetian galleys sailed out and escorted the exhausted crews and their battered vessels to safety.

---

* The most eminent professors have been unable to agree or to discover the exact ingredients of Greek Fire, nor the method by which it was launched towards the enemy. Reputed to have been invented by a Syrian in the seventh century who sold the recipe to the Byzantines, it certainly contributed to their dominance in naval warfare. The nearest that can be determined was that the liquid mixture included pitch, sulphur, quick lime, resin and bitumen, plus the 'secret' addition, and was thought to have been in some way squirted over the enemy.

8

Galata Bridge was crowded. A group surrounded a man performing that age-old three card trick, some workmen gazed down a manhole, and grilled fish from the morning's catch were being cooked on open stoves. We should have had lunch here. The gusts of wind instead of filling sails blew grit into my eyes, so that I could not appreciate the much photographed view in front of me of the Yeni (New) Mosque — seventeenth century despite its name — with Old Stamboul rising behind.

The covered Spice Market with cupolas over each bay was not far from Galata Bridge. Built in 1660 for the sale of food and spices from Egypt, now a variety of goods were offered, many inclined to the tourist trade. Besides a distinct aroma coming from the shops with exotic ingredients stored in glass jars and dried herbs hanging in bunches, there were those displaying unusual cheeses, honey and delectable sweets. We were to return to the Spice Market at the end of our holiday to buy turkish delight, the best present to take home to one's friends. The flower market occupied stalls outside but the cut blooms had already been sold; all that remained at this time of day were vegetable seedlings and container-grown shrubs and roses. Interest to the scene was added by a few owners persuasively offering their rabbits or hens to passers-by.

Taxi drivers competed for our custom but we waved them aside. The narrow streets and houses of Old Stamboul rising behind the Spice Market looked inviting, so we decided to walk. We took far longer to reach our destination for we were continually diverted down side streets when we caught a glimpse of something unusual: a protruding buttress that might originally have been part of a Byzantine Church, or a solitary minaret hiding a small mosque.

The Basilica Cistern was shut, apparently always on a Tuesday. Martin had already seen Topkapi Palace on a previous visit to Istanbul, so he went to check bus and boat times. Andrew and I walked to the Palace which is now a museum. It too was shut on Tuesdays. Undaunted we marched to the Mosaic Museum near the Blue Mosque. That was shut on Mondays and Tuesdays, and anyhow five o'clock closing time means no entry after four thirty p.m. All this proved how essential it is to call at the Tourist Information before beginning one's sightseeing. Their offices are well sign-posted and someone invariably speaks English.

We felt that it was too early to return to the Hotel. Andrew longed to go carpet hunting and here by the Blue Mosque was our chance. Development was in progress and so far only two of the arched boutiques had been completed. We went and sat down in one of them to find an elderly English couple already there with rugs scattered all over the floor. They could not decide which out of two to buy. We discussed at length the merits of both and left them in the final stage of bargaining.

We paused before a grander shop in the main street with handsome silk carpets in the window. The owner invited us inside. We explained that we did not want to buy and were only admiring his display; however he insisted that we went upstairs to view his collection and offered us tea. This refreshment was presented automatically to friends and customers alike, the ritual having developed from the Turks' natural courtesy to welcome the stranger and to give sustenance to the weary. The tea was always served in small glasses standing on saucers, with two lumps of sugar. I was getting used to the taste, without the sugar, and found it quite refreshing. If I uttered a word that sounded like "Ah-chick-chai", I sometimes managed to acquire a weaker brew, but often my pronunciation was not understood and Andrew had to come to the rescue. Exquisite carpets were unrolled for us to inspect, but we repeated that we were about to travel in Anatolia and therefore could not buy now, though we might come back and see them again on our return visit. The owner was pleasantly unpushing, probably as his mind was otherwise occupied for his wife had just produced their first baby — a girl.

Feeling well rested and knowing that we only had one more day in which to see everything in Istanbul we hailed a taxi, to save precious minutes, and alighted at the Bazaar (Kapali Carsi). I do not care for bazaars. I dislike not being able to look at what interests me for any length of time without being pestered by touts. Perhaps that was why I came to love mosques and could never pass one without wanting to go inside. They were so restful and quiet, and no-one minded how long the stranger stayed to meditate. I never met anyone else who had failed to enjoy the bazaar and indeed, some tourists spend their whole day exploring the complex. The building itself was certainly splendid. It occupied 22,000 square metres; there were eleven gateways, its ninety arched streets totalled 64 kilometres in length, and the whole of this immense site was roofed with arches and domes.

Andrew was keen to buy a suede coat — his father's fifty year old one now being in shreds — so I sat in endless small shops sipping glasses of tea while Andrew tried on and bargained. One persuasive salesman said that he was changing his stock to jewellery that night so the jacket would not be there when we returned from Anatolia. Having been followed out of the third shop with yet another final price reduction, we returned and finally made our purchase. Alas! We were not yet free to go for a Turk, who had acted as an interpreter, insisted that we went to see his carpets. Another glass of tea, admiration, explanations, promises to return, a cost price offer for one, but unfortunately we did not want the carpet.

At last we left the pedlars behind and wound our way back to the hotel. We watched some children playing football with a picturesque view of the Sea of Marmara beyond, but crossing the open space we were horrified to find, with no warning or barrier, a sheer drop of twelve metres to the road below. We were standing on part of the old Byzantine walls. This length of wall had been relatively undisturbed during the Siege of 1453 and the few attempted landing parties were easily repulsed. The Christians only realised that defeat was imminent when they received the signal that the walls had been breached on the opposite side of the city. Resistance collapsed, some sections capitulating at once in the hope of saving their houses and churches. Prince Orhan, a distant cousin of

Mehmet, was in exile in Constantinople and had decided to stay and help Constantine. He and his Turks fought to the last, knowing that if they surrendered they would certainly be massacred. Orhan in fact tried to escape by disguising himself as a Greek monk but was captured, identified by a fellow prisoner, and decapitated. On the other hand, Cardinal Isidore who was in charge of the acropolis, changed his clothes with a beggar. The beggar was taken prisoner and slain, his head displayed as the Cardinal's, while Isidore escaped having been sold to a merchant from Pera.

How welcome were our hot baths — fortunately we had been warned of an inexplicable shortage of bath plugs in Turkey so had come prepared — and how surprisingly quickly was food brought to us in a little restaurant overlooking the Sea of Marmara. Some variety of fried fish was put on the table. We had not asked for it but would have eaten anything that was offered. A huge pile of lettuce, bread, strawberries and wine also appeared. We watched a medley of boats, from small tugs to large tankers sailing by on this busy stretch of water. The reflections from the setting sun shimmered over the surface and, less than two kilometres away, the lights on the Asian shore began to twinkle evoking the excitement of the East.

St. Sophia

The Blue Mosque

Archway leading through the original Byzantine walls.

13

Back street leading
to Topkapi

Fountain of Ahmet III
and one of St. Sophia's
minarets

The sea embraces Istanbul and has played a central role in its history. It provides access for trade and has proved of value in defence, with the narrow straits of the Dardanelles to the south-west and the channel of the Bosphorus to the north-east. The Sea of Marmara laps Istanbul's southern shore, but it also divides the city, part being in Europe and its suburbs in Asia, while the Golden Horn separates Old and New Istanbul. The plentiful supply of fish gave rise to this curving inlet being named the Golden Horn; stretching for four kilometres in a north-westerly direction its deep harbour allows large vessels to dock.

On our second day in Istanbul we were lured to the waters of the Bosphorus. A ferry left at eleven o'clock; with a few hours to spare we set off for the second time to explore the Basilica Cistern, in our eagerness arriving too early. There were numerous ways in which to while away the minutes, and shoe cleaners gathered at strategic places were always ready to oblige. We persuaded Martin to have his well-worn leather shoes cleaned. The age of the boot boy varied considerably but the best one to choose was the owner of the most ornate box. These were the mark of the trade handed down from father to son, those with the greatest number of brass-topped bottles and pots were bound to be the best qualified. Different mixtures and polishes and a terrific amount of elbow grease went into producing the shiniest pair of shoes that I have ever seen.

We descended two flights of steps to reach the Basilica Cistern, or the Yerebatan Saray, the Underground Palace. Water lapped at our feet, and columns — with alternate Corinthian and Byzantine capitals — rose from the surface supporting brick arches. We could see only a fraction of them as the meagre electric light failed to penetrate the murky depths. One old rowing boat was moored to the landing stage. I could not resist transposing the scene to one of blazing spotlights, the starters flag raised and a row of canoes about to begin a bending race in between the columns: there were three hundred and thirty six of them arranged in twelve rows of twenty eight each.

Many of the palaces and monasteries during the Byzantine era had their own private cisterns, fed by subterranean pipes and aqueducts from rivers and lakes in the surrounding countryside. Part of the aqueduct built by Emperor Valens in 378 remains standing, but many of the cisterns fell into disrepair after the conquest. The Basilica Cistern was not revealed until 1545 when a shrewd observer noticed that a Turkish housewife never trudged to the local fountain for her water; instead she lowered a bucket through a hole in her cellar floor drawing water from her private miraculous source.

Having time to spare we decided to walk through Gulhane Park surrounding Topkapi Palace. It must be a delight during the hot summer months with well-established trees and patches of grass, backed by the towering walls of the Sultans' abode. A statue covered with green polythene was bound firmly with ropes, thereby preventing us from peeping underneath to discover the identity of the unknown seated figure. A zoo bordered one side of the park and, after having gazed at a camel, a lion, dogs and wolves, a cow and a bull, I became rather bored and left Andrew and Martin in order to squeeze in a visit to a mosque near our point of embarkation.

The one I wanted to see was described as the most beautiful of the smaller mosques. The architect, Sinan, had built it in 1562 for Rustem Pasha, Grand Vizier under Suleyman the Magnificent and husband of the Sultan's favourite daughter, Princess Mihrimah. I had been unable to enthuse Andrew or Martin to visit it the previous day after our walk through the Spice Market, so here was my opportunity. Needless to say the distance was far greater than I had anticipated. I had to run, but slowed down immediately I saw a barrier manned by soldiers guarding the exit from the Park. Running can be interpreted as a sign of guilt and the last thing I wanted was to be delayed by having to answer questions. Once past, I joined the busy main road which ran between the sea and the railway line leading to Sirkeci station, the famous terminal of the Orient Express. Galata Bridge seemed miles away. To jump on a bus I needed a ticket which could only be bought at main bus stops, so I was forced to jog.

A mass of people converged from Galata Bridge and the Spice Market into the open space by the Yeni Mosque. I was conscious of someone matching my strides and asking that oft repeated question: "Are you English?" As usual I ignored the person until he announced, "I am English too!" I looked up from under my hat which I always wore as protection against the sun, and sure enough he was. I said that I was terribly sorry but I could not stop to talk for I only had a quarter of an hour left to see the Rustem Pasha Mosque. He affirmed that it was worth a visit; declaring that it was too hot to try to keep up with me, he indicated the narrow street that I was to take.

A flight of steps led from the street to a spacious courtyard and to the mosque on the first floor. I kicked off my shoes, squeezed past the heavy drapings that covered the entrance, and stood stock still, staring in amazement. This was in miniature what I had expected to find in the Blue Mosque. The walls and pillars, mihrab and even the mimber were totally covered with tiles, and where the tiles had to end painted designs of green, black and brown marble took over. The predominately blue tiles had been made in Iznik and were decorated with every conceivable floral and geometric design. Fleetingly I picked out carnations, roses and cypress trees, crept past students copying and tracing their patterns, glanced at my watch and dashed. Hurrying along the narrow street was hazardous. The shops on either side displayed their goods on the pavement, and a milling throng to whom time was unimportant filled the roadway. I made the appointed rendezvous with a minute to spare, Andrew and Martin not putting in an appearance for another seven. Martin had purposely told me an earlier time, not realising that I was always punctual. The boat was already crammed with tourists, but I managed to find one

16

seat on the upper deck while Andrew and Martin preferred the relative peace of a covered section.

The Bosphorus invoked many stories from the Greek Myths. There was Io turned into a heifer by Zeus, to conceal her from the jealous Hera. Hera sent a gadfly to torment the wretched Io who, in order to escape, plunged into the waters that divided Europe from Asia, hence the name Bosphorus, meaning 'Ford of the Cow'. Jason and his Argonauts had many hair-raising adventures as they made their traumatic way up the Bosphorus, to seek the Golden Fleece in Colchis at the eastern end of the Black Sea.

Leander's Tower rose from the waters of the Bosphorus near the Asian shore, though it was not at that point that Leander swam across the Hellespont to reach his beloved Hera, but near Abydos in the Dardanelles. The Turks called the tower Kiz Kulesi, Maiden's Tower, and told a different legend. They said that a princess had been confined here by her father, to protect her from the bite of a serpent foretold by a prophesy. Predictably one was smuggled into the tower in a basket of grapes. Emperor Manual Comnenus built a small fortress on the islet in the twelfth century to which he attached one end of a chain, the other end being fixed to the Tower of Mangana below the acropolis. In this way he protected the entrance to the Bosphorus and Golden Horn, the innovation no doubt inspiring Emperor Constantine three centuries later.

Uskudar lies on the Asian shore opposite Istanbul. Formerly Chrysopolis, City of Gold, it was the starting point for the great Roman roads that crossed Asia Minor, and in Ottoman times the gathering place for the Sacred Caravan departing for Mecca. The City was frequently overrun not having a defensive wall like its European neighbour Constantinople. For a century before the Fall of Constantinople it lay in Turkish hands and no monuments from the Byzantine period remain. However mosques abound dating from the fifteenth century onwards, with three designed by Sinan. To the British, Uskudar, formerly Scutari, was famous for the hospital set up by Florence Nightingale in the Selimiye barracks during the Crimean War.

Old Stamboul disappeared rapidly from view as we chugged up the Bosphorus following the shores of New Istanbul. We passed large liners moored by the quayside of Galata while their passengers were savouring the delights of Istanbul. Galata Tower stood out well and the occasional mosque graced the waters edge, but by far the most impressive sight was the mid nineteenth century Dolmabahce Palace, a colossal white marble edifice in the rococo style looking totally out of place in Turkey. Once the site of a wooden summer-house frequented by previous Sultans, Abdul Mecit determined to build the present palace having decided that Topkapi Saray was too old fashioned. Andrew and I could not resist a visit on our last morning in Istanbul. What interested me now was the fact that it was from here, during the Siege of Constantinople, that Mehmet II, Sultan of the Ottomans, took his ships overland to the upper reaches of the Golden Horn. Thwarted by the boom which protected the entrance to the Golden Horn, Mehmet devised a means by which a fleet of seventy ships were hauled out of the water and on to wheeled platforms by oxen, then dragged up the two hundred foot hill behind Pera and down the Valley of the Springs to the water's edge.

The district of Galata belonged to the Genoese and professed to be neutral, even though a fellow countryman by the name of Giustiniani arrived in 1452 with seven hundred experienced soldiers to support Emperor Constantine. Well protected on its land boundaries by a wide ditch and strong walls, Galata nevertheless afforded easy access to the city of Constantinople across the Golden Horn, and a steady stream of information passed to and fro. The Genoese presumed that the building of the road had been purely for ease of access, and had failed to warn the defenders of Constantinople of this devastating operation. Intense jealousy existed between the Genoese and the Venetians within the city. When the Genoese of Pera learned of the Venetian secret plan to burn the Turkish fleet by now moored in the Golden Horn, they were furious at being excluded. They suspected that the Venetians would steal all the glory in the certainty of the forthcoming victory. The attack was delayed while the Genoese were allowed to prepare their ship. Before dawn and six days after the horrendous approach of the ships overland, two great transports, one Venetian and one Genoese, accompanied by a medley of smaller boats approached the Turkish fleet. The latter had ample time to consolidate their position; they had been warned by a Genoese spy of the forthcoming attack and their guns wrought due havoc. Forty Christian sailors who had swum ashore were slaughtered by the Turks later in the day in full view of Constantinople. To revenge this deed the Christians led two hundred and sixty Turkish prisoners to the city walls, and there beheaded them.

Although we were unable to drive over the new Bosphorus suspension bridge — built in 1973 linking Europe with Asia — at least we sailed beneath its awe-inspiring steel span. From afar the bridge looked graceful; from close to one was aware of the overpowering strength of modern technology. The village of Ortakoy was dwarfed by this flying structure but a mosque on the promontory stood out distinctly, designed by Nikogos Balyan who had also been responsible for Dolmabahce Palace. Our little ferry crossed and recrossed the Bosphorus, stopping every now and again on both European and Asian shore to deposit and pick up passengers. At Bebek, who should board but the English couple we had met the previous day in the carpet shop. They told me that the arrangements had been completed satisfactorily. They were also delighted with their hotel in this pleasant village away from the noise and hurly burly of Istanbul.

We sailed past the University of the Bosphorus occupying the position of the old Robert College founded in 1863 by Cyrus Hamlin, an American missionary who had baked bread and washed clothes for Florence Nightingale's hospital in Scutari. The view from the height was reputedly stunning, overlooking the narrowest part of the strait and the two castles of Rumeli and Anadolu which faced each other from different continents. Rumeli Hisar had recently been restored, and the scene was enhanced by Judas trees in full flower creating patches of vivid pink. The hillside would not have looked so peaceful some five centuries ago when terror struck the hearts of Christians on hearing that Sultan Mehmet II was building this castle on the European shore. They must have realised that a siege was imminent.

Tension had been steadily mounting between Mehmet and Constantine. Mehmet was made Sultan in 1451 at the age of nineteen after the death of his father, Murad II. He had been well trained in government and his ambition for some time had been the conquest of Constantinople. Since the fourteenth century the Turks had observed and taken advantage of the troubles in Byzantium. John V Palaeologus, in his fifty years reign from 1341—91 had been dethroned three times, by his father-in-law, son, and grandson; he managed to regain the throne on each occasion. His people had suffered from the Black Death in 1347, depleting the Empire of one third of its population, but the most damaging factor was the schism that existed between the Greek and Roman Church. The Empire could no longer survive without help from the West.

By the end of the century the Turks had conquered territory as far north as the Danube and encircled what little remained of Byzantium. In 1402, Sultan Bayezid I marched on Constantinople, but had to turn back to face the Mongol hordes led by Tamerlane. Murad II tried in 1423, but rumours of a rebellion caused the Sultan to raise the siege and retreat in order to sort out his dynastic quarrels. Shortly after Mehmet's rise to the throne, Constantine injudiciously sent ambassadors to demand the moneys due for the maintenance of Prince Orhan, the Ottoman pretender, conveniently harboured at the Byzantine Court. This infuriated Mehmet. An Italian squadron cruising up and down the strait prevented him from returning to Adrianople by his usual route, across the Dardanelles. He moved his army to the Bosphorus and landed on Byzantine territory, thereby breaking the oath signed by his father.

Mehmet crossed the Bosphorus from Anadolu Hisar, in the same place that Darius I had built his bridge of boats in 512 B.C. when marching his army of seven hundred thousand against the Scythians. Mehmet realised the advantages of this narrow strait, 700 metres wide, and made his plans during the winter. By the spring of 1452 he had gathered one thousand skilled masons and double the number of unskilled workers. Demolishing nearby churches and monasteries and using their stones as building material, he completed the fortress in four months. There were three main towers on which he placed cannons. These were joined by a wall 250 metres long itself defended by three smaller towers. Mehmet soon demonstrated his command of the Bosphorus by sinking a Venetian ship that dared to run the blockade, using a cannon built by Urban the Hungarian. Urban had first offered his services to Emperor Constantine who unfortunately could not afford his salary. The Sultan gave Urban four times the original sum asked plus all the technical assistance he needed. In three months Urban had built an enormous cannon which was brought to Rumeli Hisar. It had revealed its power and the Sultan was overjoyed, ordering another twice its size. This one had a barrel 8 metres long and the cannon balls were said to have weighed 600 kilogrammes. It was built at Adrianople (Edirne) the Sultan's capital and his headquarters for the preparation of the siege. Roads and bridges had to be strengthened for the 232 kilometre journey to Constantinople; sixty oxen were needed to drag the machine and two hundred men marched beside to keep the gun-carriage steady.

The Christian community became increasingly panic stricken. First the Emperor Constantine sent a delegation to the Sultan, to emphasise that Mehmet was breaking a solemn treaty signed by him and his father, whereby Murad had promised not to set foot on Christian soil. The ambassadors were dismissed without an audience. Constantine retaliated by imprisoning the Turks in Constantinople. Realising this was a futile gesture he released them and dispatched envoys laden with gifts, to ask that a least the Greek villages along the Bosphorus should not be harmed. Finally, in desperation, he commissioned his ambassadors to seek reassurance that Constantinople would not be attacked. The ambassadors were thrown into prison and beheaded. Mehmet advanced on Constantinople with his army and encamped for three days while he inspected the walls. War had virtually been declared.

The Castle of Anadolu (Anatolia) on the Asian shore bore a sad tale of its creator, Sultan Bayezid I. Nicknamed the Thunderbolt, Bayezid had defeated a Crusade at Nicopolis in Bulgaria in 1396 and was threatening to march on Rome, boasting that he would feed his horse with a bushel of oats placed on the altar of St Peter's. Fortuitously Tamerlane demanded his attention and defeated him in a great battle near Ancyra (Ankara). Bayezid was imprisoned — according to Marlowe — in a cage and drawn behind the victorious army as Tamerlane continued his triumphal march. Bayezid also had to suffer the indignity of watching his wife perform the duties of a slave. Unable to tolerate this gross humiliation he committed suicide by banging his head repeatedly against the iron bars that surrounded him. (One need not feel undue sympathy for Bayezid knowing that he too had been guilty of gross acts of cruelty: in order to ensure the safety of his territory while away fighting, he had ordered his own brother to be strangled). Subsequent Sultans refused to marry in case they were forced into a similar situation. Not until the middle of the sixteenth century, to the utter incredulity of Constantinople, was a marriage ceremony held. Suleyman I gave the slave girl from Russia, Roxelana, her freedom and made her his Empress.

We were a happy party aboard our boat. A running commentary had been kept up by the guide of a tour and translated into different languages, one of which was Russian. The group looked very jolly. Russians are keen travellers and there is an agreement by which they can visit Turkey every three years, with a reciprocal arrangement. Refreshments were offered at persistent intervals in the form of tea, coffee, sandwiches, orange juice and yogurt. I could not resist sampling the Turkish yogurt to which I quickly became addicted, so alien was the taste to that bland supermarket variety we find in England.

Apart from the village of Kurucesme where coal, sand and gravel deposits disfigured the waterfront, the Bosphorus was extremely attractive. Each cove presented a new scene and every village had its own identity. Arnavutkoy, the Albanian village, had picturesque wooden houses; Emirgan was named after a Persian prince, Emirgune, who surrendered to Murad IV, became a favourite and was rewarded with the gift of a palace. Fire has destroyed the majority of old wooden buildings in Turkey, but in Emirgan a rare eighteenth century yale — a wooden mansion — has survived. Many of these enchanting summer-houses once graced both banks of the Bosphorus. A floating dockyard in a natural bay dwarfed the charming village of Istinye, while Tarabya was crowded with yachts, its waterfront lined with expensive looking restaurants and hotels; a dazzling purple wisteria covered a flat-roofed taverna.

We all disembarked at Sariyer. From here it is possible to drive through the Belgrade forest to Kilyos which has some of the best beaches on the European shore of the Black Sea. After Suleyman the Magnificent had conquered the city of Belgrade, he transported a number of its inhabitants and settled them in the forest to look after the reservoirs and waterworks supplying Constantinople. Sinan designed the aqueducts and some impressive sections remain standing.

The ferry only continues for one more stop to Rumeli Kavagi where nothing much remains of a Byzantine castle, but the one on the opposite shore, Yoros Kalesi, dominates the upper Bosphorus. The public road also comes to an end where the military takes over. A boat has to be hired to explore the upper reaches of the Bosphorus which is wild and rugged. Landing is forbidden and swimming in any sandy cove is dangerous because of terrifying currents that sweep the waters. There is one that lies at a depth of 40 metres and flows north from the Sea of Marmara. Unable to escape into the Black Sea it is drawn to the surface, only to be driven back from whence it came. If fishing nets are accidentally lowered too far, the current is strong enough to pull the boats northward against the southerly surface current. Due to the sinuous shape of the channel, each indentation of the shore carries contrary currents, but a strong wind can reverse the whole situation.

The Bosphorus is very deep in parts, over 100 metres off the point of Arnavutkoy where the current is also at its strongest. The old sailing ships had difficulty rounding the point, and there is a delightful story told by Gyllius, a Frenchman who lived in Constantinople in the mid sixteenth century. He noticed that crabs too found it hard to swim so they took to land and scrabbled across the rocks, wearing away the stones by their constant procession.

The dangers that beset sailors in ancient times were horrifying. A

21

sudden blanket of fog led to many collisions and shipwrecks, while icebergs were reputed to have blocked the northern entrance of the Bosphorus. Jason's voyage took on a new realism when one appreciated some of the hazards he had to face. The most exciting was when he reached the Black Sea. Two great rocks guarded the mouth of the Bosphorus and clashed together making it impossible for ships to enter or leave the Strait. King Phineus — helped earlier by Jason — advised him to set free a dove and, if it passed through the Strait successfully, his men were to row their hardest as the rocks separated. The dove lost its tail-feathers, and the Argo scarcely made the passage before the rocks re-clashed, slightly damaging the stern.

The English couple and the tour to which they belonged, had one hour 'at leisure' in Sariyer before the ferry picked them up again on their return journey. We decided to have lunch and catch a bus back to Istanbul. Hardly had we sat down at a fish restaurant on the shores of the Bosphorus, than we were brought fresh bread and trays loaded with small dishes. Whatever was ordered for the main course these mezes were a compulsory starter. They could easily have provided a meal in themselves. One chose from a selection of salads — tomatoes, cucumbers, peppers and mounds of crisp lettuce — numerous cold vegetables including mushrooms, courgettes, aubergines and artichokes, and various types of beans. The better the restaurant, the more dishes were produced, and some took pride in their own specialities. Dolmades — vine leaves stuffed with rice — were a favourite, and cabbage leaves were treated in a similar fashion; there was always a bowl of yogurt and slices of feta, a goats cheese. Potatoes generally accompanied the main course and fruit was offered as a final flourish. We were too early in the year for peaches, apricots and grapes, and the delectable Turkish fig ripens later still. However strawberries were in season, served with a very fine sugar. They were good, but somehow lacked the flavour of the English varieties.

The bus journey back to Eminonu — the name of the district on the Old Stamboul side of Galata Bridge — took one hour and twenty minutes. After ten minutes the bus was full and Andrew and Martin, following the Turkish custom, gave up their seats to women. They were soon to regret their gallantry for they were committed to standing for the rest of the way. Martin escaped somewhere around Dolmabahce, where he took a short cut through the Beyoglu district to have a session with the Travel Agency, to check the details of the route which we, the modern Crusaders, would be taking tomorrow.

Andrew and I found a kiosk that sold bus tickets and were surprised to discover that all tickets cost the same. Hence the price of our long ride from Sariyer was equal to the five minute one we were about to take to Topkapi. This time Topkapi Saray, the Great Palace of the Ottoman Sultans, was open. When Mehmet rode into Constantinople on the afternoon of May 29th 1453, no existing building could be found worthy of the Conqueror. The Imperial Palace overlooking the Bosphorus had long since proved too much of a drain on the Emperor's diminishing fortunes. (In the twelfth century the Comneni dynasty had been forced

22

to move to the more modest palace of Blachernae.) The Latins, during their tyrannical rule from 1204—1261, had aided the general disintegration of the city, so Mehmet had no option but to start anew. He selected a deserted site on the Third Hill and built what was later to become known as the Eski Saray, or Old Palace, now occupied by the university and the Suleymaniye Mosque; but he soon realised the spectacular situation of the ancient acropolis, and in 1459 started to construct a new palace at the northern end of the First Hill.

Mehmet planned the complex mainly as an administrative centre employing about five thousand people. He reserved the Eski Saray for his wives and concubines, the Harem not being added to Topkapi Palace for another hundred years. Naturally there were many additions and alterations, and devastating fires meant that sections were entirely rebuilt, but the basic plan of the three main courts remained the same as in Mehmet's day.

The Imperial Gate led into the First Court which was open to the citizens of Istanbul. This was the service area of the Palace containing a hospital, bakery — producing superfine white bread for the Sultan — mint and outer treasury, and dormitories for guards and domestics. The Church of St. Irene enclosed within the courtyard, was used as an arsenal by the Janissaries. They were the Sultan's crack regiment of Guards, selected as young boys from Christian families within the empire and highly trained. They had their own barracks, were forbidden to marry, and their lives were dedicated to the service of the Sultan. The Church of St. Irene was closed for restoration. Founded in 300 the original building was one of the first Christian churches in the old city of Byzantium, and served as the cathedral until the completion of St. Sophia. In 346, three thousand Christians killed each other outside the church in a riot between the Arians and the Orthodox parties. The Arians considered Christ to be human thereby denying the concept of the Holy Trinity, whereas those following the Orthodox faith believed Christ to be Divine. Violent disputes continued between the two until the Second Ecumenical Council of 381, when the Nicene Creed was upheld and the Arians condemned as heretics. In its early years St. Irene suffered from earthquakes and fires, but the Church we see today is the same as the one restored by Leo III in 740.

The second gateway was more impressive flanked by octagonal towers with conical tops, typical of the military architecture of the period. Here everyone had to dismount for only the Sultan was allowed to ride beyond this point. Set into the wall on the right was a fountain where the Executioner washed his hands and sword after a decapitation. Important culprits had their heads displayed on two so called 'example stones', while those of lesser significance were placed in niches cut into the walls outside the Imperial Gate.

Colonnaded porticoes surrounded the large Second Court, the only buildings being the Divan and the Inner Treasury. There was an air of tranquillity, helped by the cool looking green grass and venerable cypress trees, one of which had a fig tree growing out of a fork in its trunk. During the heyday of the Sultan's rule when the courtyard had been filled with sumptuously dressed officials — as many as five thousand at a time and double that number when amabassadors were received — absolute silence prevailed.

The Divan was the supreme executive and judicial council of the Empire, and met four times a week dealing with all state administration. The lower walls of the square domed room were decorated with Iznik tiles, and above were traces of the original arabesque painting. The members of the Council sat on low couches covered with carpets and cushions surrounding three sides of the room, while over the Grand Vezir's seat a grilled window opened into a small room in a tower whereby the Sultans, after having retired from the meetings, could overhear the proceedings. The Records Office occupied the adjoining room which led to the Grand Vezir's office and the Inner Treasury, where the treasures of the Empire were stored as they arrived from the provinces. A collection of arms and armour was currently on display in this room.

The royal stables were beyond the west wall of the Second Court, and the palace kitchens behind the east wall. These had been restored by Sinan after a fire in 1574 and consisted of ten spacious rooms with lofty domes, each kitchen cooking for a specific section of the Palace. It now housed an incomparable collection of Chinese porcelain said to be the third richest and most varied in the world, surpassed only by those in Peking and Dresden.

The Third Gate, the Gate of Felicity, led to the private side of the Palace and was guarded by the white eunuchs whose chief, the Aga, lived in a room in the gatehouse. He was in charge of the Inner Service of the Palace, except for the Harem which came under the jurisdiction of the Chief Black Eunuch. The palace pages — highly trained castrated boys — also lived in the Third Court, and besides serving the Sultan they were allowed into the Harem. They frequently became favourites of the women and were given the names of flowers such as Hyacinth, Carnation or Narcissus. Apart from the Sultan and the Princes, the only other males admitted into the Harem were the Halberdiers-with-Tresses. They delivered firewood, and from their tall hats hung false curls or tresses which fell in front of their eyes, preventing them from gazing at the concubines.

Immediately beyond the Gate stood the Audience Chamber, a small building with an overhanging roof supported by antique marble columns. Seated on a wide throne beneath a stately canopy the Sultan would receive ambassadors and their gifts. Here too the Grand Vezir and members of the Council would report on the business transacted and the decisions taken in the Divan. Nothing was considered final until the Sultan gave his assent.

Most of the buildings around the Third Court were devoted to the Palace School which trained the Civil Service. Here again the boys adopted were from Christian minorities in the Empire and promising youths captured in war. They received a rigorous training, both intellectual and physical, in contrast to the usual Islamic education which was mainly secular. It prepared students for the administration of the Empire and was no doubt a contributive factor to the success of the Ottoman state in the earlier centuries of its existence. One of their Halls contained the Imperial Wardrobe. The costumes of the Sultans were mainly of the Kaftan type, a long robe reaching to the feet and made of silk, satin or brocade in brilliant colours and bold designs, some stiff with gold and silver thread and others edged with sable.

By far the most breathtaking exhibits were to be found in the adjacent hall, the Treasury. Jewelled turbans, weapons encrusted with diamonds and pearls, goblets, tobacco containers, writing sets, clocks, golden candlesticks — anything and everything was covered in gems, jade and tortoiseshell. The largest single stones were two uncut emeralds weighing three and six pounds, and forty-nine diamonds surrounded the eighty-six carat Spoonmaker's diamond. The most precious object was the Throne of Shah Ismail. This was a masterpiece in gold, set with countless precious stones and over twenty five thousand pearls, made in India and brought from Iran by Sultan Selim I after a victorious campaign.

A few miniatures were displayed in cabinets in the last room. The so-called minature room was closed, and also the Clock and Watch collection where the hands of the time pieces had all been stopped at five past nine, the hour of Ataturk's death. We could not easily discover the whereabouts of the Directors office; our 'professor' was not available to deal with the situation and because there was still so much to see, we did not persist with our enquiries.

The Pavilion of the Holy Mantle housed the relics of Prophet Mohammed, one of the doors of the great mosque at Mecca and some ancient Korans. The rooms were dark and crowded, with too many people attempting to gaze through a grilled door at the display. An elegant marble pavilion with lead cupolas provided a welcome contrast; set in a pleasant garden, Ahmet III had it built in 1719 as a library. The door was inlaid with mother-of-pearl and tortoiseshell, and peering through the windows one could see bookshelves lining the walls, benches, and desks covered with writing materials — a perfect room for study and reflection.

The Fourth Court took the form of an enclosed garden on various levels dotted with pavilions and koskus — from which the English word kiosk is derived. One of these, the nineteenth century Mecidiye Kiosk overlooking the Sea of Marmara, had been converted into a restaurant. A stairway led down to Ahmet III's tulip garden where, at the beginning of the eighteenth century, the annual blossoming of the tulips was celebrated with a flower festival. The affairs of state ceased while the Tulip King and his entourage took part in this ceremony. The French ambassador was so captivated by the spectacle that he introduced the tulip to Louis XIV.

On a marble terrace with a superb view of the Golden Horn, Thomas

Dallam had set up a mechanical organ presented to Mehmet III by Queen Elizabeth I. A century later Sultan Ibrahim erected a delicate gilt bronze canopy named the Iftariye — iftar meaning the evening meal taken after sunset during the holy month of Ramadan. The Pavilion of Circumcision also built by Ibrahim in 1641 was closed, this ceremony playing an important part in the Muslim calendar.

Two kiosks graced the terrace, the Rivan Kiosk built by Murad IV in 1636 to commemorate his capture of Erivan, while the grander Baghdad Kiosk reminded us of another victory. Both these follies were entirely revetted with tiles.

The Harem was shut, on this occasion not for restoration but due to the lateness of the hour. There had been so much to see. Topkapi was steeped in history of the Sultans, each one having contributed something to this immense complex. A second visit was compulsory and since we were returning to Istanbul at the end of the holiday, we would have another opportunity to visit Topkapi and the Harem.

Andrew enjoys browsing in carpet shops and decided to continue his search for the perfect rug, while I strolled through the Hippodrome wanting to see for myself this focal part of so much of Istanbul's life and history. Occupying the area to the west of the Blue Mosque, it had been laid out by Septimius Severus in 203, enlarged by Constantine the Great around 326, and was reputed to have held one hundred thousand spectators. Chariot racing was the principal sport, the crowd entertained in between races by circus acts, musicians and dancers. Theodora, the daughter of a bear keeper, danced so captivatingly before the Emperor Justinan that he made her his wife.

The supporters of the various chariot teams tended, as in modern football matches, to congregate in certain sections of the terraces, the four main divisions adopting the racing colours of their favourite teams — Blue, Green, Red and White. The popular heroes of the sport became involved in religion and politics, and led their followers into frequent skirmishes against the rival groups; the Blues and Greens eventually absorbed the other two. Dissatisfaction with the internal affairs of the government caused worse riots, culminating in the Nika revolt of 532. The screaming mob switched their fury to the Emperor Justinian. They rampaged through the city causing an enormous amount of damage to public buildings, even setting fire to the old St. Sophia. The only way that the Emperor's General, Belisarius, could restore order was by enticing the uncontrollable rabble back into the stadium and ordering their mass slaughter. Thirty thousand citizens died that day in the Hippodrome, their bodies buried where they fell.

The Hippodrome was pillaged by the armies of the Fourth Crusade. The four magnificent bronze horses next to the Emperor's lodge were taken to Venice and placed outside St. Mark's Cathedral. The vandals suffered some disappointment amidst their looting. Assuming the bright material covering an obelisk 32 metres high to be gold, they hacked it off only to find after having melted it down, that the gold content was minimal — the plating was bronze-gilt. The drilled holes that held the plating in position could still be seen on this weather beaten Colossus.

Originally many bronze and marble statues would have embellished the spina, the central axis of the Hippodrome, but gradually these disappeared. After the conquest of Constantinople by the Turks, arcades were pulled down and the columns and stones used elsewhere for building. The only remaining monuments besides the Colossus, were an Egyptian obelisk (c.1500 B.C.) brought from Karnak and erected by Theodosius I in 390, and a Serpentine column dated 479 B.C. taken from the Temple of Apollo in Delphi. Unfortunately only five metres have survived, the heads of the serpents having been broken off. One was discovered in 1847 and can be seen in the Archaeological Museum.

Depressed by these endless tales of woe and desctruction, and haunted by the thought of countless bodies buried beneath my feet, I left to return to the hotel. However, as soon as I took my camera out of its case and began to look around at different views and subjects that could be photographed, I realised how much beauty still remained. Vandalism, wars and earthquakes had failed to destroy this city. Byzantium had been founded and named after a Greek, Byzas, in the year 657 B.C.. Its site was remarkable, both secure and in a position to control the grain trades from the Euxine. Athenians and Spartans inhabited the city in turn, and Alcibiades and Lysander were its most renowned rulers. Walls were built, breached and razed to the ground. Under Alexander the Great the peoples had to acknowledge Macedonian supremacy; afterwards they suffered incursions by Scythians. Allied to Rome the city's independence was taken away by Vespasian, and later it was besieged by Severus who demolished the fortifications. He repented when the Goths sailed past unmolested and repaired the destruction he had wrought. Constantine struck by the advantages of its situation, resolved to build a new city on the site of the old. Founded in A.D.328 and inaugurated two years later in 330, it was called New Rome and, to perpetuate its founder, soon became Constantinople. It grew to be the greatest city of its time, with enormous prestige and a commanding influence over world affairs.

The shoe cleaner, Andrew, and Martin

Dolmabahce Palace

Rumeli Hisar

DAY III : BURSA

What better way to leave Istanbul than by sea. This was how we ought to have arrived. Though we were sailing in the opposite direction, out of the Golden Horn, leaving behind the Bosphorus and emerging into the Sea of Marmara, at least I saw the acropolis with its astonishing array of monuments. There on the skyline were the conspicuous domes above the kitchens of the Topkapi Palace; the squat drum of St. Irene peeping above the trees; the solid, heavy buttressed St. Sophia and finally, the soaring Blue Mosque, its light half-domes and cupolas rising layer upon layer to support the commanding central dome. The easiest way to catch this magical view is to board a ferry from Galata Bridge and visit the Princes' Islands for the day. Outward bound you could fix your gaze upon the Asian shore, and on the evening's return journey the full glory of Istanbul would be revealed.

The archipelago called the Princes' Islands lay off the Asian coast of the Sea of Marmara, about an hour's sail from Istanbul. Many were uninhabited but the largest had been used for exiled Byzantine Emperors and Princes. Hermits welcomed the relative peace, and monasteries graced the hilltops or buried themselves deep in the pine forests.

Our ferry stopped first at Heybeli Ada, formerly Chalkitis, and mentioned by Aristotle in connection with the famous copper mines. A Naval College stood on the waterfront, while another of its departments occupied the site of a Byzantine monastery on a hill to the west. The tiny chapel there was attributed to Maria Comnena, the last Empress of Byzantium, and it remained in the possession of the Greek government until confiscated by the Turks in 1942. In 1970, they also closed the principal Theological Seminary of the Greek Orthodox Church, housed in modern buildings among the remnants of another monastery.

Martin had entered into conversation with a fluent English speaking Turk who told us some interesting anecdotes. One concerned Edward Barton, the English Ambassador appointed by Queen Elizabeth I, who was buried in a Cemetery within the grounds of the Naval School. His coat of arms and a long inscription covered his tombstone, telling that he had died (of dysentery) at the age of thirty-five years in 1597, after having accompanied the 'invincible Emperor of the Turks' (Mehmet III) on his war campaign against Hungary. Ambassadors in those days had to support themselves for, though they represented their sovereign, they received no payment. They were in reality traders, and Barton was a nominee of the British Turkey Company. Ships from England brought woollen clothes, tin, pewter, lead and rabbit skins, while those returning were laden with silks, currants, oil, wine and mohair the much coveted yarn of the angora goat. Barton also presented many gifts to the Sultan from Queen Elizabeth, though in reality these were provided by the merchants hoping to flatter the potentate and advance their interests.

The second island to which we sailed was the largest, Buyuk Ada.

A rapidly expanding summer resort it has secluded coves, steep cliffs and fine woods encouraging walks or tours by carriage, bicycle or donkey; no cars are allowed to disturb the peace of the islands. General Townsend was imprisoned there during the First World War; he and his army of ten thousand having been captured at Kut in 1916 on their way to protect the Persian oil fields. The Turks, suffering a reversal of fortunes in Palestine and losing Damascus, surrendered to the allies a fortnight before the Germans. They sent General Townsend to act as an intermediary during peace negotiations.

About half the ferryload disembarked at these two islands including many students who had kept us amused with their songs. They had passed around cones made from newspaper, filled with different kinds of nuts that I had noticed for sale amongst the street vendors. We were continuing to Yalova from where Martin had originally planned to go straight to Iznik, Nicaea of ancient times and the Crusaders' first objective. However, his Turkish friend who was on his way to give a lecture on textiles at the University of Bursa, persuaded Martin otherwise. He insisted that Bursa was an ideal town in which to stay overnight, and that Iznik would be better visited by day. He had been a student at Manchester University many years ago, and recalled details of Manchester United's football matches from before the air disaster of 1958. He could also remember the names of all those who had played and their various positions on the field, so the last part of the journey was spent happily reminiscing. He shepherded us off the boat and through the jostling crowd to a line of waiting coaches. The first one to be filled was immediately off the starting line.

The object of our journey was to follow the path of the Crusaders as closely as possible. We had in fact already cheated for the Crusaders, after crossing the Bosphorus, would have marched round the coastline; though Emperor Alexius when visiting the troops sailed in comfort across the Sea of Marmara. Before beginning our journey Martin had studied Professor Ramsay's 'The Historical Geography of Asia Minor', which described the Roman and Byzantine roads in detail. Three of these ancient roads led from the southern shore of the Gulf of Izmit, across a range of high hills to Nicaea (Iznik). The first from Nikomedia (Izmit); the second from Prainetos whose importance as a landing place diminished after Constantine founded Helenopolis; and the third from Cibotos which stood on a promontory, affording the shortest crossing distance between the northern and southern shores of the gulf. From Cibotos the road passed through Helenopolis; following the river Drakon — the river of the Forty Fords — it climbed to the plateau, descended to the northern shore of Lake Iznik and finally turned east to Nicaea. We knew that the Crusading armies had taken this road, and Martin was to do the same the next day, though from the opposite direction. The ferry had landed at Yalova — west of Cibotos — probably Pylai of ancient times, which had also been the usual landing place for emperors when travelling to the East. Our bus followed the fourth Roman-Byzantine road south to Kios, now

Gemlik, a small seaport on the innermost reach of another of the count-less inlets from the Sea of Marmara. Kios was named after its legendary founder, one of the Argonauts, who had settled here after his return from Colchis. The old road continued along the coast before turning due south to Bursa, while ours became a dual carriageway making more directly for the city.

We were now in Asia, in the Province of Kocaeli, Bithynia of ancient times and the most beautiful in Turkey. Greeks had settled on Bithynia's Aegean coast since the Bronze Age. They retained their identity through-out the Roman and subsequent Byzantine epoch, regaining their superior-ity in the ninth century when their fellow country-men reigned as Emperors. Even with the rise to fame of the Seljuks and ultimate domination by the Ottomans, the Greeks were allowed to keep their communities until their expulsion in 1923. For one sad generation a vacuum was left and the old fishing villages seemed abandoned. Now the tourist trade has taken over with the accompanying fringe benefits.

The drive from Yalova to Bursa was picturesque, the scrub by the side of the road dotted with wild Judas trees. All too soon the land was brought under cultivation, neat orchards and olive groves taking over with the occasional patch of globe artichokes flaunting their decorative leaves. The steep road to the plateau had been newly laid making the going relatively easy, though in winter landslides are apt to block the route; pine trees had been planted in an effort to hold the earth and shale together. The fertile plateau was famous during the heyday of the Otto-man Empire for producing a high quality grain. Blended with goats' milk, the cooks at Topkapi produced the pure white bread enjoyed by the Sultans. The Sultan would allow each high ranking male in his Court a specific number of loaves according to his position. Those of the middle class would have the Bursa flour mixed with Greek grain, and the Court pages ate Greek black bread.

The Greeks named many of their mountains, Olympus, the most famous being in Thessaly. The one in Turkey, 2,543 metres high, domin-ated the plateau across which we were now driving. The Ottoman Sultans also appreciated this mountain; ice and snow from the slopes being packed into felt sacks, and carried by mule and ship to be buried in deep pits near Topkapi Palace. The snow iced their favourite drink, sherbet, made from fruit-juice and water. Lemon juice sweetened with honey was one of the favourite flavours and, for a special occasion, the essence from violets and water lilies provided a nectar fit for the gods — or rather the Sultans. The sherbet was poured out through a lump of snow stuck on the spout of the vessel.

The Turks renamed this mountain, Uludag, or Great Mountain, and have designated it a National Park. Snow still covered the upper peaks and during the winter skiing has become a popular sport. Half a dozen 'T' bar lifts haul the enthusiasts to the top of the runs, the snag being that no abonnement system exists and a separate ticket has to be bought for each ascent. I envisaged the scene to be much the same as in the bus terminals — which I shall describe later — where each lift owner has a team of hired men waving their arms frantically to try to lure the skier to use his lift. Hikers take over in the summer, strolling through the sweet smelling pines which cover the foothills of the mountain. A 35 kilometre twisting road leads to the summit, but a cable car only takes ten minutes.

The approach to Bursa was rather spoilt by large factories. Our Turkish friend pointed out, with a certain amount of pride, car assembly plants for both foreign and national models, and textile factories producing mainly towelling and raw silk, a trade established since ancient times. Due to industrialization the outskirts have spread and Bursa is now the sixth largest town in Turkey. Nevertheless, the old city retains its attraction nestling on the lower slopes of Mt.Olympus. Bursa was originally called Prusa after its founder King Prusias of Bithynia in 183 B.C.. Pliny the Younger, the distinguished geographer, governed during the Roman occupation, and its Byzantine era was concluded when captured first by the Seljuks and finally by Orhan Gazi, Sultan of the Ottoman Turks in 1326. He made Bursa his capital, and his four successors also ruled and were buried in this lovely old town, their mosques and tombs dominating strategic points on the hillside.

The Ottomans were obsessed with expanding their empire, and Orhan's son Murad I was perpetually at war in the southern Balkans. He died at the battle of Kossova having crushed the forces of King Lazarus of Serbia. Tamerlane caused consternation by capturing Bayezid — Murad's son — and bringing him back to Bursa as a prisoner. Having gained so much territory and marched so far to the west, it has always remained a mystery as to why Tamerlane suddenly abandoned his campaign. When he left Bursa he could not resist taking a souvenir, the great doors of the Byzantine cathedral. Covered in silver gilt, and with blue enamel reliefs depicting scenes from the lives of St. Peter and St. Paul, they were carried back in triumph to grace his golden city of Samarkand.

After ten years of dispute as to who had the right to administer the Divan, Mehmet I gained the throne in 1413, to be followed by Murad II, the last of the Sultans to be buried in Bursa. His son was Mehmed II nicknamed the Conqueror. He made Adrianople (Edirne) his capital before transferring his seat of power to Constantinople in 1453.

––––––––––––

The bus station was large and busy, open twenty-four hours a day. Our lecturer, fully in command of the situation, ushered us to a nearby restaurant where we ordered the speciality of the region, doner kebabs. The kebabs in Turkey were nearly always made with lamb; forever rotating on a long spit they were tender and served with either gravy or yogurt. I preferred to forget the other speciality, the tripe soup with which I was persuaded to start the meal; a very old recipe, it was steeped in garlic, and was said to have been a cure for drunkenness.

A hotel was recommended, a taxi acquired, and with warm farewells we sped on our way. We climbed to Cekirge a delightful suburb above the old town.   Our hotel was in the process of being redecorated.   The manager apologised for the 'restoration' and produced rooms with a splendid view over the distant plain.

We were back in the town centre immediately and made straight for the oldest of the royal mosques, the Orhan Gazi Camii.   Built in 1336 by Orhan I, the conqueror of Bursa, it was significant for being the earliest example of the Bursa-style of architecture.   The basic form of the 'Bursa' mosque consisted of a rectangle divided into two by an arch, each section covered with a dome of equal size.   The room we entered first, the central hall, was flanked by two eyvans — domed areas recessed from the central court — in fact, additional rooms.   Wide steps led to the main eyvan, the prayer room, where I discovered a grandfather clock made by Charles Hill of Leicester.   Many of Bursa's mosques have suffered from earthquakes, the Orhan Gazi Camii in the fifteenth and eighteenth centuries, but both times it was faithfully restored.

Because of the Sultans' campaigns and Tamerlane's interruption, the Great Mosque, the Ulu Cami, begun by Murad I in 1379, was not completed until 1421 during the reign of Mehmet I.   Facing Bursa's main street it was built of honey-coloured limestone from Mt.Olympus and covered by a myriad of domes, twenty in all.   They in turn were supported by twelve great piers dividing the interior into numerous arched aisles.   A sadirvan occupied one of the sections inside; the dome above used to be open to the sky but now glass and a grill keeps out both birds and the elements.   Calligraphy covered every conceivable wall space.   The playing of the fountain and the Turks murmuring their prayers helped to create a unique atmosphere.   The architecture of the Ulu Cami was a development from that used by the Seljuks for their mosques in Anatolia. Later, as demonstrated in the Blue Mosque, the whole conception changed and instead of a mysterious interior with numerous pillars and archways, light and space became supremely important.

We chose to walk to the imperial mosque complex of Mehmet I for, though some distance away, one absorbs the atmosphere of a town so much better than when confined in a vehicle.   We passed the familiar figure of Ataturk, this time seated upon a horse.   His statue graced every town or village square for he was worshipped as the saviour of the nation. A wedding had just taken place and guests thronged the pavement.   We caught a glimpse of the bride and bridegroom; she was pretty, though rather heavily made up, and wore a classical white lace dress, while the groom sported a smart new suit.   They and their friends swept into the hotel for the reception and we spied them again on our return, grouped on a terrace for photographs.

A bridge spanned a gorge, at the bottom of which flowed the River Gokdere bringing the melted snows from Uludag (Mt. Olympus).   We walked steadily uphill and eventually reached the Yesil Turbe (Green Mausoleum), perfectly situated on a knoll surrounded by cypress trees. Sadly, two serious eathquakes, at the end of the eighteenth and the middle of the nineteenth centuries, had damaged this charming octagonal

34

structure with its domed roof. Originally covered with iridescent green tiles — the unique and revered green of Islam — now only a few sections were faced with imitation ones made in Kutahya. The interior was a revelation: blue ceramic tiles containing gold calligraphic inscriptions enveloped Mehmet's sarcophagus, and different coloured tiles made a striking feature of the mihrab.

Mehmet I died in 1421 and his mosque — close to the turbe — though commissioned on his rise to the throne in 1413, was not finished in his life time and lacked its entrance portico. Adopting the Bursa style of architecture there were side rooms, the main prayer area being reached by four wide marble steps where a magnificent tiled mihrab commanded obeisance to Mecca. The Imperial loggia above the entrance, used as the Divan, was also covered in sumptuous tiles. Two screened balconies on either side were reserved for the women, while in the middle of the central court a sadirvan reflected the brilliant colours from stained glass windows. A gigantic oriental plane tree dominated the garden. On closer inspection it turned out to be hollow, reminding me of our 'London' plane in Warwickshire which also has an alarming cavity.

Besides a mosque and a turbe, the Sultans included in their building complexes the statutory medrese (a place for learning), an imaret (a soup kitchen for the poor), a hamam (a bath) and sometimes a hospital. Mehmet's medrese was originally a theological school, though modern times have turned it into a museum of Turkish and Islamic art containing precious rugs, tiles and handwritten Korans.

Our Turkish friend of only a few hours past had told us of a popular drink called aroma which came in various flavours: cherry, apricot and peach. While tasting all three in a café nearby we gazed at the sensational view of Bursa, its hills rolling beneath us to meet the sudden flat plain. Bayezid's mosque complex shared this view, imaginatively positioned on the skyline of the next ridge and surrounded by cypress trees.

Andrew and Martin wanted to visit the Bedestan, the market place. The old Bedestan had been authorised by Bayezid, and was now used to store and display the most valuable goods: jewellery, objects of gold and silver, and brocades. Next to it Mehmet I built a covered bazaar. Crowds thronged the pathways lined with the usual booths and stalls, and I escaped the jostling shoppers having spied, through an archway, a secluded courtyard with the ubiquitous fountain in the centre. Two tiers of rooms surrounded the four sides, an arched gallery protecting them from direct sunlight. They were the old han, or inn, but on closer inspection the building looked conspicuously new. I discovered that the whole market place had been gutted by fire in 1955 but was quickly and meticulously restored. I lost Andrew and Martin at some stage. I had been intent on exploring for there were a number of these courtyards, and I had lingered in one for a considerable time admiring the domes of the Ulu Cami which filled the skyline. I had no clue as to which direction to start searching; nor could I remember the name of our hotel. That feeling of mounting panic had almost begun, when I caught sight of the two, six foot Englishmen deep in conversation, having obviously forgotten all about me. The purchase of a straw hat revived my spirits. Nowhere in Istanbul had I spied a hat of any description, for Turkish women only wear shawls. I expect these were only for men, nevertheless one served my purpose, but I wished Andrew had been brave enough to buy the splendid topee that he tried on for fun.

Our hotel, in the Cekirge suburb was not within walking distance. Buses were elusive and taxis extravagant. The answer was a dolmuss which appeared to have a monopoly in Bursa. A dolmuss is a shared vehicle, either a type of dormobile for the country or a car for town work. They had their own stops with the ultimate destination marked and the cars themselves had notices on their windscreens. One waved frantically when the correct dolmuss appeared, jumped in quickly and handed over the fare at some stage during the journey. This turned out to be less than half the price of a taxi and, what is more, the dolmuss stopped right outside our hotel.

Bursa was renowned for the hot springs that bubbled from the depths of Mt. Olympus. Vestiges of Justinian's imperial baths were incorporated in the Eski Kaplica (the Old Spring Bath), while the Yeni Kaplica (the New Baths) had been built by the Grand Vizier of Suleyman the Magnificent who was cured of gout by bathing in the waters. By a stroke of fortune, or by good planning, one spring rose beneath our hotel. Channelled into the basement it provided a private Turkish bath for the hotel guests for which one only had to remember to book a time. The changing room and pool area were tiled throughout, and I felt like a Sultana as I descended wide marble steps leading into the three metre square bath filled with excessively hot water. In the ante room cold water ran continuously into marble basins and splashing oneself was meant to be invigorating; but I found the extremes of hot and cold uncomfortable and barely endured ten minutes.

Lying in bed I could appreciate the reason the Sultans built their complexes on the hills above the city. Unfortunately none of their palaces have survived — constructed of wood they were susceptible to earthquakes and fires — but the air of tranquillity remained. The scent of pines drifted through the open window and for the first time I heard the much famed song of the nightingales. Their romantic melody, the pleasant fragrance from the evergreens and the listlessness I felt after the hot spring bath, combined to send me into a blissful stupor.

DAY IV : IZNIK

Today we were going to Iznik, formerly known as Nicaea, steeped in history and the site of the Crusaders' first major battle. Soon after the five a.m. call of the muezzins, I roused myself to read of their exploits. The Crusaders' ideal was admirable, but the method of its achievement was often barbaric and filled with personal motives and greed. At other times they displayed outstanding bravery and chivalry which, to a certain extent, compensated for their arrogance.

Until 1071 the Arabs had shown tolerance to the Christians allowing freedom of worship, and relative peace prevailed. Unfortunately, fierce Seljuk Turks then captured Jerusalem, took Anatolia and Nicaea, and threatened Constantinople. Emperor Alexius appealed for reinforcements from the West, offering as bait aid to reconquer Jerusalem and hinting at his willingness to heal the schism that existed between the Greek and Latin churches. Pope Urban II made a rousing speech at Clermont, and the fifteenth of August 1096 was chosen as the date of departure for the First Crusade. Some of those who joined had a genuine desire for pilgrimage, others were the younger sons of the French aristocracy who, expecting no inheritance at home, saw the Crusade as an opportunity to gain territory. Famine and pestilence were rife which increased the desire to emigrate, and the Pope, as an added incentive, promised forgiveness of sins to those who died in battle.

Peter the Hermit was greatly moved by Pope Urban's speech and in turn, by his own compelling preaching, gathered a following of twenty thousand. Most of them were peasants, with some townsfolk and the junior members of knightly families, but their numbers included brigands, criminals and tramps. Peter was impatient to start and left Cologne in April leading the way on a donkey. The journey passed without incident until, in southern Hungary, a dispute took place with a local tradesman over the price of a pair of sandals. Riots flared instantaneously, resulting in the death of four thousand Hungarians. The army subsequently pillaged and set fire to Belgrade, and marched on to Nish where they demanded food. This was provided on the understanding that the mob left as soon as possible. A fractious group of Germans foolishly set alight some mills, so another fight ensued, but this time the Crusaders were duly routed and scattered. Their army, greatly diminished in size, eventually reached Constantinople and joined forces with a similar group led by Walter the Penniless. Emperor Alexius decided to forgive the so called People's Crusade their crimes. He fed them, and allowed small groups at a time to enter the city walls and gaze with wonder at the buildings, but in the end he was forced to send them on. They had caused havoc in the suburbs, breaking into palaces and villas, and even stealing lead from the roofs of churches.

The rabble was ferried across the Bosphorus, straggled through Nicomedia and back along the southern shore of the inlet, setting up camp at Cibotus.   Their behaviour grew worse; they ransacked the countryside rounding up any flocks of sheep or herds of cattle.   Groups penetrated inland as far as Nicaea, capturing its outlying villages and committing appalling atrocities; they tortured and massacred the inhabitants, many of whom were part of a large Greek Christian community.   Finally, lured by the prospect of booty and treasure in Nicaea, and also hearing news of the Turkish army's approach, they decided to set off together from Cibotus.   (Peter had by this time lost his authority over the army and had returned to Constantinople, hoping to gain support from the Emperor). The Crusaders marched noisily and carelessly, their road taking them through a narrow wooded valley alongside the river Drakon.   Having planned an ambush the Turks waited silently and, at the appropriate moment, launched their attack.   Confusion reigned.   Those that could fled back to the camp but they were all slaughtered in the end.   A few managed to blockade themsleves in a castle by the sea, Alexius organising their rescue by sending a ship from Constantinople.   The People's Crusade was over.

Emperor Alexius then faced increasing problems for now the main armies of the Crusade were approaching Constantinople.   When he asked for aid he had no idea that he would be inundated by these vast armies. Estimates as to the size of the army ranged from sixty thousand to six hundred thousand, but these included countless camp followers: servants, traders, and the usual hangers on both male and female.   Besides feeding them he had to placate their leaders.   Of the numerous princes and knights three groups were pre-eminent.   The first led by Godfrey of Bouillon, Duke of Lower Lorraine, accompanied by his brother Baldwin, marched his army along the road taken by his ancestor Charlemagne and also by Peter the Hermit.   A rumour spread that Godfrey had vowed to avenge the death of Christ with the blood of the Jews.   With this blackmail he raised a great deal of money from terrified Jewish communities.   Though they survived this ordeal, thousands were massacred at Worms and Mainz by subsiduary armies with blood lusting leaders.   The Bishops and inhabitants of the towns tried to protect their Jewish friends, but often without success.   Because of the havoc wrought by the People's Crusade, the Hungarians demanded Baldwin as a hostage before allowing Godfrey's army to cross their country. Discipline lasted until the Sea of Marmara was reached, where the soldiers went berserk and ravaged the countryside for eight days.   Order was eventually restored and they reached Constantinople in December, 1096.

Prince Raymond of Toulouse, together with Bishop Adhemar of Le Puy, led the second group of Provencals down the Adriatic coast and then due east to Constantinople.   They had an equally hazardous journey, beset by Slavs in Dalmatia and finding themselves desperately short of food in the midst of winter.   At the frontier they were met by envoys and imperial troops who were to convey them across Thrace. The Crusaders resented the restrictions imposed by the escort, necessary for keeping these large visiting armies to the main routes and preventing the plunder of the countryside. Relations between the two factions grew worse and skirmishes eventually gave way to a full blooded battle. The Crusaders were taught a severe lesson, and this subdued and crestfallen army reached Constantinople towards the end of April, 1097.

The third division was led by a Norman from southern Italy, Bohemond of Taranto. He invited his nephew Tancred to accompany him and, in front of his congregated army, tore his rich scarlet cloak in pieces to make crosses for his captains. His was the most disciplined, best equipped and well organised army. He took them by sea to Dyrrhachium (now Durazzo in Albania) and thence overland to Constantinople, forbidding them to pillage and plunder in Christian lands.

Alexius proved a wise but firm Emperor. As each leader arrived in Constantinople he persuaded them to take an oath of allegiance, whereby they promised to restore back to his rule any former Byzantine province recovered from the Turks. By May the last of the armies had been transported across the Bosphorus and, beginning their march across Asia Minor, they left Constantinople in peace.

Now we move on to Nicaea, the first of the cities in Turkish hands to be captured. The Crusaders marched cautiously up the valley still littered with the bones of the former catastrophe. The Seljuk Sultan, Kilij Arslan — nicknamed the Lionheart — had left Nicaea after the defeat of the People's Crusade and was away fighting on his eastern frontier, but he returned hastily upon receiving news of yet more approaching Crusaders. The Crusaders reached Nicaea first and surrounded the land walls, whilst the Sultan arrived soon afterwards and fought hard to try to re-enter his city. Godfrey and Bohemond were unable to leave their sections of the wall unguarded, so Raymond took the brunt of the attack. After a hard day's fighting the Sultan was forced to retreat into the mountains and leave the city to its fate.

The western side of the city that bordered the lake allowed free access to messengers and supplies, and created a problem for the Crusaders. They were obliged to ask the Emperor for help and he successfully transported a flotilla overland. The small garrison of Turks seeing the Byzantine ships on the lake, with no hope of rescue from their Sultan and knowing that a general assault was imminent, surrendered directly to the Emperor. They knew that Alexius treated his prisoners reasonably well, whereas they were likely to suffer à fate far worse in the hands of the infidels from the West. Both sides called each other 'infidels', the word spat out in utter contempt.

The Crusaders were furious at this arch trickery for they had hoped to take hostages themselves and pillage the riches of Nicaea. Instead they were only allowed into the city in small chaperoned groups, and these frustrations led to feelings of resentment against the Byzantines. However, the Emperor was diplomatically generous. The leaders were presented with gold and jewels from the Sultan's treasury, and a gift of food was offered to every soldier.

From Bursa our bus went back along the road to Gemlik and then turned inland to Lake Iznik. This ought to have been the route chosen by the Emperor to convey his ships overland to the lake. The terrain was flat, though further in distance than the mountainous way it was suggested they took. Martin retraced the Crusaders' route later in the day and reported that the road was indeed steep. The effort required to haul the ships – albeit on rollers – up the 'valley of bones' to the plateau and then down to Lake Iznik, must have been prodigious.

The scenery in this small area between sea and lake was most surprising. If I had been asleep and suddenly opened my eyes, I would have sworn that we were in English parkland; good pasture was interrupted by fine specimens of Turkey Oak and by the lake poplar and silver birch predominated. The road traced the shore winding through small villages seemingly unaccustomed to buses, even though they pass several times a day. Young school children, girls in their black dresses with white collars and boys in black jackets, were taking their break by the water's edge. We could see across the width of the lake to the hills rising behind, but its length – 30 kilometres – meant that it was some time before the city situated on the eastern shore came into sight.

The best view of Iznik was undoubtedly from a distance, the ancient defence walls and massive towers giving the illusion of its former greatness. Founded by a general in Alexander's army, Antigonus the One-Eyed in 316 B.C. and renamed Nicaea after the wife of Lysimachus, King of Thrace, it was subsequently occupied by Romans and Byzantines. The Seljuk Turks took possession in the eleventh century but were ousted by the armies of the First Crusade: as a result of the Fourth Crusade Iznik became the capital of the surviving remnants of the Byzantine Empire. Following a prolonged siege Orhan Gazi – the Ottoman Sultan – captured the city in 1331, and at the beginning of the following century Iznik was plundered by Tamerlane. Resilient as ever, the city again became famous for the ceramic tiles it produced during the height of the Ottoman Empire, but when the industry was transferred to Istanbul in the eighteenth century its decline began, the final devastation occurring during the Graeco-Turkish war of 1922.

Another example of the Turks' natural desire to help was demonstrated at the bus station. ' We asked for the Tourist Information as soon as we arrived and a dolmuss driver insisted on taking us there himself, refusing payment. The girls in the office were helpful too, one speaking a little English and Andrew being able to communicate with the other in German. They gave us a map on which they encircled the town's most important features.

The Hospice of Nilufer Hatun was the nearest. Murad I commissioned it in 1388 in memory of his mother, a Greek princess who had married Orhan Gazi, thereby cementing the Byzantine-Ottoman alliance. This accomplished woman administered the Empire when the Sultan was away on campaigns. The hospice, now a museum, contained a wealth of

Roman relics as well as coins and pots and old Iznik tiles.* A sarcophagus with clear bas-reliefs took pride of place in the centre of the hall,
but the most captivating Roman fragments were to be found in the
garden; columns, stones, small decorated arches and more sarcophagi
were laid in rows inviting inspection. Even more diverting was the sight
of a stork nesting in a decapitated minaret. Storks loved Iznik for there
were many of these crumbling minarets providing perfect nesting places.
The one belonging to the mosque opposite was intact, built about the
same time as the neighbouring hospice. Unfortunately, due to earthquakes and war, the original turquoise ceramic tiles had been destroyed
and the ones now providing the decoration were inferior imitations from
Kutahya.

Apparently there were no tiles within the Yesil Mosque, but that did
not deter me from wanting to peep inside. I bent down to take off my
shoes and realised that I would have bare feet. That morning as the day
promised to be hot, I had put on canvas shoes and shed my tights,
completely forgetting the procedure required before entering a mosque.
When Muslims pray they bend forward repeatedly, placing their foreheads
on the floor, so the reason for making everyone remove their shoes was
purely a matter of cleanliness. A sadirvan for the purpose of ritual
washing was to be found outside every mosque and was generally an
object of beauty in itself. The larger mosques often had a row of taps
with a stone seat conveniently placed in front of each spout. Perhaps I
ought to have felt guilty for not washing my feet in respect for their
religion? Anyhow, I squeezed my toes together and ventured inside. A
cleaner was brushing the carpets after having first sprinkled them with
water; it felt as if I were walking on dew, a pleasant sensation, and I
relaxed. The cleaner proudly showed me his carpets, the decorated
mimber and two enormous candles either side of the marble mihrab.

Nicaea (Iznik) was laid out on the Roman plan. There were four
main gateways with two long straight streets crossing at right angles in the
centre, the others running parallel to each other. Three of the gates
remained standing. Yenisehir Gate, the first we encountered on arriving
from the south was impressive, though the road no longer went through it
but between a gap in the walls at one side. A similar by-pass method was
used for the north Istanbul Gate, a sensible idea allowing a free flow of
traffic and enabling one to walk unmolested under the old arches and
admire various details. The eastern Lefke Gate was still being used by
traffic, which resulted in chaos caused by lorries and tractors and trailers
carrying goods and farm produce. Because of the narrow gap only one
could pass at a time, therefore, in order to inspect the outside walls, I had
to dodge hooting vehicles and was nearly suffocated by the dust. The

---

* The early tiles were of a special quality, famous for their turquoise, blue, clear
yellow and coral-red. The distinctive coral-red was only used for about forty-five
years from the mid sixteenth to the early seventeenth century, when the secret of the
ingredients died with its inventor.

diesel fumes were dreadful as the drivers revved their engines impatiently, and the whole scene discouraged lingering.   Later, when making my notes, I could not remember much about this gateway, nor whether its arches contained any special features.   The Istanbul Gate was easy to recall for I had spent some time admiring the solid central arch with its two side alcoves.   The recess in the archway above had once portrayed a scene depicting an historical event, and the beginning of a third arch, higher still, presumably framed a statue.   I consulted our two guide books that evening to check the facts, only to be thrown into total confusion. The first one said, 'The Lefke Gate was built in honour of Hadrian's visit in A.D. 120.'   The second contradicted this by stating that the Istanbul Gate had, 'a central triumphal arch erected to commemorate Emperor Hadrian's visit in A.D.123.'   (They never agreed about dates).   The first book described the Hadrian's arch mentioned in the second guide book, as having been erected by Vespasian.   All rather bewildering!

We wanted to see the Ulu Cami, formerly St. Sophia and Nicaea's most important monument.   Two Ecumenical councils had been held there, one in 325 convened by Emperor Constantine and the second in 787 by Empress Irene.   From the Lefke Gate the street stretched before us without even the lake at the end in sight.   Large silver limes and chestnuts provided welcome shade for there were no buses in the town nor any waiting taxis, and we had to use Shanks' pony.

St. Sophia by the central cross roads was a sorry sight, a mere fraction of its former glory.   At one time restored by Sinan, the final destruction had been wrought during the fighting in 1922.   The iron gates were padlocked and a passer-by, besides retrieving Andrew's pen which had fallen out of his back pocket, pointed to a notice displaying opening times.   St. Sophia was shut between twelve and two o'clock and our watches showed four minutes past midday.   We could practically see everything from the gate so open were the ruins, except for a mosaic and a fresco said to be there.   When Andrew and I returned later in the afternoon, it was still shut.

Smart houses bordered the road that led from St. Sophia to the lake, their gardens full of blossom and colour and roses expertly trained to cover bare walls.   Acacias which flower sparsely and irregularly with us, were laden with sweetly scented hanging racemes.   The lake was more than a lake, the impression gained being that of the Mediterranean; gently lapping waves broke onto a shore edged with pine trees, fishing boats remained stationary on the water, and the varying blues of lake and sky met on the horizon giving no hint of land at the far end.   We noticed a few hotels set back from the road, but though their positions were perfect they seemed neglected and almost derelict.   The motel in which we had originally planned to stay looked more promising, with individual chalets and pine trees in the garden.   Appearances are often deceptive; dining room tables were laid but no one was eating.   We ordered drinks outside and they were brought to us by a waiter with conjunctivitis.   All at once I felt distinctly chilly, not only because a breeze was blowing from the lake, but also because the atmosphere was depressing. The others sensed this too, and we were glad that we had followed the advice of our Turkish friend on the ferry and were returning to Bursa for the night.

We decided to have lunch at the more promising of two lakeside restaurants and chose our food from the display counter — a selection of mezes and fish. Andrew complained that his smoked variety tasted peculiar but his half bottle of local wine must have drowned any misgivings. Martin had beer to drink and I chose a refreshing fizzy mineral water called Maden Su; with fruit to finish the whole meal was remarkably cheap. We were entertained by the antics of the owner and a friend who, with some difficulty owing to the increasing wind, were attempting to put up an awning, and also by some boys sitting patiently on a low wall trying to catch fish.

After following the shore for about a kilometre we turned inland across a field and meandered beneath the ancient walls. Fig trees grew out of the towers their branches laden with fruit which would swell and ripen later in the year. Although I adore figs, I wished that I could make them wither at a glance, as had occurred in the Gospel story, because eventually their roots would destroy these splendid towers and add to the decay of the city. In this south-west section another arched gateway, the Saray Gate, enabled us to enter the safety of the garrison, though barking and snapping dogs made us glad of our rabies injections. There were fewer houses in this area and each had a piece of land including a vegetable garden. Not a single weed was visible amongst the rows of healthy looking plants. The Turks appeared to be tidy; we never noticed any rubbish lying about and their store of wood for the winter was always neatly stacked.

The Roman Theatre we had come to visit was a disappointment. Only the grading of the grass-covered depression indicated the seating area, nevertheless, one could still appreciate its magnificent setting. At the back where a few arches remained standing, one tunnel had survived with an entrance to the arena. This evoked the excitement of bygone spectacles and Andrew and Martin were convinced that lions and bears had been kept in the tunnel for entertainment. Their imagination was running riot as both guide books agreed that this was a theatre built by Pliny the Younger when he was governor of Bithynia, and not an amphitheatre.

Back at the autogar (bus station, and also known as the garagi) our ways parted. Martin wanted to travel the Crusaders' route over the hills and down the 'valley of bones' to the coast. I had noticed on a postcard for sale in the main street, a picture of two elegant peacocks. They were in a tomb outside the city and this I very much wanted to see. Andrew chose to come with me. Besides his gallant concern for my welfare, I had a feeling that the peacocks held sway over the Crusaders' tramping feet. He had left his Berlitz behind and because I pretended that I knew exactly where I wanted to go, promising it would only take an hour, I had to make the arrangements. With the tourist map in hand I approached the

manager of the autogar. I pointed and talked slowly.
"Here to the museum. Key — I demonstrated turning the lock —
from museum guardian. Museum to Istanbul Gate and catacomb. Catacomb back to museum and autogar." He picked up the telephone and
after a rapid conversation quoted a price. I was delighted at my success
and forgot all about bargaining.

Andrew approached the museum keeper at The Hospice of Nilufer
Hatun, whom we had already met earlier in the day.

"Why did you not ask to go this morning?" he complained, "I am so
busy this afternoon. Look, a coach has just arrived." Despite his
grumbles a guide was spared with a key.

The fifth century tomb had only been discovered in 1967. Seven
kilometres away — the final stretch along a dusty road — it turned out to
be simply a hump barely visible in the surrounding countryside with an
iron door at one end. The guide unlocked the door and we went inside.
It took a few minutes for our eyes to adjust to the darkness and then to
realise with horror what exactly had caused this totally unexpected scene
— vandals. Chisel marks had ruined the heads of those majestic peacocks,
the despoilers trying to get behind the far semicircular wall to find
treasure. Flagstones had been ripped up, with wax still showing where
candles had stood giving the hooligans light to perform their dastardly
deeds. They had forced their way into the tomb by hacking at the stone
above the door. Two peacocks with open tail feathers on either side of
the entrance also had their heads obliterated. Our taxi driver was equally
shocked. He and the guide talked in subdued voices repeating, "Yeni,
yeni," which we found out afterwards to mean "new".

I suppose we were fortunate to have been allowed in here at all, so
we inspected what was left. Much still remained and, had we not known
that the paintings were intact until fairly recently, we would have been
loud in our praise. They were undoubtedly very beautiful and happily
not as garish as their picture reproduced on the postcard. The barrel
vaulted ceiling was decorated entirely with flowers and motifs in alternate small squares, and a geometric frieze gave a three dimensional effect.
The murals on the side walls were exquisite. The principal paintings
showed an acanthus base supporting a large bowl filled with pears, on top
of which was perched a partridge. Could this be the origin of 'a partridge
in a pear tree'? These pictures alternated with panels of geometric
design. Two charming french partridges filled the space above the door
and we left them guarding their treasure, hopefully with more care in the
future.

Andrew thanked the keeper of the museum and enquired about the
sad affair, but the wretched man could only hang his head in shame and
would not answer, apart from that fatal word "Yeni", so it was with a
certain degree of sadness that we left Iznik in a dolmuss bound for
Yenisehir. This meant that we returned to Bursa by a different route,
always more fun. I was sure that the dolmuss was being driven in the
wrong direction, and this was so, but only in order to collect a passenger's

wife.   She was escorted from the house by her husband: presumably it would have been undignified for her to have walked to the autogar. They were both young and smartly dressed, he in a well-cut suit and she in a coat despite the warm weather, and with a scarf covering her hair. We wondered whether their marriage had been arranged?   Though strongly denied that this practice still exists, it undoubtedly remains the custom outside the principal cities.   An older couple occupied the front seat next to the driver and in each case the woman sat by the window, for it was against Muslim tradition to come into any form of contact with a man other than her husband.   I found subsequently that when coaches were full I was asked to move from my seat next to Andrew, in order to sit with a woman and prevent her embarrassment.

We climbed through olive groves, the dolmuss lurching round hairpin bends when, for no apparent reason, the driver suddenly stopped. He turned round and asked whether I would like to take a photograph? I was amazed at his thoughtfulness and, as none of the passengers seemed to mind waiting, climbed out to make a record of this last view of Iznik looking so lovely at the head of the lake.   I changed my mind and wished now that we were staying for a night, for then I would have had time to walk around the city walls, visit other mosques and climb into St. Sophia to see its mosaic and fresco.   I might even have caught fish in the lake or, best of all, found a bear in the tunnel under the Theatre — another time perhaps?

We still had a long way to go.   The dolmuss stopped in Yenisehir and we had to change for Bursa, the last dolmuss leaving in twenty minutes.   The guide book said that Yenisehir possessed a fine mosque, but there comes a stage in the day when one must call a stop to sight-seeing.   Anyhow, the time factor was against us and I wanted to keep the Roman tomb uppermost in my memory.

We both dozed on the journey and climbed stiffly out at Bursa.   A dolmuss — dormobile — was definitely not as comfortable as a bus on a journey of more than one hour.   The centre of the town was a long uphill struggle from where we had been deposited.   There we found another type of dolmuss, this time our shared car of yesterday, which climbed more easily to our hotel.   The Turkish bath was invigorating, and at dinner in the second and best of the two neighbouring restaurants, Martin recounted his adventure.

He had succeeded in following The Crusaders' path albeit in the opposite direction.   His dolmuss had dropped him half way along the northern shore of Lake Iznik by a turning which led inland.   He had hitched a lift on a truck which unfortunately came to its journey's end in a village on the plateau.   There he sat in the local café for two hours, carrying on disjointed conversations with the villagers and sipping three glasses of tea.   They all knew from whence he came and where he wanted to go.   At half past five the owner of the only village car, having woken from his siesta, arrived with his vehicle prepared to take Martin to the coast from where he could catch a bus back to Bursa.   A hair-raising drive ensued down a steep twisting road, and from his description we agreed that the Crusaders would indeed have found the ascent arduous. They should have crossed the pass from Yalova taking the fourth Roman road, the one we had followed in our coach the previous day which was not nearly as precipitous. By the time we had finished our bottle of wine we had reorganised the campaign, and reckoned that the Emperor too was utterly incompetent if he had not instructed his ships to sail further along the coast to Gemlik, and used the easy route — the parkland which we had driven across that morning — for the overland passage of his ships to Lake Iznik.

A stork nesting on a ruined minaret, Iznik

Istanbul Gate

DAY V : BURSA TO ESKISEHIR

We arrived too late: the dolmuss to Bilecik was already full. We had been delayed at the hotel unable to retrieve our travellers cheques and passports because the manager, who kept the key to the safe, failed to turn up. Panic ensued and a boy was sent to try to find him after a telephone conversation revealed that he had left his home and, irritatingly, decided on some other port of call. By the time we reached the bus station the tickets were sold out and we had no alternative but to buy ones to Eskisehir; even then we barely managed to secure seats on a coach that left at half past ten.

The autogar was large and busy. Five different companies covered the main routes each with their own booth plastered with signs and the names of the towns they served. At least three men sat behind each desk, and a fourth darted backwards and forwards bellowing the names of his company's towns, and pouncing on any new arrivals to persuade them to travel on his bus. Ideally one should compare the prices offered, but this is difficult to do when being hustled and harrassed amidst the noise and shouting. Tickets were cheap, and there was no doubt that this was the most economical way of seeing Turkey. The coaches were comfortable too, some with reclining seats and the grand ones even having air conditioning. Coaches connected main towns, buses ran from towns to villages and dolmusses served less popular routes. Every form of transport left punctually, the only tiresome point was the inability to book an onward ticket. If one wanted to get off the bus to do some sightseeing, there seemed to be no way of finding out at the departure terminal whether a connection existed. Invariably there was some form of transport, providing we did not leave it too late in the day, but it would have helped considerably if only we could have known before setting out.

Quite soon after leaving the conductor would come round pouring eau de cologne into passengers' cupped hands. I found it refreshing and the smell soon disappeared. Bottled water was available kept in a cool box at the back of the bus. This was a great innovation and I always accepted a drink for, besides quenching my thirst, I enjoyed the variation of taste to be found between the local springs.

The drivers were experienced, though some drove too fast. I did not mind unduly provided we were not given the best seats — those immediately behind the driver — where I could see and anticipate illusory accidents on the road ahead. The driver or the conductor would frequently turn on the radio or play tapes, so we were regaled with a miscellany of music ranging from western pop to the wail of the East. One of the joys of travelling by bus was that one could read. Andrew frequently studied his Berlitz and muttered sentences that sounded Greek to me, but I think Martin just stared at the passing scenery, imagining that he was charging into battle on the back of a Crusader's horse.

We were leaving Bursa.   Mt. Olympus, the summit still covered with snow, rose majestically to our right, the road crossing the plain to Yenisehir shortly branching off to our left.   Groups of women dressed in brightly coloured baggy trousers gathered at the waist and ankles, and shawls over their heads, toiled in the fields.   With short-handled inverted hoes they worked backwards hacking away at the rock-hard soil, breaking it up and removing any weeds.   The only men we ever saw were invariably sitting on tractors.   To be fair, on the smaller farms they guided ploughs pulled by oxen, often over land that looked so stony and dry that one wondered whether anything could grow.   They sowed by hand, scattering the corn from left to right in the old biblical tradition, while at the other end of the scale sophisticated equipment was used for spraying crops. Irrigation was another major land investment that evidently, by the resulting yields, was immensely successful.   Turkey is entirely self-supporting, a fact of which they are understandably proud.

We left the plain behind and drove through a forest of lime trees which presently became interspersed with pine, the two shades of green providing a striking contrast.   Eventually pine took over completely, the altitude affecting this subtle change; and soon we were on the plateau with another fertile plain stretching before us leading ultimately to Eskisehir.

Having had time to consult the guide books I read that there was nothing of note in Eskisehir itself, the chief places of interest necessitating day excursions.   .Arriving in the early afternoon we would waste half a day so, borrowing Martin's map, I schemed.   Martin had wanted to go to Bilecik because the Crusaders had been there.   After leaving Iznik they had marched east along the old Byzantine road that crossed Asia Minor. On the banks of the River Sangarius (Sakarya) this road was joined by another coming south from Nicomedia (Izmit).   It continued south to Linoe (Bilecik), south-east to Gordoserba (Sogut), and eventually descended to the plain and Dorylaeum (Eskisehir).   I saw that if we left the bus at Bozuyuk, we would surely be able to get another to Bilecik and rejoin the Crusaders on the final stage of their march to Eskisehir.   The bus was full and I was by now sitting next to a mother and baby, so it meant passing the map back to Andrew and Martin.   When no immediate exclamation of delight was forthcoming, I squeezed past some standing passengers, repeated my suggestion, and remarked rather petulantly that I thought that it was pretty feeble to give up so easily, and anyhow *I* would like to tread the path of the Crusaders.   They kindly said that they would take my suitcase on for me; fortunately they were only teasing, for when I nervously climbed down from the bus at Bozuyuk, they came too.

Luckily we only had to cross the street, wait for a quarter of an hour and a mini bus appeared bound for Bilecik.   The road branched north and we followed the River Sakarya up a delightful valley where wild acacia and pyracantha grew, both covered with white blossom, and garden restaurants served fresh trout.   The bus climbed, the dirt surface and

50

surrounding countryside becoming more dusty when rounding a corner, we spied Bilecik nestling against the hillside. The guide book said that there were gracious Ottoman houses, half stone and half timber with their own gardens and also, down a ravine, the Orhan Gazi Cami one of the most ancient of the Ottoman mosques. Both of these I had to see.

The autogar was below the town. Martin went into the office to make inquiries about transport, returning with the news that there were no buses to Sogut and the dolmuss was fully booked; so he opened discussions with a taxi driver. I hovered as I did not want to miss my mosque, and occasionally interrupted by mentioning its name. We were not making much progress, the prices suggested by the Turk appearing too high. Not being fluent in Turkish each sum mentioned had to be written down on a piece of paper, crossed out, and an alternative one offered. Then the names of the towns, Sogut and Eskisehir would be repeated and the whole rigmarole would recommence. My grandmother used to say in her slow musical voice, "Something will occur," and sure enough a young Turk who spoke excellent English came to our aid. He discovered that the taxi driver had no desire to drive the whole way to Eskisehir, which was why he was raising the price, but was willing to take us to Sogut from whence, he suggested, a bus would complete the journey. Unfortunately, no one knew the time of that particular bus. We thanked our friend profusely and I quickly went to buy some rolls and aroma juice for lunch, from one of the numerous counters that were always to be found at bus stations.

We had some difficulty explaining to the taxi driver that first of all we wanted to walk round the town, leaving our suitcases in his car. The complication of fixing a time to meet, plus the realisation that the town was further than we had anticipated, made us decide to drive there instead. The driver immediately plunged down an earth track into the ravine.

"What about the town?" I cried.

"Cami, cami," came the reply.

The mosque was probably built in the first half of the thirteenth century, plain both inside and out except for some 'z' carving round the eaves. Two nineteenth century minarets stood sentinel, while the stump of the original jutted from a nearby rock. I climbed up to it and found a happy gathering of women. One prayed, kneeling on the grass facing Mecca, while the others were sewing and chatting. It was the first time I had been close to such a natural group and they smiled at me and I smiled back, bowing my head according to the custom of the land. By the end of my visit to Turkey I found this action quite natural, a polite way of saying hello and goodbye and thank you, and all the words I had not learned or could not pronounce in Turkish. One of the women approached and presented me with some home-baked bread wrapped up in a newspaper. I bowed and thanked her in English, but we understood each other perfectly. She had such a kind face.

Other women were making their way along a narrow path leading to a tomb which contained two coffins covered with drapes, one bearing the name of Orhan Gazi. He was the son of Osman Gazi, the son of Ertugrul Gazi the founder of the Ottoman Turks. Orhan captured Iznik and Bursa, and married the Greek princess whom I mentioned in the previous chapter. His official tomb was in Bursa so I cannot begin to explain the presence of this second tomb. The women were treating it with great reverence. Having left their shoes outside, they raised their hands to Allah and then bowed their heads and crossed their arms over their breasts, murmuring all the while. I looked up and down and around, without the movements and mutterings, inspecting the tiny monument. The women did not appear to mind my intrusion, behaving naturally because there were no men about. Andrew and Martin had remained near the mosque, wisely leaving the women to their hallowed ground, and were talking to three military gentlemen with guns slung over their shoulders who seemed fairly surprised to see tourists in this area. When any Turk discovered that we were English he entered into conversation. He invariably either had a friend who owned an English dictionary or an English book or better still, he had a friend who knew someone in England, more often than not working in a hotel in a totally unexpected town like, in this instance, Scarborough.

The taxi driver was waiting patiently, but as soon as we clambered aboard he roared off keeping to the valley and leaving Bilecik above us. "The town, the town," I cried. Slowly we deciphered his babble. He was tired and wanted to deliver us to our destination and return home to sleep. I was all for thrusting some money in front of his eyes and I am sure he would have about-turned sharply, but Andrew and Martin said that it was late and we still had to catch a bus from Sogut; besides, I had had my quota of sightseeing for the day. I opened my parcel of aromatic bread which tasted delicious. Stuffy Martin and Andrew would not even sample it, so I gave them the stale rolls I had bought at the bus station and munched my way through the gift from the woman, consoling myself with thoughts of my private encounter.

The landscape was attractive with scrub oak covering the hillside up to the level of the open plateau. I spotted some hellebores peeping from beneath the oak, my first wild flowers. They must have been the variety orientalis, but before I could extricate my camera from the rucksack, we had sped past. One more missed opportunity. I never saw another hellebore. That time it was my fault, I should have shouted, "Stop, stop!"

Despite the driver's anxiety to return quickly he parked unprompted at a cemetery. A row of busts stood outside with identical faces but wearing different headgear. Their name plates told us that they were Attila the Hun, Genghis Khan, and the most famous Seljuks, Mongols and Ottomans who had arrived from the East and had conquered and ruled in Asia Minor. Ertugrul Gazi had made Sogut his capital, and was buried in the restored turbe set in pleasant surroundings with young cedars, old oaks and pines.

The driver left us at the bus station where we discovered that we had a two hour wait for the bus to Eskisehir. That, incidentally, was the longest delay we were to experience in Turkey, and an example of how useful it would have been if only we could have found out times at the bus station in Bilecik which, after all, was only 29 kilometres away. I never minded waiting for I always had my diary to write, guide books to check where we were going the next day – making sure that I would not miss anything – and Steven Runciman's 'The First Crusade'. A Turk approached our table and surreptitiously showed Andrew an ancient coin, but it was so worn that he was unable to decipher the Latin inscription.

I could not leave Sogut unexplored so went for a stroll along its cobbled streets. The houses built of stone and wood were presumably in the same style as those that I had missed in Bilecik, but smaller and without flower gardens. The men sat around in groups, while the women were undoubtedly busy in their houses or working in the fields. Two enormous trees, a silver poplar and an oriental plane, dwarfed a nineteenth century mosque erected on the site of the original built by Ertugrul.

As I sauntered into the bus station I was greeted with a change of plan. It transpired that the bus to Eskisehir was fully booked, but why we had not been told in the first place was inexplicable. The reason may have been that Martin's original question was,

"When is the next bus to Eskisehir?" and after the reply,

"Five o'clock," had not followed it up with,

"Three tickets, please." Since we sat down to wait, it must have been obvious that we were planning to take that specific bus, the only one due to leave Sogut. Not until Martin produced money for the tickets a whole hour later was he told that they had all been sold. A Turk with a car was forthcoming and after the inevitable haggling over the price, condescended to drive us to Eskisehir.

The descent from the plateau was not unduly steep and, for the Crusaders camping on the last day of June, 1097, this fertile plain with its fresh springs must have been a welcome relief from the hot dusty hills. The army had split in two purely to ease the problem of supplies, the second section due to follow a couple of days later. Bohemond was leader of the first, Raymond of Toulouse of the second.

Meanwhile the Sultan, Kilij Arslan, after his failure to relieve Nicaea had withdrawn eastward and made peace with the Danishmend Emir. With his own troops, his new ally and his vassals the Cappadocian Turks, he lay in ambush near Dorylaeum (Eskisehir). At sunrise on the first of July, with blood-curdling yells he swooped down over the hills. The Crusaders quickly formed a circle, the women and those unable to fight in the centre, while a messenger was dispatched to the remainder of the army, urging them to hasten to the rescue.

Bohemond told his troops to remain in their places and to fight a defensive battle. One knight disobeyed his orders and charged with his forty men, only to be driven back humiliated and covered with wounds. The Turkish army was huge and showers of arrows fell continuously on

53

the Christians. They knew they had to fight to the bitter end as either way they would be killed or massacred. The women proved their worth by bringing water to the thirsty soldiers and coping with the wounded. At last, around midday, their comrades arrived and managed to force an entry to the camp. The Crusaders formed a long front line and began to take the offensive. The crushing blow to the Turks came from an inspired manoeuvre planned by Adhemar, the Bishop of Le Puy. He had not joined the main army, but hired guides who led his soldiers to the hills from where the Turks had launched their attack. They appeared over the brow and the Turks, realising the battle was lost, took flight to the east. Being nomadic tribesmen they had journeyed with their entire possessions and treasures. In their hurried departure everything was left behind, so their ultimate defeat was emphasised by the capture of their great white tents.

Although many lives had been lost, the Crusaders admired the way the Turks had fought against them. They preferred to give praise to their enemy rather than acknowledge the part played by the accompanying Byzantine army whom they now despised. This was aggravated by the fact that the regained territory now had to be restored to the Emperor, to whom they had sworn an oath of allegiance in Constantinople. There was no doubting the greatness of the victory and, more important, it ensured the safe passage of the Crusaders across Asia Minor.

All too soon we were back to the noise and bustle of a modern city, Eskisehir being the fifth largest in Turkey with a comparatively new growth in industry. In the foyer of our hotel, in which long-term business men had also opted to stay, we met a Scot and a Finn. The Scot was full of fun and always on the point of going out to meet Turkish friends for a meal, invariably carrying a plastic bag concealing a bottle of some kind of liquid refreshment. He was there for nine months helping to set up a factory for Fords, while the Finn was similarly organising the running of a chipboard factory; but more of him later.

We were anxious to see our rooms, and as we emerged from the lift we thought that we had entered a prison. The bedrooms on each of the three floors were arranged round an open space, though the absence of safety nets and the addition of carpets and potted plants relieved the dour impression. Our room was hot and stuffy, windows in hotels always being kept permanently shut. That was easy to cure, the joke being the washing area in one corner where the lavatory, basin and a hand shower were in a minute square separated from the bedroom by a plastic curtain. I could not see an outlet for the water from the shower, though on experimenting traced the flow to a hole hidden behind the loo; and the drains stank.

Martin has a knack of making helpful friends, the first being the lecturer on the ferry from Istanbul to Yalova; now he had entered into conversation with a middle-aged Turk. Martin wanted to visit King Midas' tomb the following day so had ventured as usual to the bus terminal to seek information; for some unknown reason he'd had no success. His new friend helped him solve the mystery. First we had to find our way to Seyitgazi, 44 kilometres south-east of Eskisehir, and then complete the journey by taxi. The bus for this small town was tucked away in a back street which Martin admitted he would never have found without his guide. Having learned from the mistake of the dolmuss, he bought tickets there and then.

We celebrated the successful conclusion of arrangements with a drink, Andrew and the Turk ordering local beer, Martin his usual gin and tonic also made in Turkey, while I asked for a double freshly squeezed orange juice with ice that I had seen the Finn drinking. It turned out to be far the most expensive item. The conversation was enthralling. The men discussed for at least half an hour the merits and failings of various football teams. Like our friend on the ferry this Turk knew all our players. He also boasted of his home town's success against Trebizond, the mighty Trebizond who had recently beaten Liverpool.

We dined in the restaurant next door which was full of Turks, always a recommendation for good food. Decor was obviously unimportant, the large room painted white, but the babble of voices and a band playing western-type music provided an amusing contrast. At all the tables the Turks sat not alternately man and woman, but the men on one side facing the women on the other. The young women were attractive, well dressed but like the bride in Bursa, rather made up; the older women tended to plumpness, while the men looked contented and prosperous.

I always took two bottles of plain water up to our bedroom, for I did not like the idea of having to drink tap water if I were thirsty during the night. I just remembered to do this but was too sleepy to write my diary, the endless buses, dolmuss — no, that was wrong, we had missed the dolmuss — taxis and minibuses were all spinning through my mind and causing total confusion. We had clambered in and out of so many during the day that I would have to sort them out the following morning. However, I could still taste the herb bread and see vividly the kind bright eyes of the Turkish woman who had been so friendly.

DAY VI : KING MIDAS

Many a splendid legend surrounds Midas, King of Phrygia. He mixed wine with the water of a spring and succeeded in making Silenus intoxicated. Silenus — a companion to Dionysus — was thus induced to teach King Midas the secrets of wisdom. Dionysus, as a reward for having Silenus returned to him, allowed Midas a wish. Midas wished that everything he touched would turn to gold; as this included food he nearly starved, and pleaded that the gift might be rescinded. In order to achieve this, Dionysus bade him dive into the river Pactolus which has had gold in its sands ever since.

Midas was made to judge between the divine lyre of Apollo and the pipes of Pan. He decided in favour of the latter which understandably made Apollo furious, and in his wrath he caused Midas to grow asses' ears. Midas was able to disguise his growth from everyone save his barber who, bursting to tell the secret, was driven to digging a hole in the ground and whispering the terrible story to the earth. Then he quickly filled it in, but reeds sprang upon the spot and swaying in the slightest breeze took up the tale murmuring, "King Midas has asses' ears!"

We were off to see King Midas' tomb. It had been discovered in 1800 by a party of Europeans, amongst them a Captain Leake who had attempted to decipher the inscription. He recognised a phrase that read 'to King Midas' and presumed the rock to be his tomb. No one has ever succeeded in penetrating the rock face in order to verify the truth, so the original interpretation has persisted, though subsequent investigations have recognised it to be a sanctuary to the Phrygian goddess Cybele. She was the earth goddess, the mistress of wild animals, protector of mankind and guardian of the dead; her cult was adopted by the Greeks and Romans, and was officially established in Rome in 204 B.C..

To reach King Midas' tomb above the village of Yazilikaya, we had been escorted by our friend of the previous evening to the elusive bus station. Arriving in plenty of time we were given glasses of tea and ushered to the seats reserved for V.I.P.'s, the ones I most disliked being directly behind the driver. Our friend would have joined us for he had never seen the tomb, but he had a more important engagement; he was going to watch his home town Eskisehir play Kayseri.

Once beyond the sprawling outskirts of Eskisehir, we found ourselves being driven across an arid plain with rising foothills on the horizon to relieve the monotony. From my vulnerable position I could see an obstruction some distance ahead; on drawing closer it turned out to be an accident, an overturned car, a body of a child covered with an overcoat, and the inevitable onlookers. Andrew and I stayed in our seats but at least half the occupants of our bus toppled out to gawp at the unfortunate incident; what had started as a family outing on a Sunday, Ataturk's adopted day of rest, had ended in tragedy.

56

An hour's drive brought us to Seyitgazi. Andrew and Martin went into the garage office to enquire and haggle over taxi fares. They were a good team by now and together managed to secure transport at reasonable prices, though it often took some time. I went in search of a loo. I was getting used to those holes in the ground; they were really very clean and more hygienic than many of our European counterparts. There was always a tap with either an old tin can or plastic jug, plenty of running water and basins. The only snag was the absence of any hand towels; but I noticed that other women produced their own, so it was I who was remiss.

Back at the bus station earnest discussions were still taking place. I noticed a small boy eating something that smelled delicious; many hours had passed since our early breakfast so I had reason to feel hungry. In sign language I asked him where he had bought his food, and he politely escorted me to a shop down a side street. The owner was kneading dough. He flattened a portion, sprinkled the top with a mixture of mince, tomatoes and onions, and placed it on a long-handled wooden platter which he thrust into an open oven; the finished product was wrapped in newspaper. I also bought some bottles of the fizzy mineral water, Maden Su, whose springs were in the locality, and three baclavas, for we had not as yet sampled this Turkish delicacy. The taxi was by now procured and we were off. Both Andrew and Martin declined to share my pizza-like concoction. When travelling I have noticed amongst fellow companions this reluctance to sample local food. Perhaps they fear upset stomachs, though modern medicine has provided pills to cope with such emergencies. It is impossible to learn everything about a country solely by looking at its buildings and scenery. Ideally the tourist should live with the people but nowadays the annual holiday is too short for that luxury.

I often wish that I could have attempted journeys such as those described by Freya Stark, and I would have loved to have ridden Aunt Dot's camel south from Trebizond described so amusingly by Rose Macaulay. Gertrude Bell was another intrepid explorer in Asia Minor travelling extensively at the turn of the century. She organised the hire of guides, porters, mules and horses, and although she took a certain amount of food with her she always either bought or accepted offerings from the natives, often grateful for curd, eggs or the occasional scraggy chicken.

Our dirt road took us along the Doganli valley. The ridges were covered with pine, and a great deal of effort had been spent clearing the fields and rendering them fit for ploughing. This back breaking job had been given to the women and I saw them bent double, heaving at the rocks and stones and putting them into piles, later to be moved by horse and cart. Two oxen driven by an old man were ploughing the eternally stony ground. Farming was hard work, even more so now for the young men had been lured by the expectance of higher wages to the towns, the ones from these villages to work in factories surrounding Eskisehir.

Whenever we approached a village barking dogs would leap towards the car. They looked extremely ferocious and I wondered if they would have shown such aggression had we been on the back of a horse.

Another curiosity was the absence of people in a village. Here, in the poor districts of Anatolia, no one had any time to loiter; even the children were put to work tending their goats or precious cows. None of them returned Andrew's wave, either they were not used to seeing tourists or it was against their religion to communicate with strangers. This will soon change for the road was being repaired — with stones from the fields — and in Yazilikaya a large black Mercedes was parked at the beginning of the walk to the acropolis. Our driver ascertained that the Minister of Tourism was amongst a group of dark-suited gentlemen, and was about to leave having examined the potential attraction of the site.

The City of Midas was in the heart of ancient Phrygia which covered most of central and north-west Asia Minor. The immigrant population came from Macedonia and were at the height of their power from 1500—1000 B.C.. Homer relates that they had helped King Priam during the siege of Troy in return for aid he had given to them in a battle on the banks of the river Sangarius. Their last King, who according to Greek historians reigned from 738—695 B.C., was the first foreign ruler to dedicate offerings to Apollo at Delphi. Shortly afterwards the Phrygians took the full force of an invasion by a Thracian people named the Cimmerians. By the time they had disappeared Phrygia was greatly enfeebled and fell under the domination of its neighbouring kingdom Lydia, which in turn was overrun by the Persians. Finally Alexander the Great passed through Gordion — their capital — in 334 B.C., where he was shown the Gordion Knot and told of the legend. An oracle had declared that the first man encountered approaching the Temple of Zeus was to be made King of Phrygia. Gordius, a peasant, arrived opportunely and having been crowned King dedicated his wagon to the god. The famous knot was the one which fastened the yoke to the pole; so artfully was it tied that the myth arose that whosoever unloosed the rope would gain the empire of Asia. No one throughout the countless centuries had succeeded. Alexander cheated: he drew his sword and slashed the knot in twain.

The Phrygians built their villages on the slopes of hills beneath rocky summits out of which they carved their rock tombs and ornamental facades. We found King Midas' tomb on a protruding spur of rock standing 32 metres high. A 20 metre square section was decorated with a meander pattern imitated from tapestry work and surmounted by a pediment above which were two volutes. This immense rock face stood out against the blue sky and dominated the countryside. The setting was magnificent with a wide valley skirting the acropolis. A decided nip in the air despite the sun made me glad of my cardigan; Andrew, climbing down a stairway chiselled out of stone, found hard packed snow in a cave. Part of the steps leading upwards had been worn smooth and were impassable, but higher up they continued before disappearing in a tantalising way behind a vertical crag. We explored many rock hewn sanctuaries and found another facade, but this time only the upper section of the pediment had been carved.

A handsome walnut tree was on the point of breaking into leaf and silver pears grew wild, their white flowers covering the branches with startling effect. Oreganum was beginning to spread over the stony surface, and the dried up spikes of last year's verbascum having shed their seed, would grow anew later in the season. There was much to expect from the coming summer months, the most important for the villagers being a good harvest. I wished King Midas' spirit would bless this land with, if not pure gold, at least a good crop of golden corn.

Every Turk we met or saw, smoked. Our driver was no exception; he lit up immediately he took his place behind the wheel and courteously offered Andrew and Martin a cigarette — though not to me assuming all women to be non-smokers. None of us smoked, but this was the precise situation where the duty free cigarettes Andrew had bought as presents would have proved invaluable, helping conversation and as a gesture of good will. We had repacked in Istanbul leaving behind a suitcase in order not to have so much to carry on our journey through Anatolia. Through some misunderstanding the cigarettes languished in the abandoned case. I handed around the baclavas. Martin and the driver refused but I managed to persuade Andrew to taste one; cut into small oblong pieces they were made of the thinnest flaky pastry soaked with honey and walnuts. He agreed that they were delicious and had a second! Thus revived we left Martin in Seyitgazi to drink his eagerly awaited beer and book seats on the bus back to Eskisehir. The driver whisked Andrew and me to the group of buildings on the citadel.

The main feature of this mosque complex was the tomb of Seyit Battal Gazi. He commanded one of the numerous Arab tribes that raided Asia Minor, and had died in 740 during a fierce battle against the Byzantines. The great warrior was much revered, but it was not until many centuries later that the mother of the Seljuk Sultan, Alaeddin Keykubad, had a dream which revealed his resting place. She found Battal's remains enshrined in a Christian convent, together with a Byzantine Princess who had died for the love of her slain hero. She immediately commanded a grand turbe to be built for them both. His coffin, covered in an embroidered green cloth was eight metres long symbolic of the valiant soldier, while that of his princess lay alongside draped in black. Alaeddin's mother also built a mosque in his memory, and Ottoman Sultans added a medrese, a minaret, other tombs and kitchens, for this shrine became the ninth resting place on the pilgrimage to Baghdad and Mecca.

We took a short cut back to the village, scrambling over walls and down a steep stony field to find the bus waiting in the village square. Martin had been able to secure the last remaining seat for me, a stool was produced for Andrew, while Martin and a couple of other men sat on the wide dashboard. Even so there was always room for more passengers, and anyone waiting by the side of the deserted road was automatically given a lift.   The overturned car was in the same position, an unnerving warning of the danger of speed.   However, there was no cause for anxiety, our driver was meticulous and would have passed any test with flying colours. As we approached the outskirts of Eskisehir those propping up the dashboard were asked to crouch low down, for around the next bend was a police car.   Apparently it was against the rules to overload a vehicle, and there were too many standing passengers to escape the notice of the law. The driver had to show his papers, but after a lot of amicable chat and the acceptance of a packet of cigarettes, we were allowed to continue our journey.

The football stadium was empty but everyone knew the result — Eskisehir had won 2—0.   We all felt exalted.   Andrew and Martin went to celebrate; I said that I would find my own way back and dived into a mosque.   Imposing and modern, it copied the traditional Ottoman style being tall, spacious and light.   Arabesque motifs decorated the dome and the walls were painted to simulate tiles.   I stood quietly at the back listening to the drone of chanted prayers and waiting until the congregation left before carrying out a closer inspection.   An imam approached and, opening his hands in the gesture of peace, said, "Welcome."

I wandered along an attractive part of the town where the river had been channelled into a canal and market stalls set up in the adjoining street.   Fountains were placed at intervals and, by the main road, miniature lakes with ornamental rockeries made an imaginative scene.   Back at the hotel I plucked up courage to operate the hand shower.   I really had no cause to complain for the water was hot and I could wash my hair. What impressed me more than anything was that the adaptor on my hair drier conformed to Turkish electrics.   We would have had none of these luxuries had we been riding; they were certainly preferable to ducking in an icy cold stream, but then I suppose we could always have waited until we reached a town and paid a visit to the local hamam.

Our friendly Scot was on the point of dashing out with his sagging plastic bag.   He and Andrew discussed places to eat, the guide book being unreliable as restaurants changed quickly according to managment and finances.   The Emet II to which we walked had been opened for three months, and it produced an excellent selection of mezes one of which was a local speciality, pounded chicken breasts mixed with chopped walnuts. My chicken kebab was incredibly tender, as too were Andrew and Martin's lamb variety, and much discussion went into the choosing of the wine. On the whole we found the red to be superior; some of the best came from Cappadocia and were burgundian in character.   One of our favourites had the somewhat improbable title of 'La Dolce Vita', while the most attractive white that we tasted was called Kulup.   My only criticism of this restaurant was the decoration.   Instead of enlarged posters displaying the wealth of Turkey's heritage, there were gawdy photographs of the Rocky Mountains and Texas.   I felt that I ought to summon the Minister of Tourism to issue a decree banning these scenes.   Even in the waiting room at the bus station there had been a picture of the Eiffel Tower instead of an elegant minaret.

At one of the tables a young couple talked animatedly.   A third person — possibly a younger brother — looked increasingly bored.   We suspected that he must be the chaperon for, though a seemingly modern town, old customs still existed.   An unhappy spectacle was the Finn to whom we had talked the previous evening in our hotel.   He was dining alone so we invited him to join our table.   He regaled us with a long and sad saga.   He worked for a chipboard firm and had travelled the world helping to set up factories.   By far his longest stint was here in Turkey. For eighteen months he had tried to organise a factory and teach the Turks to run it themselves.   His problems were endless, more so because the Turks hated taking orders from foreigners who were infidels.   The work force supplied had come from farming communities, and he had to teach them the basics including which way to tighten screws.   The hours were long and all the workers wished for was to earn enough money to buy a coloured television set.   He also had troubles at home. for leave was infrequent and his wife independent.   We had seen two extremes, this sad and troubled Finn weighed down with his anxieties, and the carefree Scot gaining the utmost satisfaction from his job abroad and making friends with the Turks, in fact the perfect ambassador for his country.

Mosque complex at Seyitgazi

Ploughing the stony fields in the Doganli valley

King Midas' tomb

DAY VII : AESANI

Andrew and Martin had not merely celebrated Eskisehir's victory the previous evening; they spent a considerable time organising today's sightseeing. Their investigations had started badly. Trying to discover the whereabouts of the Tourist Information, two policemen sent them in the opposite direction. When they finally located the bureau they made enquiries as to how to reach Aesani. I had heard Aesani described as, 'the best preserved Roman sanctuary in Asia Minor' and, because we had a day to spare, I had no difficulty persuading Andrew and Martin that a visit was essential. A session at the autogar had followed where they rejected a 7 a.m. start and voted for the midday bus.

We had to change buses in Kutahya which I longed to explore. Even though none of the ancient town of Cotyaeum existed, there were two Seljuk mosques one of which had been converted into a library; also a mescit — a small mosque equivalent to a chapel — and a medrese built in 1414 as an astronomical observatory and a school of science and mathematics, now a local museum showing examples of Kutahyan ceramics and Turkish arts and crafts.

Bayezid had married a Seljuk heiress and it was actually in Kutahya, on Tamerlane's way back to Samarkand, that he had committed suicide. The Ulu Cami, built in 1411 by his son Mehmet I, was dedicated to his memory. The best Ottoman mosque, the Huseyin Pasha Cami, was designed by Sinan and the town included the usual baths and a covered bazaar. The inevitable Byzantine fortress extensively repaired by the Seljuks and Ottomans dominated the acropolis but Kutahya's chief fame lay in its production of ceramic tiles. Persian craftsmen had been forced to settle in the town after Selim I's victorious campaign, and the tiles they produced were predominantly cobalt blue and milky white. They were second only to those manufactured in Iznik, eventually dominating the market after their rival's decline and adopting their colours, the renowned Iznik green and turquoise.

The autogar was on the outskirts of the town so that was all I saw of Kutahya. If we had caught the early bus we could have had the morning to explore the town, but Andrew and Martin were not sufficiently enthused by mosques to make the effort. The other alternative that I had tentatively suggested was to stay the night in Kutahya, for Aesani was 60 kilometres south-west of Kutahya, and we had already travelled 80 kilometres from Eskisehir. This idea however did not link with the march of the Crusaders. The following day we had a six hour journey to Konya, and Martin wanted to travel the route the army had taken starting from Dorylaeum (Eskisehir). This steered a south-easterly course across the arid plains of Anatolia. The road from Kutahya to Konya went south to Afyon before turning east to Konya. I would see many Seljuk mosques and medreses in Konya where we were to stay for three days, and also have a chance to inspect Kutahyan tiles in the Harem of Topkapi Palace on our return to Istanbul, so it was not worth making an issue of the matter and anyhow, we were as I had wished, on our way to the Roman remains at Aesani.

To my relief Andrew and Martin enjoyed the afternoon's sightseeing immensely. There was not a single fellow tourist at Aesani, the only other person being a Turk in uniform whom we found sitting disconsolately on a Roman tombstone. He jumped up when we arrived, his dark wrinkled face breaking into a welcoming smile anxious to show us every detail of the site. He only spoke a smattering of English, but Andrew and Martin were happy to practise their Turkish and followed his explanations with comparative ease.

The Temple of Zeus built around A.D. 125 in the reign of Hadrian, stood on a vast rectangular terrace. The neighbouring village of Cavdarhisar was scarcely visible behind rows of poplars, yet the temple could be seen for miles, while the backcloth of snow-capped mountains rose at the far end of the plain adding grandeur to the whole scene. An earthquake in 1970 had caused a considerable amount of damage dislodging the pediment with the head of Zeus, but the majority of corinthian columns remained standing. A remarkable feature was the existence of a large high-ceilinged chamber beneath the Temple floor to which we descended by means of a perilous iron staircase. Dedicated to the Phrygian goddess Cybele it contained her broken statue and stone fragments with a mass of Latin inscriptions. Andrew and Martin relished this form of calligraphy and vied with each other in making speedy translations. In the poor light the inscriptions were difficult to decipher; they had an easier time in the outdoor museum. To enter this the caretaker ceremoniously produced a key to unlock an iron gate, but the remaining security arrangements appeared somewhat innocuous, consisting of a double stranded barbed wire fence with a low wall on the fourth side. Within this area well preserved doorways and arches, fractured statues, capitals, stones with decorative carvings were placed in rows, and also some tablets laid out alluringly for Andrew and Martin's competition.

The baths and gymnasium were a field's distance away, a few broken walls marking out the basic plan. The caretaker became our guide and pointed out the various rooms and a tunnel where fires had been lit for heating the water. Scouring the floor he presented me with a collection of tiny coloured stones. He said that they were from the original mosaics; one was covered with gold leaf. I put them carefully into my purse, not realising that in the inevitable process of being knocked against each other the gilt would be scraped away and, by the end of the day, I was left with one that had changed from a glittering treasure to a dull white chip.

The Stadium and Theatre were even further away. We crossed a field sprouting this season's corn, followed a lane bordered by a wall combining the odd recognisable Roman stone, and crossed the smooth turf of the arena. How inviting this appeared; the stage was set and I fully expected to see horses charging out of the arched starting gates, their hooves thundering over the wide expanse of green with the cheers of the crowd urging their heroes to victory. The Stadium and the Theatre at the far end each had places for nine thousand spectators, enabling the local population to be accommodated. Part of the Theatre's side walls were intact and also quite a few sections of the stone seats. I slipped away to try to capture with my camera this haunting site.

The men sat idly on the lower benches no doubt discussing the merits of the Theatre. After a while they enquired about bus times and discovered from the guide that the last one to Kutahya was due 'any minute'. I was hailed, but they had no need to shout for I could hear very well, the acoustics after well nigh a thousand years still working perfectly. Watches were pointed at and we became the participants of a race running back the way we had come, alas, without the aid of horses and the only sound coming from our huffing and puffing. On reaching the side road the guide jumped on his bicycle, and raced to the main road in the centre of the village to try to delay the bus. I hailed my chariot in the form of a sedately chugging tractor. We climbed aboard sharing the trailer with two women who tittered behind their shawls at this unusual request. We stopped to let them off half way to our destination. I thought that we would have to leave our tansport too but the driver waved, indicating that we should remain seated, and set off with greater rapidity to the cross roads. He refused a tip but accepted a glass of tea. We had no time to drink ours for the bus lurched to a halt responding to our guide's signals, who anyhow was blocking its way by standing in the middle of the road. We shouted our thanks and clambered inside an already overloaded vehicle. Courtesy prevailed and I was offered a seat into which I gratefully sank.

Our fellow passengers, mostly children returning home from school, tried to converse. Their questions were always the same.

"What is your name?" "Do you speak English?" and, "Where you go?" We answered, named the list of towns we had visited to the accompaniment of the proverbial exclamations, and repeated the questions back to them. Giggles and only occasionally were answers forthcoming. We had to be careful what we discussed between ourselves, for invariably there was someone within earshot who had a surprisingly good command of the English language. .

The journey back seemed to pass more quickly for we were travelling downhill all the way. We crossed the ancient river Rhyndacus (Kocasu) by one of the Roman bridges so well constructed that many are still in use today. We left the plateau winding our way through juniper scrub to the valley below, and drove alongside the river Goksuyu whose waters were the colour of turquoise. One could be justified in thinking that the origin of the word came from this exquisite shade of blue-green, a feature of the rivers and lakes of Turkey. In fact it takes its name from the 'Turkish stone' – the turquoise – found originally in Turkestan. We changed buses again at Kutahya and arrived in Eskisehir at eight o'clock.

A vote of two to one meant that we had a good walk to the second of the restaurants suggested by our Scotsman, but I was promised a taxi for the return journey. Each building we passed had placards or posters in the windows up to two storeys high advertising the profession of its occupant. Besides endless lawyers, I have never seen so many doctors in residence. We debated whether it was the accepted procedure to call on a selection and discuss the price of consultation before treatment. The most amusing shop window besides displaying highly fashionable sports clothes, showed a model dressed in a khaki safari suit complete with topee, identical to the one Andrew had failed to buy in the Bursa market.

Martin was in a rather grumpy mood and we eventually discovered the reason. He had taken a great deal of trouble to explain to the washing lady in the hotel that he would like his favourite grey flannel trousers pressed, and only pressed. Obviously wanting to please she had decided to give them a good wash, with the result that they had shrunk. To aggravate the tension the restaurant was shut. Luckily the Emet II, where we had dined the previous evening, was quite close and we were soon cheered by another excellent feast, this time undisturbed by the neurotic Finn who had transmitted his despair the night before.

The enlarged posters of the Rocky Mountains with the emerald green lake in the foreground continued to annoy me. The Turkish turquoise was infinitely superior. Why not display Turkish scenes? After all the country offered superb scenery and a wealth of interesting places to visit. The Turks ought to make more of their historical achievements; they only have to look back to the greatness of Suleyman the Magnificent during whose reign the Turkish Empire was at its zenith. At that time Henry VIII ruled England, Francois I France and Charles V Spain. However none of these could compare with Suleyman. His territory was vast; he occupied Greece, his boundary stretched north to Budapest and he even threatened Vienna; he owned part of Russia, Georgia, Armenia, and land south to the Persian Gulf, Syria and Egypt were within his domain which continued on through North Africa including Libya, Tunisia and Algeria. Suleyman's army was superior to any of those in Europe and his navy controlled the Mediterranean. His architect, Sinan, rivalled Michelangelo who was struggling to raise the dome of St. Peter's. The splendours of his Court outshone all others and his domain included six of the seven wonders of the world. With this formidable achievement, a land rich in ancient dynasties each one contributing to the splendour of Turkey, surely something better could be found with which to decorate a restaurant than just a reproduction of the Rocky Mountains and views of Texas.

Head of Zeus

Temple of Zeus - Aesani

DAY VIII : AFYON

I preferred the bus of the previous day which had been full of school children to this one, the 7 a.m. to Afyon, crammed with farmers off to market. It was not the farmers I minded but the fact that each one smoked incessantly. Both Andrew and I found the atmosphere exceedingly unpleasant, especially at this early hour. The bus, of an older vintage, rattled its way along the straight roads to the accompaniment of racking coughs and squawking chickens in cardboard boxes.

A solid six hour journey from Eskisehir to Konya had not sounded especially tempting; a slight detour meant that Andrew and I could break our journey in Afyon and from all accounts the town appeared to be worth a visit. Martin had chosen to take the direct route to Konya to be certain of following the path of the Crusaders. Shortly after leaving Eskisehir I noticed a rather surprising signpost pointing ahead to Ankara. I had presumed that in order to reach Afyon we would have to drive through Kutahya which I knew was in the opposite direction to Ankara. By a strange coincidence our bus driver had taken the longer but possibly superior road to Afyon, and I realised that we too were travelling along Martin's road.

There were a number of roads the Crusaders could have taken from Dorylaeum (Eskisehir) to Iconium (Konya), and the one they chose was determined by a process of elimination. The military road to the east was out of the question because it ran into country still controlled by the Danishmends whose power had not been broken. They could have started out on this road which kept to the banks of the river Tembris (Porsuk), turned south-east after 40 kilometres passing beneath one of the old warning beacons * on Mt. Aigilos, finally crossing the salt desert to Iconium; but the army was too large and too slow moving to consider tackling such a long stretch of country without water, even though this was the quickest route. They had no option but to take the longer road south, and then turn east following in the shadows of the range of mountains that bordered the desert. This was the Pilgrim's way to Jerusalem constructed by the Byzantines after the founding of Constantinople, and we had driven along a section on our bus excursion to King Midas' tomb for it passed Seyitgazi, Nakoleia of ancient times. Today's modern tarmac took a line between the salt desert and the Pilgrim's way, passing through Emirdag, and it joined the Byzantine road further south at Bolvadin, formerly Polybotus.

In spite of the guides provided by Emperor Alexius the Crusaders had difficulty finding the way. For many years the country had been in a continuous state of war harassed by invading tribes; villages were

---

* A long line of these beacons spanned Byzantium starting at Loulon — a fortress commanding the pass through the Cilician Gates — and ending at Constantinople. When lit they provided a practical telegraphic communication, and the Emperors of Byzantium would know quickly of a Saracen invasion.

destroyed and fields uncultivated, wells had dried up, bridges collapsed, and the roads were in a bad condition. The frightened population fled at the approach of the army so it was impossible for the Crusaders to gather any local information. Taticius, the Byzantine general and his guides were under constant criticism. If anything went amiss the Crusaders suspected the Greek guides of treachery, while the Greeks became embittered by the Franks' ingratitude.

They set out from Dorylaeum on July 3rd 1097, this time the whole army together to avoid a recurrence of the disaster they had so nearly suffered on the plains before the city. They found their way to Polybotus, where fifty years later Emperor Manuel Comnenus built a fortress for protection against the attacks of the Seljuk Turks, and centuries later Sinan repaired and modified the Kirkgoz Bridge. We would meet the Crusaders again at Cay, 13 kilometres south of Polybotus. Meanwhile our bus, after setting off towards Ankara, branched south making for Emirdag where we had a twenty minute stop. The autogar was thronged with many types of vehicles arriving for market, and by the time we left we had a new set of passengers. Martin's bus left Eskisehir an hour later and he too called at Emirdag, but his was a grander coach travelling a greater distance and it carried a superior clientele. The road we took to Afyon turned west, while Martin's continued south to Bolvadin.

We reached the edge of the plain and began to climb rolling foothills covered with scrub pine. Higher up the hillside large areas had been fenced and important looking notices erected. Impressive replanting schemes were attempting to replace the great pine forests of antiquity, mercilessly felled by the Seljuk nomads for the grazing of their flocks. Goats had continued the damage by eating every young sapling that appeared above ground and preventing any regeneration. Their wool was much prized but, unlike sheep's wool that can be cut with shears, mohair has to be pulled out, each strand individually in order to keep its softness.

The pass provided a superb view of both plains, the one to which we now descended containing Afyon. The owner of the bus company had told Andrew that we would arrive at 9.30 a.m., but it was three quarters of an hour later that we rolled into the bus station. Andrew promptly secured our onward tickets. The young men in the first booth asked an extortionate price for two seats to Konya, but the second company he tried sold him tickets for considerably less, the Turk behind the desk allowing us to leave our luggage in his office. We found out later that a code of pricing existed to which the bus owners had to conform. Heavy fines were meted out to those attempting to break the barrier, so no wonder the original ticket sellers slank away when we returned to the bus station in the early afternoon.

We had a good three hours to explore Afyon. After three minutes I thought that we had made an appalling mistake. We spied our usual Tourist Information sign and trudged in the direction the arrow pointed. The street was wide and dusty with half completed concrete blocks on either side; there were areas of wasteland, the end was out of sight and,

70

though we were at a height of 1,000 metres, it was hot. A housing estate with high rise flats prevented us from seeing the great Black Fortress, the Kara Hisar which had lured us to make this detour, and was supposed to be the feature of the town towering above it to a height of 270 metres. Steeped in the usual history of Turkish towns, Afyon, once Akroenus, had been ruled successively by the Cimmerians, the Lydians and the Macedonians; it became part of the kingdom of Pergamum, was incorporated into the Roman Empire, and eventually fell under the sway of Byzantium. At one period it had even been overrun by Arabs.

Suddenly everything changed. A clatter of hooves made us pause, and we watched a pony pulling a small painted cart on top of which was balanced a door. The driver sensing our fatigue, slowed down and offered us a lift. We accepted with alacrity. Soon the boring street came to an end and we moved onto cobbles. There was the rock and we pointed to its summit, exclaiming and making signs. Our desire to reach the top was understood, but first we had to deliver the door to a house secreted amongst a warren of narrow back streets.

Even though the driver lived in the town he had obviously not climbed the peak and he frequently had to ask the way to the beginning of the ascent. At last he drew to a halt when the poor pony could no longer cope with the uneven stones and we too were beginning to feel battered and bruised. We walked through an old woman's back yard scattering the hissing geese. Houses ceased and the rock face loomed above. Our driver attempted to follow us but soon gave up quite out of breath. He indicated that he was hungry. With many gesticulations and pointing at watches, Andrew arranged to meet in the same place in an hour's time.

The way was steep. We found traces of a footpath but often Andrew had to haul me up rocks too difficult to climb on my own. The Kara Hisar was protected by a sheer cliff face and we began to doubt our driver's indications that this was indeed the correct way to the top. We trudged on compensated by the thought that invading armies would have been equally bewildered. Then totally unexpectedly and hidden behind a jutting crag, we were confronted by an archway cut out of a natural piece of rock with a massive block of stone at one side ready to bar the entrance. We had reached the acropolis and the view was fantastic. We could see for miles, the charming old town huddled beneath us, the ugly sprawling outskirts and the never ending plain. I could not see the poppy fields supposedly hidden behind gigantic sunflowers, but then we were too early in the year for them both to be in flower. Afyon was the centre for the strictly supervised production of opium, the seeds of the poppy being shipped to laboratories in the United States and the Netherlands to meet the pharmaceutical demand.

The fortress was originally built by the Hittites, and their successors added to and repaired the fortifications. The remaining brickwork was mostly Byzantine, though the charming conical tower was unmistakably Seljuk. We walked the circumference of the battlements, climbed up steps hewn out of the rock, inspected a couple of rooms and noted water catchments hollowed out of natural stone. We were both delighted with the achievement of having found and reached the top, and agreed that the day's detour had been well worthwhile.

The driver was waiting for us at the rendezvous and I was even more pleased when I saw that he had removed the pony's bridle and had bought some clover for it to eat. I had noticed bunches of clover hanging outside shops without realising their consumer potential. Perhaps it was the pony's stomach the owner had been worried about and not his own? Andrew had observed how well the Turks looked after and cared for their animals, and how healthy they all looked.

The last hour of our visit to Afyon was not as successful. We asked to be taken to two mosques, the Imaret Cami which turned out to be shut because a service was taking place, and the Ulu Cami (the Great Mosque) said to date from 1271. We could see nothing 'great' about this mosque and questioned our driver, repeating the name Ulu Cami and he continued to nod and grin. The only part that appeared to belong to the thirteenth century was a stone doorway. Even the hamams that we had rattled past earlier with steam escaping from beneath their domes, showed greater antiquity.

The driver kept on repeating, "The Park", so we consented to be driven there. I think he was showing us off to his friends, for there were frequent hand waves and shouts as we jolted over the cobbles. He had given me his own small sack filled with straw for a cushion, which certainly saved a lot of bruises. We noticed groups of drivers with similar carts waiting patiently by the roadside, and gathered that they too were for hire for any suitable job or errand that happened to materialise.

The Park turned out to be a well kept garden on two levels, with a monument strategically placed on the higher ground commemorating the victory of the Turks over the Greeks. The large sculpture showed a fierce naked Turk trampling on a fallen despairing Greek, and was supported by a plinth with four bas reliefs depicting scenes of the war. The final victory had taken place at Dumlupinar in 1922, some 40 kilometres to the west of Afyon.

We were immediately surrounded by a group of school children in the middle of their lunch break, who asked if we were German.

"No, English," we replied firmly, so naturally they wanted to practise their school book phrases. Andrew tried to find out from them the whereabouts of a Seljuk bridge. He is good at acting, but his signs for 'bridge' and 'river' failed to bring any ray of recognition to their blank faces. We were stupid not to have a dictionary — inadvertently left behind in Istanbul — and the Berlitz had no phrase to cope with the question, "Where is the Seljuk Bridge?" The Tourist Information was the obvious solution, so I helped the driver pick up the remains of the clover produced for the pony to eat on lengthy stops, and we jumped aboard. He was reluctant for us to leave without first having visited the Archaeological Museum situated at one end of the square, but since the guide book stated that it contained, 'a collection of antique coins and some particularly ugly Roman statuary', we decided to give it a miss.

We left the old town and were back on the smooth main roads of the outskirts, but with the added discomfort in the form of fast driven cars and lorries with foul smelling exhausts. Our first stop was at some government office with the national flag hanging limply from its standard. The driver disappeared and he looked, on emerging, as if he had solved the problem for we set off at a spanking trot, only to draw to a halt at the railway station. We gave up and asked him to take us back to the roundabout by the autogar where we had seen the original 'Tourist Information' sign. He seemed pleased with Andrew's tip and waved goodbye, though his grin was not quite as wide, aware that in some way he had failed to satisfy these peculiar foreigners.

Andrew was determined to find both the Tourist Information and the Seljuk Bridge. The sign also said, '200 metres', so this elusive bureau could not be far. A boy on a bicycle led us to a window front but the room behind was deserted. After lengthy discussions a helpful passer-by confirmed that the office had moved, but whither, no one knew. The Seljuk bridge remained a mystery.

The bus was late, but there was a good excuse for it had come from Izmir, a distance of 329 kilometres. To Konya was a further 226 kilometres; the road was straight and the driver, determined to make up time, completed the journey in three hours twenty minutes. There were two police stops en route and at both our large coach was waved through. Lorry drivers were being checked for permits which they are obliged to carry for the transport of goods around the country. They take a great deal of pride in their vehicles and paint them with imagination, either with garlands of flowers or a landscape.

The agricultural scene provided a good contrast. The first 62 kilometres followed the direction of the Akar river so the land was fertile, with groups of women – from four to fourteen in number – toiling in the fields. The old men were watching the cattle allowed to graze on the banks and verges of the new road, care being taken that they neither wandered in the path of the traffic nor disturbed the newly sown corn.

After 62 kilometres we came to Cay and crossed the Crusaders' path. The Crusaders coming from Polybotus continued south, trudging over the high Sultandagi mountains to Antioch in Pisidia, modern day Yalvac, which we were to visit in a couple of days. The land, well protected by these mountains, had escaped devastation by the Turks and the army had been able to replenish its dwindling supplies. They recrossed the Sultandagi and rejoined the main road at Philomelion (Aksehir). We had driven straight to Aksehir from Cay, a distance of 46 kilometres, and for the final stretch to Iconium (Konya) we followed the same path as the Crusaders. This was to be the worst part of their march so far. By now it was mid-summer and the heat was intense. There was no water – apart from the salt marshes of the desert – for the Turks had polluted or destroyed the Byzantine cisterns, and the whole army suffered dreadfully. They chewed branches of thorn bushes, the only available vegetation, in a desperate attempt to find moisture. The horses died first and the heavily armed knights were forced to march on foot, while all available sheep, goats and dogs pulled the baggage trains.

Iconium (Konya) had been deserted by the Turks who had fled to the mountains with their movable possessions. Fortunately the valley of Meram survived, and its fresh streams and orchards provided a haven of refute for the weary soldiers who arrived in the middle of August. Kilij Arslan* ultimately made Konya his capital, for it held an important position lying at the junction of several great trade routes. Today Konya is the fourth largest city in Turkey.

We found Martin on the point of leaving our hotel, He looked rather shaken and was off to find a stiff drink. The hotel's failure to serve alcohol made us realise that we were in the depths of Anatolia, where the imam had more power and spirits were banned. A larger hotel better equipped to cope with tourists obliged, and colour began to creep back into Martin's cheeks. He warned us to be prepared for the state of the bedrooms and indeed, when with trepidation we later entered ours, his suspicions were confirmed. The beds were damp, but worse was the smell of the drains which came from the familiar curtained off cubicle in the corner.

The hotel only served breakfast but a local restaurant was recommended. Invited into the kitchen to choose our dinner, we peered into steaming cauldrons and watched the cooks placing skewers on a grid over an open fire. Meat was hard to obtain and the kebabs were made with mince, but I enjoyed the local yogurt soup and we had pitta bread for the first time which allayed our hunger.

Martin had passed an uneventful day in his coach, the only section of road that differed from ours being the 52 kilometres from Emirdag due south to Bolvadin and Cay. However, he was one step ahead for he had already visited the Mevlana museum.

Andrew and Martin went for a walk after dinner but I found it too cold. I missed my anorak which I had left behind in Istanbul so as to have less to carry, supposing the Turkish climate to be temperate; but on the high Anatolian plateau (Konya stood at 1016 metres above sea level) the temperature dropped sharply at night. I also shivered trudging to the bus station in the early morning. However the days were perfect and the sun always seemed to shine. I returned to the hotel and decided to unpack. On inspecting the shelves I immediately shoved everything back into my suitcase. For the first time I wished that we were camping with warm sleeping bags in the valley of Meram, where the air would be pure and the surroundings infinitely preferable to this squalid habitation.

---

* Kilij Arslan was the son of Suleyman, a cousin of the great Alp Arslan. Suleyman founded the Rum dynasty of Seljuks in Cilicia, which subsequently dominated most of Anatolia.

74

Our transport in Afyon — the driver warding off the evil eye

Decorated lorry

75

DAY IX : BINBIR KILISE

What a dreadful night.   Andrew had not been in bed three minutes before warning me that he had been bitten.   We unpacked our inner sheets, a clever innovation discovered at a camping shop.   They could equally well be made up at home, for they were simply plain sheets folded over and sewn together at the bottom and side.   However suspect the bedding we were cocooned in our own clean linen.   Dawn broke earlier now, so the muezzin's alarm call came at four thirty a.m..   The mosque was quite close to our hotel and its resident muezzin started the wail. The replies from his compatriots echoed in the distance, and I began to feel that sense of heaviness drawing me into oblivion when, bang! — our neighbouring muezzin blared forth again.   Eventually their sounds died away and silence fell on Konya.   It was only to be the stillness that settles before the great bombardment.   The dogs opened fire. I had not noticed them in the town when we arrived but they certainly had their field day now.   We were on the first floor overlooking a main street, and the follow-up came from enormous lorries that thundered past with crashing gear changes specifically reserved for our stretch of road.   I suppose I must have dozed in between for by the time I crawled out of bed, the normal daytime sounds had taken over.

Andrew had disappeared for his habitual morning's walk.   He used to go for miles often scouting out possible restaurants for the evening at the same time.   I tended my bites and went to have breakfast.   The Turks, like the French, enjoy fresh bread and they bake throughout the day;   even so, the larger hotels and those in the cities invariably produced stale bread for breakfast.   This unprepossessing hotel offered the most delicious breakfast.   The bread was fresh, instead of the usual carton of jam local honey appeared on the table, also slices of goat's cheese and a mound of olives.   I managed to acquire a whole jug of hot water, so eked out countless glasses of tea and began to revive, even having time to write those long overdue postcards.

Andrew and Martin during their meanderings the previous evening found out where the dolmuss stopped, so we caught one to the bus station and bought tickets to Karaman, a town 107 kilometres south-east of Konya.   The road was straight, crossing a flat but fertile steppe — the word used in Turkey to describe the wide treeless plains.   We took a long time to reach the mountains on the horizon, the uniformity of the landscape relieved briefly by a magnificent array of storks on a piece of marshland; as we raced by they rose majestically into the air.   The occasional white splotches in the distance were made by the tents of Yuruks (nomads).   It would have taken days to ride across the steppe and I could see no sign of a village where we might have rested for the night.   Perchance the Yuruks would have let us share their tents and given us a drink of goat's milk to quench our thirst.   We had bottled water on our civilised method of transport, and sweets were offered as well.   Only two bus companies competed on this particular route so competiton was fierce.

At the time of the Crusaders' march this vast plain had neither been reclaimed nor irrigated and they were advised, by a small population of Armenians, to carry sufficient water for their journey. After a good rest at Meram they had recovered their strength. Godfrey, who had been wounded while hunting bear was fit again while Raymond, gravely ill upon arrival and having been offered extreme unction, was now able to march with his army. They continued from Iconium (Konya) to Heraclea (Eregli). Nowadays there is a direct road that runs between these two towns but in 1097, because of the desert, the Crusaders took the longer and more southerly route towards Karaman heading straight for the range of mountains dominated by Kara Dag (the Black Mountain). They would have been welcomed by the Christian community in the hills at Barata (Binbir Kilise and now renamed Maden Sehir) and when fed, watered and refreshed, continued north-east to Heraclea.

Karaman had a modern bus station. While Andrew and Martin went in search of a taxi, I discovered a large clean self-service lokanta (restaurant) which provided various types of rolls and mineral water for our lunch. I found Andrew and Martin in a smart office where the Director had recommended the taxi that he normally used himself, and a fee was quickly negotiated. This must have been due to Andrew muttering, "Herr Professor," and Martin looking so distinguished. Martin had become quite fluent in Turkish and managed to discard his Berlitz, which undoubtedly was a contributing factor to his diplomatic success. Our host insisted that I drank my glass of tea before leaving.

As frequently occurred our taxi driver had no idea of the whereabouts of our destination, so he had to stop and ask the way. Presently we turned onto a dirt road with a sign warning us that it was in bad condition and impassable after rainstorms. Luckily the sun was shining and we soon spied a ruin of what appeared to be a half buried chapel. The roof was barrel shaped and covered with earth and grass, and I discovered the clue to its identity when, descending a few rough steps and bending my head to enter a low archway, I found the interior filled with stagnant water. The Byzantine Greeks had built many of these cisterns, the poisonous looking water beneath the greenish scum possibly being cleaner in ancient times.

Turks, basically a nomadic race, have never been able to understand water, and Gertrude Bell noticed that in villages it was always a Greek who maintained the water supply. Here on the slopes of the Kara Dag the Greeks cared for their water meticulously; by means of dams, aqueducts, terraces and cisterns, they conserved the precious liquid for the long dry summer months. With the departure of the Greeks in the middle ages, the system deteriorated. In 1909 a torrent rushed down the west side of the mountain ruining crops and covering fertile fields with gravel.

Our driver was more concerned with the plight of the apricot trees, a frost having nipped their blossom. Gertrude Bell had also visited Binbir Kilise in May, but 1905 must have been a late spring for she rode through patches of snow to reach the top of Kara Dag.   She was surprised to discover a huge volcano, its crater three quarters of a kilometre across with a ring of rocky peaks around the lip.   She found snowdrops and crocuses, and lower down the slopes orange-red tulips and deep yellow-brown spotted fritillaries.   According to the custom of hospitality she was offered a hut in a village, where she stayed for four days and started exploring the churches.   In one she copied a faded inscription which she showed to Professor Ramsay whom she met a few days later in Konya. From this he was able to date the building and the result inspired them both to carry out a detailed survey in 1907.

The Kara Dag had always been revered.   From its lofty summit men could commune with the gods and survey the whole land, while the great holes in the mountain leading to unfathomed depths helped the image of the mother earth.   The climate was delightful and vineyards and orchards filled the Lycaonian plain.   Nilus, a hermit, lived on the slopes before A.D. 400.   Others joined him and the population grew until Barata became the veritable Byzantine city of Binbir Kilise flourishing from the fifth until the eleventh century.   The Seljuk domination began in 1073 and churches were converted to mosques, but the Christians were allowed to remain and tended to congregate in villages higher up the mountainside. The Seljuks in turn lost their power and the population mysteriously faded away.   With internal wars and the insecurity of travel, roads deteriorated and the district became less accessible.   A traveller recounting his visit in 1836 described the area as being deserted, but by the time Gertrude Bell arrived a number of Yuruks had installed themselves and, using stone from existing buildings to construct their own dwellings, accelerated the process of ruin.

We arrived at the village of Maden Sehir 30 kilometres from Karaman, to find an obviously poor but enlarged community with more houses and fewer churches.   However two churches still dominated the countryside.   In the first one only the apse, half the nave and a section of the narthex remained standing.   A donkey grazed amongst the ruins and beans had been planted to within centimetres of the north wall.   The level of the ground had risen to one metre from the top of the pillars, but under the arches I could just make out some faint traces of painting. Gertrude Bell had been able to recognise the busts of saints their heads surrounded by halos, and some folds of drapery.   During the eighty intervening years the elements had hastened the decay.

Gertrude Bell had taken photographs and detailed measurements of every church she found.   She described this one as being a basilica, the nave higher than the aisles and five round headed windows piercing the upper storey of the north wall — the south having collapsed.   We were so near to the couch of the apse that we could easily observe the way it had been constructed, small stones radiating from a central Byzantine cross to fill the whole area.   Originally it would have been plastered and decorated with frescoes.   The centre core of the wall was filled with rubble and mortar, and the outside finely faced with blocks of stone individually cut to shape, each fitting precisely into its allotted place.

Beyond the village, a gravelly football pitch and more grazing donkeys, we came to the site of the second romantic ruin. The apse alone retained its grandeur with Maden Dag, one of the peaks of the Black Mountain, forming an appropriate back cloth to the set. A few crumbling walls stood forlornly at the western end but at least the soil had not encroached. The columns of the nave had disappeared, removed to enrich some other building, the only evidence of their former existence being rows of broken bases now pathetically decorated with dry wispy grass.

We were told by one of the villagers gesticulating in the direction of a pass on the horizon, that there was another group of ruins higher up. I knew this to be true both from Gertrude Bell's descriptions and also from historical sources. Binbir Kilise (Maden Sehir) had suffered greatly from Arab marauders who from 660 onwards swept over the Anatolian plains once or twice a year. The inhabitants had moved 500 metres up the hill to Deghile, a site high on the north-west spur of Kara Dag, where they felt safer. From 850 conditions improved and the churches at Binbir Kilise were restored or rebuilt.

Our taxi driver became increasingly worried as the road deteriorated and, sure enough, we had a puncture. Rather than sit and watch the wheel-changing operation, I said that I would carry on walking to the brow of the hill. The road twisted and turned hugging the contours of the hillside, and I made good progress before the silence was shattered by repeated hoots from far down the valley. What seemed like a noisy black beetle crawled up the road to join me. Andrew, Martin and the driver emerged from the car and I was told that the spare tyre was rather bald, so it would be foolhardy to attempt to proceed any further. We were practically at the ridge and I persuaded them to park the car and take some exercise. I endeavoured to enthuse them by saying that we might find something stupendous on the other side.

I had long lost patience with Andrew and Martin's ambling gait. I find walking slowly much more tiring, therefore, striding out ahead I took a short cut to avoid a hairpin bend and reached my view point. What a disappointment. The ruined building perched on the skyline was yet another valley away. With a sinking heart I estimated that it would take an hour to reach the summit, and we had to be back in Karaman in time to catch the four o'clock bus to Konya. To our surprise a shepherd boy we questioned reckoned it would take only fifteen minutes and confirmed that there were indeed other ruins. That piece of information settled any argument and the men staunchly agreed to have a go.

The taxi driver, who out of curiosity had come with us and had originally walked with Andrew and Martin, obviously disapproved of a woman leading the way so he joined me instead. He wore the most unsuitable shoes, a type of sandal with a heel presumably to make the most of his height. Martin's leather shoes had lost their shine and he never took off his jacket, while Andrew looked more sensible in an aertex shirt but his suede boots were distinctly out of place. I was very pleased with my walking boots. They were a good protection against rocks and dust, comfortable for sightseeing and when I had to remove them for my mosque visits, at least I was certain to be wearing socks and would not have to walk barefoot.

Our jolly driver was quite chatty and we enquired about each other's family. Not speaking a word of Turkish except for weak tea and hot water — I still found please and thank you eluded my tongue — it was amazing what could be conveyed through sign language. He offered to carry my knapsack which was very kind for my camera, lenses and books had become quite heavy.

The hillside was uncultivated, covered in scrub oak with scarcely any grass that I could see for the boy's sheep. All at once we found ourselves above the treeline, and the church which had led me inexorably on was suddenly quite close; leaving the dusty road we joined a rocky path. I stopped to take a photograph of Andrew and Martin making the final ascent, but a steep gradient becomes flattened by the camera so the result was disappointing. Andrew and Martin took the lead but the driver, sensing my competitive instinct some of which he had caught himself, led me straight up the hill so that we reached the top first and only one minute beyond the shepherd boy's estimated time. I saw some ruined buildings but also people and a dormobile. The couple and a baby were French and I asked them at once if they were driving in the direction of Maden Sehir?

"Yes."

"Could you possibly wait and give us a lift back to our taxi?"

"Bien sûr, pas de problème!" I gave a sigh of relief and passed on the welcome news.

Now I could concentrate on the object of our exertions. At first I saw only stone walls and dwelling places for a few inhabitants of the village, but as I walked along grassy pathways, pillars, naves and apses emerged. Ducking under a doorway I came across a hidden chapel, and through an archway saw yet another one. Churches abounded, some large and easy to identify, others less discernible. Climbing out of aisles I disturbed turkeys from their scratchings making them gobble and flap their wings. Sheep and goats dozed beneath crumbling walls. The soil level varied in height but one church had been protected against invading earth and converted into a mosque. I saw a hole in the hill a field away and, running across to see what it contained, discovered a chapel carved into the rock. The final ruin to which I clambered was on the skyline, the one that had drawn us to the site. Standing at its western entrance, I looked down the nave of this basilica. The solid pillars on each side were intact with side aisles beyond, and a pair of arched windows fitted into the curved wall of the apse. This church deserved to be the most complete, for its position at the summit of the pass dominating both valleys was spectacular.

I had counted seven churches of varying sizes. Gertrude Bell and

Professor Ramsay in their joint book entitled, 'The Thousand and One Churches', described one basilica, six churches, three chapels and four monasteries, two rock tombs and a mausoleum, and dated them to between the ninth and eleventh centuries.   One of the small chapels Miss Bell had measured and drawn in 1905 had been converted into a Yuruk dwelling by the time of her second visit in 1907, and the tower of part of a monastery into a cowshed; whilst a complete arcade and the remains of the upper storey of the narthex of one of the larger churches had been blown over, the columns and stones lying on the ground as they had fallen — like a pack of cards.   The cards had subsequently been gathered and redealt by the Yuruks, the convenient building material having been put to an alternative use.

Binbir Kilise means one thousand and one churches.   It is doubtful whether that number of churches ever existed, but the surrounding hill-sides held many treasures.   One villager who assumed the title of local guide, said that St. Paul had preached in a church "a fair walking distance away," although dates made this assertion somewhat improbable.   St. Paul was known to have visited Konya and many towns and villages in the surrounding countryside, but there is no evidence that a community existed here as early as the first century.   The story more likely arose from an inscription found in a church on the summit of Kizil Dag.   It recorded that a certain man by the name of Paul had built this church in memory of his father.

The Frenchman showed us a large stone with Hittite carvings.   The reliefs were hard to recognise, but after a while I could make out the figure of a farmer sowing corn, a cow, and a second man holding a stick. We were to study many clear Hittite figures in the museum in Ankara, but how much more thrilling to see one in situ.   Gertrude Bell also found some Hittite carvings on a great rock near the summit of Kara Dag.   In one of her letters she tells of the excitement at discovering these strange drawings and showing them to Professor Ramsay who immediately recognised their importance.   He had hoped to unearth a Hittite settlement, and on another peak the strange juxtapositon of rocks confirmed his suspicions.   They took longer to solve the mystery of curious cuttings in the rock face until Gertrude Bell remembered coming across a similar invention in Syria.   It was a wine press.   The sides were cut sloping to a hole which conducted the liquid into a receptacle placed beneath, while over the back of the press square holes in the rock held the end of a lever by which pressure was exerted on the grapes.   The French couple had also seen a wine press and they too were a fund of information.   The husband told us that many wolves still prowled the steppes of Anatolia, and the sheep dogs wore iron collars with vicious spikes for protection, as a wolf always made for its adversary's throat.   We had already seen some of these terrifying looking dogs: they were a cross between a dobermann and a lurcher.   The Frenchman's task during his lengthy visit to Turkey — he and his family had been there for three months already — was to catch some falcons.   His wife presented coffee to the villagers as a token of

81

thanks for the hospitality shown to them during their overnight stay, for money would not have been acceptable.   With a natural and charming gesture they reciprocated by giving her some eggs.

After the welcome lift back to our car we were driven, considering the state of the spare tyre, far too fast back to Karaman.   Nevertheless we gave the driver more than the agreed price to compensate for the burst tyre, and he smilingly escorted us to an even grander office than the one in which we had sat earlier.   The tea was of a superior variety too, much paler in colour and tasting rather like tilleul — a lime tisanne.   The manager graciously invited us to stay in his new hotel.   We explained that we already had rooms booked in Konya but if we ever returned to Karaman we would certainly pay him a visit.   There would then be time to investigate more of the hidden sites and to walk to St. Paul's Church; and also to explore the town where there is a twelfth century citadel, a mosque and a dervish monastery with tombs of several members of Mevlana's family, about whom I shall write later.

Travelling by coach was very restful and I was glad that we had not brought a landrover nor hired a car.   We had none of the worries as to who was to drive or map read or where we were to park at night with safety, and by the time we had reached Konya my energy was restored. At the bus station we transferred to a dolmuss which I left by Alaeddin Hill promising to be back at the hotel in two hours.   I started walking over the Hill, the ancient acropolis, now transformed into a delightful park with numerous cafés.   Hitherto the only people I had seen sitting down together were groups of men.   Here at last whole families were out to enjoy the evening, partaking of glasses of tea and lurid coloured drinks of juice.   I had failed to obtain a map from the Tourist Office because we had left Konya before opening time and returned too late in the evening, so it took me twice as long to find my way about frequently having to retrace my steps.   I came across one building which I thought must be the French Church of St. Paul.   Noticing my interest the guardian was summoned by an ever watchful Turk; after ushering me inside the wizened old man locked the door.   I felt most uncomfortable, disliked the interior and had to listen to his explanations and look at the visitor's book.   Other Christian denominations used this Church besides Roman Catholics, amongst them Protestants and Greek Orthodox.   I was shown a plate for donations; contributing generously I also tipped the guardian well to ensure my exit.

Alaeddin Street connects Alaeddin Hill with the Mevlana Museum, and bordering this wide avenue were a good selection of mosques.   The first I approached, the Iplikci Cami (the Merchants' Mosque) was Konya's oldest structure dating from 1202, looking Arabic in style with plain reddish-brown brick walls and tiny windows.   The Serafettin Mosque about half way down the street was founded by the Seljuks, rebuilt by the Ottomans in the seventeenth century and restored in the nineteenth. Now it was again closed for repairs.   The glimpse of a minaret topped by a delicate open loggia reminiscent of Venetian architecture, enticed me

82

down a side street. It belonged to the Aziziye Cami where I was asked to cover my bare arms, even though my shirt had short sleeves. A cardigan also carried in my knapsack came in useful and, since I was wearing my Turkish straw hat, I lent my scarf to a woman who had been refused entry having no head covering.

Some authorities say that the huge Selimiye Mosque at the end of Alaeddin Street was designed by Sinan. It certainly displays that dramatic feeling of space: large pillars and arches supported the dome, and windows encircling its base allowed light to pour into the building. There is nowhere to sit down in a mosque, but the carpets were soft to the feet and the peace and serenity could not fail to revive the spirit.

Returning to the hotel by the appointed hour I discovered that Andrew and Martin had not been idle; through talking to the organiser and the guest lecturer of a smart tour, they had obtained seats on their private coach the following day, so we attended the regular evening lecture given to members to enlighten them on what they were about to see. Andrew had also wrought miracles with our room. Having complained bitterly in the morning we now had clean sheets and blankets and the dust had vanished. Unfortunately he had no luck with the hot water. The manager simply refused to turn on the boiler before eight p.m. even though Andrew pointed out that he had an important group staying, some of whom were fairly elderly, and that they expected hot water when they returned from a full day's sightseeing; indeed hot water at six or even seven o'clock was essential for the success of the hotel.

Andrew warned us that there were not many restaurants in Konya. On our way to his choice for the evening we passed one that appeared reasonably inviting and were tempted inside. Unfortunately, by the time we had inspected the kitchen it was too awkward to leave. The mezes were unimaginative and the adana kebabs, a local speciality made with minced meat, turned out to be highly spiced. A television blared from one corner commanding people's attention; it showed a football match between Aberdeen and Real Madrid, surprisingly won by Aberdeen. Outside, a colour television set in a shop window was also switched on and a group of enthtralled spectators cheered excitedly. One man, obviously drunk, gripped Andrew's hand for ages and became rather a bore. Although the Muslim religion forbids the drinking of wine, raki, a cloudy white aniseed based concoction usually diluted with water, appears to escape Mohammed's censure.

The water was still cold when we returned to the hotel. Andrew stormed down to the desk and the receptionist came to inspect, discovering that the hot tap was undeniably cold, but that the cold tap was hot. We still kept our inner sheets, though the bugs appeared to have been swept away with the dust and we escaped any further bites.

A donkey tethered in the ruins of the basilica, Maden Sehir

A lonely apse framed by the peak of Maden Dag

DAY X : YALVAC

Martin's principal reason for wanting to go to Yalvac, apart from the fact that the Crusaders had been there, was that St. Paul had visited and preached in the town. After Herod died some of the disciples met in Antioch (Antakya)* where the Holy Spirit entered Paul and sent him to spread the word of God in Cyprus. From there he returned to Perge on the mainland and accompanied by Barnabas continued to Antioch in Pisidia, modern day Yalvac. He gave a great oration in the crowded synagogue. On the following Sabbath even more people gathered to hear him preach. When the Jews saw the multitude and that many of them were being converted, they were filled with jealousy and roused the leading men to persecute the followers of Christ. Driven out of the city Paul and Barnabas shook the dust from their feet and hastened to Iconium (Konya). They stayed for some time inevitably creating dissension until, threatened with stoning, they moved on to Lystra and thence to Derbe. There Paul was stoned and left for dead but he recovered, performed miracles and many conversions. He then returned once more to Iconium and Antioch in Pisidia, continuing to Perge and finally sailing back to Antioch (Antakya).

There was no morning bus to Yalvac, and because it was so far away the only one scheduled for the afternoon was out of the question, so we were delighted at the tour's early start. The instructions issued to them were: "breakfast from six o'clock, suitcases outside bedroom doors at six fifteen, departure seven fifteen prompt." After Yalvac the tour was continuing to Antalya, making for a very long day. One of the questions from a lady the previous evening had been, "Would the hotel in Antalya be of a higher standard and would the water be hot?" To be fair to the organisers they had been double booked at the best hotel in Konya, and had no alternative but to sink to ours.

There were quite a few empty seats in the coach but we waited until the passengers had found their favourite ones before taking ours. The drive was full of scenic beauty, the snow-capped Taurus Mountains forming a perfect background, especially the peak behind the lake of Beysehir. We stopped at the town of Beysehir for the passengers to stretch their legs, but most were asleep. I took a photograph of the charming old Seljuk bridge, sauntered to the lake and watched an old man drive his pony and cart into the water to enable the animal to drink. Fishing boats were moored on the opposite shore and beyond them I saw a mosque, a turbe and a medrese. The tour organiser was taking photographs and I asked if I had time to visit them.

"Only ten minutes," came the reply, so I gave my knapsack to Andrew and ran over the bridge, past the fishing boats to the mosque.

---

* Numerous cities founded by the Seleucids bore the name of Antioch; the original was in Syria, but it is now within the Turkish border and called Antakya.

85

The door was padlocked and I had to be content with a quick appraisal of the arched portico and squat black cupolas; however the exquisitely carved entrance to the Seljuk turbe was well worth my energetic venture. Glancing at my watch I saw that I only had one minute to go. In a panic I rushed towards a motorised three-wheeler and cart facing in the right direction, pointed over the bridge and at my watch and gasped, "Bus!" I was prepared to climb into the cart but found a plough taking up too much room. The farmer, rallying to the situation, beckoned to a friend with a truck who very kindly drove me to the coach. Uncertain as to whether this man would accept any money from a woman, I hesitatingly proffered a tip; I need not have worried for it was accepted with equanimity. After all that effort the coach was empty. The tour organiser apologised; his passengers had woken up and the Turkish guide, an invaluable addition to their party, had organised tea in the cool shady garden by the river.

We continued driving in a northerly direction keeping to the eastern shore of the lake. A water buffalo grazed alongside cattle and a young camel looked incongruous. None of the olearia in my garden survived the cold winter of 1981–1982, but here wild bushes grew to a height of 5 metres. Poplar were by far the most cultivated tree in the part of Turkey we crossed. Their wood, valuable for match making and timber production, gave a comparatively quick return and I saw numerous varieties growing in lines, in squares, in vegetable gardens and plantations. They also make excellent wind breaks and were planted around fields and in areas of reclamation.

We drove straight through Yalvac to the Roman site a kilometre north of the modern town. Formerly Antioch in Pisidia it had once been an important city. A great main road had stretched to the west ultimately reaching the Aegean, and another to the south – the way we had come – through Karallia (Beysehir) to the Mediterranean at Side. A branch road ran east from Beysehir to Konya. Our complete circuit this day was on Roman roads, the journey so far taking four and three quarter hours, counting our half hour stop at Beysehir.

The tour was to be conducted by its guest lecturer round the immediate remains, but he suggested that we walked a kilometre further on to the aqueduct since it was the best preserved ruin in the vicinity. The Romans were an amazing nation: besides creating a sophisticated road network which covered the whole of their Empire, they built prodigious water systems, in this case from a spring in a mountain some distance away. The aqueduct was definitely worth closer inspection, a substantial part having withstood the ravages of time. May was too late in the year for spring flowers which carpet these high altitude slopes, but walking back towards the main site I was thrilled to find growing in the rough ground, a knapweed, with hardly any stem and succulent leaves to help it survive the long dry summer.

The ancient city had been built on the side of a hill, and the temple in which we found ourselves was at its highest point commanding a

86

dramatic view over the surrounding countryside. Tiny figures climbed into their bus far below. The members of the tour had been so kind and some were worried at leaving us in this deserted area, but we had assured them that we would be all right. A couple had even wrung our hands as if in grave doubt as to our ability to survive on our own. We meandered through the Propylea, along a wide causeway and peered down the steps of the theatre; the baths were to one side and the entrance gate on the other, facing Yalvac. Not much was left standing, nevertheless the jumble of fallen columns and stones that lay by this gate provided us with an amusing interlude. We discovered some excellent carvings of flowers and acanthus scrolls. Our search rapidly became a treasure hunt with each one trying to find something better. "Look a shield!" scored five points for it was half covered with earth; a double headed eagle upside down should have been the winner at plus ten, but I claimed victory for identifying a fragment containing only the buckle of a belt and the hilt of a sword.

We could not linger too long for we had no idea of the time of our bus, nor if an onward one existed, so we made our way through Yalvac passing the plain square mosque with its Seljuk portal and noting with amusement the number of carved Roman stones incorporated in the walls. At the bus station beyond the town only a couple of vehicles were parked at the far end of the large empty space. Not a promising sight, but luck was on our side. We did not have to take the later bus the long way back through Beysehir to Konya as we had feared, for in twenty-five minutes a dolmuss left for Aksehir. We even had time for something to eat in the small locanta. Andrew and Martin chose cucumber, tomatoes and bread, while I had a tub of yogurt and something that looked like cold soup, but turned out to be chestnut puree!

The dolmuss of the dormobile type was full and our young driver fairly sped along the valley road. This was most satisfactory for we were again on the route of the Crusaders. The army had a welcome rest and found water and food in Yalvac. Now they marched 16 kilometres southeast before swinging north-east to cross the formidable mountains of Sultandagi and rejoin the Roman road at Philomelion (Aksehir). I did not envy them, but then I doubt if they would have swapped their situation for ours. As we climbed the pass the road deteriorated but it made no difference to the driver's technique, his foot was permanently flat on the accelerator. A woman behind was sick into her plastic bag and her husband asked the driver to stop so that she could throw it out of the window. The driver continued for a kilometre before putting on his brakes. He explained that a bus had recently parked on the former bend, the passengers had scrambled out to look at the view when suddenly the road collapsed and the bus disappeared into the ravine.

We touched the snow line at the top of the pass and the descent was even worse. We were now extremely nervous, especially Martin who was on the side of the precipice; he admitted afterwards that he had never been so frightened in his life. I disliked the way the driver took his eyes off the road to look at his companions when talking to them, and I strained my eyes for him, praying that there would be no approaching vehicle. Andrew remarked that by visiting so many mosques I had become a firm believer in kismet.

Miraculously we survived and were soon speeding along the valley towards Aksehir. There must be a three o'clock bus to Konya for most departure times from main towns appeared to be adjusted to the hour. We had ten minutes to go. A long straight road ran through the outskirts of the town and if there were a speed limit our driver took no notice. Suddenly there was a screech of brakes and he swerved to the right down a side road, nearly knocking over a cart and causing a woman and child to jump back in alarm. Urgent discussions with his companions took place as he turned to right and left, but this was brought to an abrupt halt by the piercing note of a siren. A policeman on a motor bicycle made the driver follow him to a check-point on the main road. So this was what he was trying to avoid. The driver had to get out and show his papers which were out of date. The seconds ticked by and then the driver, realising his trump card, turned and pointed at us. The police are helpful to tourists therefore as quickly as the drama had started it ended. We were off again making a dash for the bus station. As we drew to a halt we leapt out, beating the pundits at their game and shouting, "Konya, Konya." They shouted, "Konya, Konya," back even louder and pulled open the door of a bus already on the move. We had just made the autogar as the clock struck three.

The journey back to Konya from Yalvac took a total of two hours fifty minutes, a considerable improvement on the outward one. There was time for some more sightseeing. Andrew wanted to visit the Mevlana museum and was determined to find a good restaurant for our last dinner in Konya. Martin decided to go to the Church of Saint Helena at Sille and, as I would have time for my mosques and museums the following morning, I decided to accompany him.

The local bus left from the centre of the town in twenty minutes; while Martin went to buy the tickets I muttered that I would go in search of a loo. There was always one at bus stations but apparently not here. I was undoubtedly hunting for something and a Turk asked if he could help. I replied that I was looking for the tuvalet. Beckoning me to follow, he plunged into the narrow twisting back streets lined with shops and full of people. This was not what I had expected and I thought that he must have mistaken my request; but on the contrary, he had understood my Turkish pronunciation and continued his determined lead. I did not want to appear rude, but on the other hand I began to feel apprehensive. I tried again, this time pointing to my watch and back to the bus station.

"Evet, evet," ("Yes, yes") he replied. He stopped at an archway which revealed a line of basins, and through a swing door a row of closed doors, and at the far end another chamber. There were several men though no women, and I was extremely embarrassed. I could not even back out for my guide was holding open a door. It was becoming farcical for he even offered to hold my book and hat while I entered the cubicle, and was still lurking when I came out. He directed me to the basins with a bow and offered his handkerchief with which to dry my hands. Outside he shook hands and said goodbye. I mumbled my thanks before rushing in the direction of the bus station. I met Martin who looked extremely angry. He had not heard me say where I was going and after buying the tickets realised that I was missing. On enquiring as to my whereabouts, someone had told him that they had seen an English lady entering the market with a Turk. He was understandably anxious, wondering how he was going to explain my disappearance to Andrew. So relieved was I to emerge into the sunlight and civilisation, that I broke out into helpless laughter and could not begin to explain to Martin what had happened.

Sille was eight kilometres north-west of Konya and we only had to ask the way to the church for a Turk to lead us there. The main cobbled street of the village wound alongside a small river crossed at various points by a splendid mixture of footbridges. Though the river itself was contained within concrete banks, the workmen had carefully avoided disturbing an old stone humpbacked bridge decorated with two lions' heads. Another bridge was made of wood, while the one we finally used before reaching the open country consisted of swaying planks.

The Church beyond the village was said to be the oldest in Anatolia, built in the simple style of the Byzantine Cross in 327 by Helena, the mother of Constantine. She was the daughter of an innkeeper in Bithynia and married Constantius Chlorus a Roman general. He was persuaded to divorce his low bred wife when he was declared Caesar, and married Theodora the stepdaughter of Emperor Maximian. Helena had already given birth to Constantine (to become the Great) at Nish in Serbia. Constantine always had a deep regard and affection for his mother, and after her death conferred upon her the title of 'Nobilissima Femina' and changed the name of her birthplace to Helenopolis.

Constantine was proclaimed Caesar by his troops on the death of his father in York in 306 — after having repelled an invasion by Picts and Scots — and eighteen months later he became Emperor. He was converted to Christianity before the battle of Milvan Bridge in 312, as he approached Rome. He had a vision of the Flaming Cross which appeared in the sky at noon with a script 'By This Conquer'. Helena, influenced by her son, adopted the new Faith at the age of sixty-three years and devoted the rest of her life to the service of Christ. She used the treasure of the Empire for alms, built numerous churches and enjoyed assisting at services. At eighty she took charge of rebuilding the Church of the Holy Sepulchre in Jerusalem.

Sille had been a Greek village from pre-Christian times. St. Paul most likely preached there, converting the inhabitants who continued to live happily until the Graeco-Turkish war of 1920–1922. Following the Treaty of Lausanne signed in 1923, Orthodox Greeks in Anatolia were exhanged for Muslim Turks in Macedonia. On entering the village we

89

had seen some derelict houses in the Greek style. They and the Church were a reminder of how it had once been possible to co-exist after acts of aggression. The Turks originally defeated the Greeks in the eleventh century, but the war in the twentieth century had finally wrought sterner retribution.

The Church had been restored in the nineteenth century. Without care and attention the frescoes were fading and the ornate screen, cutting off the altar and side chapels from the congregation, was in bad repair. However the basic structure was sound with yet more familiar lions' heads combined in the outside walls. In the once hallowed ground a couple were planting rows of maize between the inevitable poplar saplings. They probably lived there too, in the little room I had noticed above the entrance door which originally housed the bells.

We strolled back along the far side of the river. The rock face rising from the path was pierced with caves or chapels, but we had no desire to explore them for we knew that we would be visiting many better ones in Cappadocia. In any event, most of them were used as shelters for animals and chickens; some had doors and padlocks for the storage of more precious items, grain and hay, while others appeared to be inhabited. How different from when Gertrude Bell had visited the village in 1905. Arriving on a Sunday she had witnessed a service being held in one of these rock cut churches which she presumed to be even older than the Church of St. Helena. She had returned the following day to map them both, and had also been invited into the house of a Greek family to inspect their carpets, for the village thrived on this industry. She and her escort, the German Consul in Konya, had been offered as refreshment, jam and water.

Rounding a corner we nearly bumped into a shuffling black-hooded figure; the woman immediately shied away raising her arm to shield her face as she cowered against the wall. I felt dreadfully sorry that we had upset her. We were not contaminated, just infidels, but coming into such close contact with Martin, a member of the opposite sex, had caused this reaction. Many women gathered in the main square waiting for the bus, all covering their heads and half their faces with black shawls. They squatted on the ground looking like a bevy of crows. I longed to take a photograph, but the pointing of the evil eye in their direction would have caused an uproar.

Martin and I sat together four rows from the front of the bus, but as it filled Martin offered his seat to one of the women. He and the other men were forced further and further to the rear as each in turn gave up their seats and, by the end, Martin and his male companions were squashed together at the back of the bus. He told me later of the curious picture that took shape before him: wave upon wave of swaying black mounds were interrupted by an incongruous white straw hat.

No hot water, not even from the cold tap. Andrew had walked miles and we were cheered by the fact that he had found a modern hotel which served a dinner of excellent quality. The delicious hot pitta bread had been baked in a long thin oval shape, and after the mezes we were offered a lamb casserole with rice. Turkish rice whether stuffing vine leaves or peppers, or as an accompaniment to meat always had a delicate flavour due to the subtle use of herbs and pinenuts; sometimes raisins and finely chopped pieces of liver were added. There was also a pudding, small squares of shredded wheat of a finer variety than ours, with chopped nuts and soaked in honey. The hotel had a pleasant atmosphere and was full, popular both with Turks and tours, two parties of French sitting at long tables chattering away. The waiters took the opportunity to practise their English, one of them having a friend who actually worked in London.

We agreed that it was too far to walk back to our hotel and, besides, we thought that we had earned a treat at the end of a long day. Discussing our sightseeing in the taxi we came to the conclusion that we must indeed belong to the race of mad Englishmen — and women. We had sat in buses for a total of well nigh seven hours in order to see one Roman site, and a town famous only for the fact that St. Paul had preached there. However none of us would have missed a kilometre of the day, and how could we tell if we would ever be here again or have a second chance to visit Yalvac?

Beysehir

Seljuk bridge at Beysehir

Aqueduct at Yalvac

Church of St. Helena, Sille

DAY XI : KONYA

From excavations on the acropolis, Alaeddin Hill, archaeologists found proof that Konya had been occupied as early as 7000 B.C. Hittites, Phrygians and the usual succession of conquerors had ruled in their turn. The Romans called the city Iconium, but the most illustrious period was during the twelfth and thirteenth centuries when the Seljuks reigned supreme. They governed the greater part of Anatolia and with their power and wealth they turned Konya, their capital, into a centre for culture and learning. They were prolific builders developing a distinctive style of architecture, flamboyant but with a subtlety of ornamentation displaying their love of beauty and design. After the Seljuks came the Mongols, Karamanids and finally the Ottomans, but it was Seljuk art that dominated Konya.

The Seljuks had come from Mongolia, that mystic land which has given birth to so many hordes who, with monotonous regularity, have invaded the West. They were attracted by the nourishing grass covering the steppes of Asia Minor, ideal for their large herds. Having forced their way through Persia they invaded Byzantium. Their confrontation with the Emperor's army took place at Manzikert in 1071, where they achieved total victory and captured Romanus IV, also called Diogenes. The Seljuk leader, Alp Arslan, asked his prisoner how he would have been treated if their roles had been reveresed.

Diogenes replied brazenly, "I would have run you through with my sword."

Arslan smiled softly and said, "I would not be guilty of such a cruel act, one so contrary to what your Lord Jesus Christ would have recommended:" and he set Diogenes free. On returning to Constantinople Diogenes found that Michael VII Ducas had usurped the throne. Diogenes suffered the fate of the fallen by having his eyes put out, the deed performed in such a savage manner that not surprisingly it caused his death.

Our taxi driver of the previous evening was parked opposite the hotel. A devout Muslim he wore his close-fitting cap and forever fingered his beads; he was the first and the only Turk we met who actually drove slowly and with care. We hired him for the morning — the only way of insuring that I could visit all the important mosques and medreses — and went together to the Archaeological Museum where I hurried round the showcases, knowing that in Ankara I would see the best of the excavations unearthed from nearby sites. Nevertheless, there was a good collection of coins, some delicate Roman glass and a Minoan vase and bracelet. The most outstanding items were three Roman sarcophagi, one of A.D. 250 showing the ten Labours of Hercules, the second of about the same date from Pamphylia and the third with a frieze depicting hunting scenes; I could pick out a man fighting a bear, a wolf, a dog chasing a hare and a solitary partridge.

Having found a safe driver Andrew and Martin were prepared to let me venture on my own — though I suspect they were secretly relieved not to have to visit the mosques as well. Andrew had acquired a map so I could plan my itinerary. With a quick look at the ornamental Seljuk doorway of the Sahip Ata Medrese next to the museum, I jumped into the taxi and we were off — at a snail's pace — to the Sircali Medrese. The tour's guide had warned me that many mosques were shut for restoration and, sure enough, this now proved to be the case. However through a grilled iron gate I could see the glazed tiles of the interior (Sircali means glazed). Built in 1242 by the tutor of Alaeddin Keykubad II, this was the first large scale structure to be decorated with tiles, and it now housed a collection of tombstones from the Seljuk, Karamanid and Ottoman periods. The portal was magnificent with fine reliefs of stylised flowers on the stone pilaster surround. Additional embellishments included rose motifs, columns with zig-zag decoration, and heavy keystones of alternate types of material providing a striking contrast over the rounded doorway. They fitted together with interlocking bulbous protrusions, rather like a jigsaw puzzle. Above them a script dedicated the medrese to the study of Islamic law.

The next stop was at the Karatay Medrese which I had passed on numerous occasions going to and from the autogar. I had attempted a visit when on my walk, only to be told that I was too late and would have to wait until the following day. Today it was also closed. I studied the decorative carvings on the monumental doorway considered to be one of the finest examples of Seljuk stonework in Turkey. Built as a theological college in 1251 the Medrese was now a museum for ceramics. I desperately wanted to go inside, so inveigled the help of the taxi driver and we both approached and banged on the door. It swung open and two museum keepers appeared. My driver explained that I was a tourist, I said 'please' and the ruse worked! I was ushered into the main room of the medrese covered with tiles, and the effect was stunning.

The bright shining peacock-blue hexagonal tiles on the side wall attracted one's immediate attention, and above stretched a broad band of blue tiles with black calligraphic designs highlighted in gold. From these great fan shapes of geometric patterns soared to the circular drum beneath the dome with more Islamic scroll decoration; finally, crowning the whole scene, there was the dome adorned with brilliant blue tiles depicting the firmament. The sun's rays poured through a lantern; dazzled, I was forced to look down catching sight of a pool immediately below. Centuries ago the sound of a playing fountain must have soothed the working students. Restoration was being carried out so the medrese was uncluttered, without its showcases and displays that would have detracted from the natural ornamentation. Other parts of the medrese had equally outstanding wall pictures made from tiles; one in particular caught my attention where the rose motif was barely discernible, blending with the intricate pattern.

In a small turbe connected to the main room I found the simple coffin of the founder of this building, the Emir Celaleddin Karatay. He had been the trusted adviser of Keykubad I, served as vizier under his son Keyhusrev II and was appointed regent for his three sons. Leaving behind the tranquillity of the medrese I rejoined the Konya's bustling thoroughfare, but not before handing a tip to the hovering museum keeper.

Across the road, protected by a modern concrete canopy, stood the last remaining fragment of the ancient defence wall and behind, on the hilltop, the largest mosque in Konya. Designed by an architect from Damascus during the reign of Mas'ud I (1116—1155), its Syrian style was unusual for Anatolia, and not until the most illustrious of the Seljuk Sultans, Keykubad I (1219—1234) rose to power, was it finally completed. Closed on my first inspection it was closed again today, reconstruction having been in progress for several years. This time there was no one about and no hope of entry. I squinted through every crack, chink and keyhole. I scrambled up a bank rising from a side path to gain height and, through a half shuttered window, was able to see a flat timbered ceiling with beams (similar to one I was to come across in the Ulu Cami in Kayseri). Apparently forty-two columns taken from Roman ruins supported the roof. From another angle I observed a large courtyard and the top of an octagonal turbe; the second hidden turbe was decagonal. It has been suggested that the conical tops to these mausoleums were inspired by the Seljuk tents, and certainly they were similar in shape to the tents of the nomads we had noticed on the steppes of Anatolia.

A wide road encircled the park — across which I had walked the other evening — and traffic raced around the one-way system. My driver gingerly edged his way to the outside lane stopping before the Ince Minare Medrese. The adjoining mosque was in ruins and the minaret, having been struck by lightning in 1901, was only half its original height. Believe it or not, this medrese was also closed for restoration. I consoled myself with the notion that the portals were the most important feature of mosques and medreses, and anyhow it was amusing to compare and contrast their different characteristics. This one was very grand and elaborate and much photographed, being an outstanding example of Seljuk architecture at its most fanciful. Like most sightseers I took my photograph and the keeper noticing my interest discreetly beckoned; producing a key he unlocked the door.

The main room of the medrese was a museum of stonework, but due to restoration most of the exhibits had been moved outside and only four of the most precious slabs of stone were placed against the walls. Carved on the first was a double-headed eagle the symbol of royalty, on the second two separate eagles faced each other with some calligraphy in between. Two sheep grazed on the third, and the last showed a rather curious gentleman. He was sitting crossed-legged wearing baggy trousers, a close fitting tunic with a narrow belt, a dervish hat and holding delicately in his left hand between thumb and little finger, an apple. The interior walls were faced with thin brick, and again those impressive fan shapes led from a point in each corner of the room and branched to the base of the dome. Each rib of the fan was decorated with narrow ceramic tiles and these, in varying shades of blue, were also interwoven with the brick work of the dome. Both this medrese and the one by the museum, the Sahip Ata, were commissioned by the Emir Sahip Ata Fahrettin Ali who was the greatest builder of his time. He succeeded Celaleddin Karatay as Vizier during the triumvirate of the three sons of Keyhusrev II, continued under Keyhusrev III, but was excecuted in 1277 after the Mamelukes captured Konya. * He and Celaleddin had been the two most eminent Viziers in Seljuk history.

The final building I visited that morning was the one for which Konya is renowned, the Mevlana Museum. Mevlana Celaleddin Rumi (1207—1273) was born in Afghanistan. Well educated he accompanied his father on the ritual pilgrimage and settled in Karaman — where many of his family were buried — later moving to Konya where he taught in one of the medreses. He soon became involved with a dervish called Husameddin Celebi; abandoning his career he joined the sect. Dervishes were Mohammedan friars vowed to a life of austerity and poverty, and Mevlana became their leader developing an ideology far ahead of the strict order of his time. He advocated equality of the sexes and monogamy, tolerance, love, charity and humility. The Tekkes (Dervish monasteries) were closed on Ataturk's orders in 1925 but, although disapproving of dervish practices, he at least adopted some of Mevlana's teachings.

Mevlana's two most famous works were the 'Mesnevi', a collection of several thousand odes ranking second to the Koran in Islamic literature, and 'Divan El Kebir', poems and prose written in Persian but subsequently translated. His teachings were closely linked to music, this being the best medium for freeing the soul from earthly bondage and abandoning oneself to God's love. The Rite of the Whirling Dervishes was performed after prayer and meditation, the men wearing conical hats and cloaks, each movement of the hand and each whirl conveying some religious nuance. Now the dance is only performed in December during celebrations commemorating Mevlana.

The taped dervish music droned incessantly adding to the dramatic scene in the museum, where row upon row of tombs stood sentinel as I tiptoed on precious carpets down a broad isle. The tombs were of varying sizes draped with coloured rugs, and at the head of each was placed the turban formerly worn by its occupant. There were sixty-five consisting of Mevlana's immediate family and the most illustrious of his disciples. His own tomb and that of his eldest son were on a raised platform immediately under the Green Dome, so called because of the vivid tiles of its exterior. This was a sacred shrine visited by worshippers from every part of the country. Some placed their foreheads, as a sign of devotion, on one of the two silver steps that led to the tomb; one old woman had

---

* The Seljuk Sultans of Rum regained their capital and ruled until the Mongol occupation in 1308.

97

tears in her eyes. The murmured prayers and the whispering of the tourists, the dim light and heavy atmosphere precipitated a feeling of dizziness, and I knew that unless I moved quickly I would soon become a swirling figure falling none too gracefully to the floor.

I recovered in a large domed chamber where the Whirling Dervishes performed their intoxicating dances. The musicians played at one end of the room, their instruments now shown in cabinets together with delicately carved Koran lecterns. A similar room that once had been a mosque contained a permanent exhibition of choice books; many of the Korans were beautifully decorated with gold leaf scrolls and flowers painted in the finest detail. For those who admire calligraphy there were many supreme examples especially in the reading room at the entrance to the tekke. The quotation above the silver door translated, "He who enters incomplete here, will leave complete."

Having spent a long time in the museum, I hurried round the courtyard noticing a group of Ottoman turbe of the sixteenth century. Though Mevlana's original turbe was Seljuk, a Karamanid Emir had added the fluted drum and conical turret with dazzling emerald green tiles. Dervishes' cells took up two sides of the courtyard, each one topped by a small lead cupola. A· few were furnished and, with the addition of wax models, presented scenes from their everyday lives. The calming sound of a fountain was delightful, but once beyond its hypnotic influence I dashed back to the hotel. Our adopted chauffeur was waiting patiently, and this time, accompanied by Andrew and Martin who had collected the cases, settled the bill and seen to all those boring and time consuming chores, we headed for the autogar.

We were soon in a bus bound for Nevsehir, deserting the Crusaders whom we would meet again in a few days at Nigde. We travelled on a Roman road that cut straight across the barren Anatolian steppe to Aksaray (Archelais) and Nevsehir (Soandos). This Great Road (Ulu Yol) was also constantly used by my new-found friends, the Seljuks, being the main caravan route between Konya and Kayseri. Caravanserais were built at frequent intervals, the merchants paying an annual tax to the Sultan to permit them free access to these inns when travelling from town to town. Caravanserais also fed and supplied the Seljuk armies when on the march during times of war, and served as a place of refuge when on the retreat.

The first one we passed, Horozlu Han, was eight kilometres out of Konya, but after an hour and a half we left the bus for a closer inspection of Sultan Hani. Founded by Keykubad I in 1229, this royal Caravanserai was the largest in Anatolia. Recently restored and back to its former height, its conical dome and imposing rectangular walls dominated the countryside. The entrance faced Mecca appearing twice the size of the mosque and medrese portals in Konya. I was entranced at finding the familiar Seljuk motifs on this secular building: the rose tracery, the zigzag columns, the geometric designs, the ornamental calligraphy and various marbles providing contrast and decoration.

We collected the key from the Tourist Information for the great door was barred against modern travellers. The warm sun welcomed us into the silent interior, so different from the thirteenth century when shouts and calls, orders and confusion greeted the arrival of a caravan. The horses and camels would have been led straight through the courtyard to a large covered area consisting of a central aisle, with a dome over a cross-section two thirds of the way down; on either side four more aisles were divided by rows of pillars. The smell now came from pigeon droppings, hundreds of these birds providing their form of welcome to twentieth century tourists.

The owner of the caravan would have prayed in the mescit, a chapel on the first floor of a tower in the centre of the courtyard. He could then have organised a vet to see to any of his animals, visited a physician if he needed medical treatment and bought stores for the next stage of his journey. There were bakeries and a kitchen, sleeping quarters, in fact everything that he could possibly have needed either for himself or for the maintenance of his caravan. He would have been allowed to rest for three days. We were off in three quarters of an hour, but not before drinking a well earned glass of tea offered to us by the brothers looking after the Tourist Information.

The imperious blare of a horn coming from a coach that had drawn up outside the entrance to the Caravanserai, demanded instant attention. One of the brothers hurried off to cope with the situation and Andrew followed out of curiosity. Leaving Martin to try to find out when the next bus might, with luck, be passing on its way to Aksaray or even Nevsehir, I went in search of subjects to photograph. I was soon surrounded by children urging me to take their, "picture, please picture." but as soon as I raised my camera they stood in a straight line with serious faces. "Cheese" or "Smile" made them look even more glum. Others rushed across to try to sell me brightly coloured woollen stockings and to ask for sweets. Realising that I could not help them, they scampered off to the coach to try their luck with the group of tourists emerging from the Han (caravanserai).

The surrounding houses — some with mud walls painted white and thatched roofs — were set well back from the village's sole attraction. It was difficult to imagine how the inhabitants earned a living for the land offered virtually nothing apart from a meagre sustenance for sheep. On the bus we had passed flocks tended by lone men, the fortunate riding donkeys but each one accompanied by his faithful companion, the steel-collared dog.

I sat on a stone wall dreaming of caravans, and my eyes must have half closed for the distant walls of Sultan Hani shimmered in the bright sunlight like a mirage; a spot detached itself from the side and moving quickly spoiled the image. I heard my name being shouted and saw Andrew running towards the Tourist Information to collect Martin. Andrew had organised a lift on this coach carrying an English tour bound for Nevsehir! Apparently he had met with some opposition because not all the occupants wanted three strangers in their midst and a vote had been taken. I climbed aboard and whom should I see sitting on the front seat but the carpet and ferry couple from Istanbul.

As usual in an organised tour the coach stopped for refreshments, halting a few kilometres before Aksaray at a motel with a modern self-service restaurant. By then it was four o'clock and we were extremely hungry, so Andrew and I shared a large slab of rather disappointing chocolate cake and I sampled a drink called Ayran, beaten yogurt, which I found to be very refreshing. We exchanged travel gossip with our friends. Their tour had left Istanbul and followed the Aegean coast south, continuing east to Antalya before turning north to Konya, roughly the opposite direction to that taken by the Yalvac tour. They spent one morning in Konya and the only building they had time to visit was the Mevlana museum followed by an hour 'at leisure'.

Our luck had not yet ended. A few miles east of Aksaray the tour stopped at Agzikara Han, another impressive Seljuk caravanserai. The monumental gateway included the jigsaw puzzle key stones over the arch-way — as in the Sircali Medrese in Konya — and the inner portal was also decorated. The han was not in such a good state of repair or as large as Sultan Hani, the livestock area having only three aisles each side but, owing to the absence of a roof, it was far less smelly. Children were clamouring for sweets and 'stilos'. A couple could not understand what they were saying so for once I could interpret. The woman hunted in her handbag and produced a biro which she gave to a little boy. It might have been a jewel from the Sultan's turban for it caused his face to express infinite joy. Five minutes later, as we left, I saw the same face stricken with grief, the precious stilo having been snatched from his hand by a bigger and stronger boy.

We passed other caravanserais but they were in ruins and we did not stop. The highlight of the last hour of our journey was the sight of a troupe of gypsies clattering along at a fair pace. The fleeting impression was of a happy group of families, their worldly goods piled high upon carts pulled by good looking ponies, with hunting dogs keeping pace prepared to attack the bus if we dared to slow down.

By a strange coincidence we were all staying at the same hotel in Nevsehir. The tour's guide looked distraught as he fended off the inevitable complaints, and was grateful to Andrew who waded in and expressed delight at the high standard the hotel seemed to offer. To us it was luxury and we even had a bath — minus a plug — with hot water promised immediately. While Andrew and Martin visited the Tourist Office to arrange our next day's sightseeing and to sip their preprandial drink, I washed the dust from my hair and clothes, wrote my remaining postcards and half caught up with my diary.

The dinner provided by the hotel was unbelievable. As we entered the dining room we were greeted with a display of mezes laid out on a long sideboard; it looked as if the chef had entered a competition and had cooked every dish in his repertoire. He had produced mousses and spicy

100

meat balls, stuffed vine leaves and peppers, small pieces of liver, numerous varieties of beans, cold meats, aubergines and salads. The main course — brought to our places — consisted of thin slices of veal with rice, while the dessert was arranged at one end of the sideboard. This was the first time that we had found a selection of puddings in a restaurant, the reason probably being that the hotel catered for hordes of hungry and greedy foreign tourists. A crumbly sugary substance turned out to be halva — crushed sesame seeds — slices of sponge were covered in syrup some deceptively shaped like pears, and I noticed the occasional orange and apple disappearing into ladies handbags or pockets for the following day; but the final tour de force was a mound of Turkish delight. Andrew discovered another good local wine. As soon as I possibly could, without appearing rude, I left the others to chat to our fellow travellers and went upstairs. Imagining that I was riding a camel I floated past the glistening white corridor walls and approached my resting place for the night. Feeling like a whirling dervish I sank gratefully into my bed.

Karatay Medrese

right: Sircali Medrese

Caravanserai
at Sultan Hani

"picture, please
    picture"

DAY XII : CAPPADOCIA

We nicknamed the contraption in which we were to spend the next two days, the Flying Coffin.   It was a very old vehicle indeed – one of the forerunners of the dormobile – with three rows of seats, but the windows were so low that in order to admire the scenery we had to bend our heads or slide down into our seats, either contortion resulting in aching necks and backs.   A French woman joined us, and another Turk posing as a driver took his place behind the wheel.   Two plastic alligators crouched on the dashboard fitted with sham leopard skin; they faced each other, their necks swaying in mock battle according to the equilibrium of the van.

Until now German had been the second language of the Turks, but in Cappadocia French predominated for they had been amongst the first antiquarians from the West.   Apart from the accounts of occasional travellers, the treasures of Cappadocia remained virtually unknown until the visit of Father Guillaume de Jerphanion in 1907.   He devoted his life to their study and exploration.   For many years before and after the second world war it became increasingly difficult to visit the remoter areas of Turkey, and not until 1950 was a major survey carried out in the Peristrema Valley by Nicole and Michele Thierry.   The French had also been responsible for a great deal of the restoration of frescoes and churches in the region.

Our guide gabbled away in French.   His peculiar enunciation made some of his lengthy and involved stories quite hard to understand.   Nevertheless he knew where to take us and was determined that we should see as much as possible in the day, doubling the itinerary covered by the tours.   We soon realised that the first item on the day's agenda had to be reached before the arrival of the coaches.   We sped south out of Nevsehir, our driver hogging the centre of the road thereby preventing the coach behind from passing, but not having enough power to pass the one in front until a sneaky manoeuvre at the car park put him ahead.   We had arrived at Kaymakli, the first of two underground villages.   No one knows when they were originally hewn out of the soft rock.   The early Christians used and enlarged them as places of refuge from the endless invading hordes of Arabs from the south and later 'Turks from the east, and the local population went underground in 1833 to escape from the army of Mehmet Ali, the Egyptian pasha.   Now they have been re-opened as a tourist attraction with electric lights and arrows to point the way. Our guide ignored the latter plunging down passages and through narrow archways revealing numerous small rooms used either as sleeping quarters, chapels, burial chambers, cooking areas or for storage.   Everything was included that could possibly have been needed in such a community. Ventilation shafts disappeared to great depths gathering air from some obscure source and fresh water was drawn from wells.   In case of invasion entrances could be blocked by heavy millstones, and each of the eight or more storeys could similarly be sealed from one another. Gingerly we crossed ill fitting iron grids covering gaping holes. Some were used purely as access to lower levels, while others were part of a cunning defence system down which trespassers tumbled. These holes acquired the name 'oubliettes', for the unwanted bodies were conveniently forgotten, carried away by a subterranean river.

The caves were filling with streams of shuffling tourists of every shape and size, some far too big and whom I feared would block our exit. At one stage the five of us squashed into the angle of what must have been the longest tunnel, while the contents of a panting coach load squeezed past. The stench of garlic and human exertion was revolting in the extreme and, though I have never had claustrophobia, I can now appreciate its terror. The others felt the same and thankfully we soon emerged, blinking and squinting in the strong sunlight. I could never be a troglodyte.

Kaymakli was joined by an underground passage of nine kilometres to its sister village of Derinkuyu, and above ground by the main Nevsehir-Nigde road. By a unanimous vote we agreed to give Derinkuyu a miss and took a cross country dirt road to Uchisar.

Now at last we were approaching the true Cappadocian landscape. Thirty to sixty million years ago the whole of this region had been the scene of fierce volcanic activity. The three chief volcanoes, Hasan Dagi (3252 metres), Melendiz Dagi (2963 metres) and Erciyes Dagi (3916 metres) erupted, tossing lava, ash and boulders for tens of thousands of years. The gradual accumulation of volcanic ash meant that the province of Nevsehir came to be situated on a plateau 1,200 metres above sea level, and eventually this soft stone, or tufa, was scoured into canyons and gorges by the river Kizilirmak (Red River) and its many tributaries. Strong winds, rain and occasional earthquakes contributed to the process of erosion, and the weird landscape slowly gained its unique quality. These curious formations varied from valley to valley, as if local artists had staked their claim to a plot and left behind their individual style of decoration. Some of the rocks were cone-shaped or twisted in extraordinary ways, others were tall and thin, or squat and disfigured. Fantastic crags or plain spires sprung from the ground many topped by black hoods, these emanating from a basalt strata which once lay above the tufa. In fact every shape that one could possibly imagine decorated the landscape providing a veritable display of outdoor sculpture.

The colour of the rock also varied, the basic tones being ashen white or grey, but in certain areas brick red predominated, whereas in a neighbouring valley it had faded to rust or ochre. The whole scene could change dramatically according to the light or the time of day, distant ranges taking on either a pinkish hue or, with darkening skies, becoming a deep violet.

The region proved an ideal place of refuge for those small bands of persecuted Christians. Rather than build houses they found it easier and safer to burrow into the cliffs. By the Edict of Milan in 313 Christianity was tolerated within the divided Roman Empire, Constantine governing the West from Rome and his half sister's husband, Licinius, the East from Byzantium; but even with family connections the two Emperors failed to rule harmoniously. In 325 after numerous battles Constantine defeated Licinius and made Byzantium into the new Christian capital of the Roman Empire. In the ninth century a Macedonian ascended the throne by means of the usual intrigues and assassinations, and Greek replaced Latin as the official language. However a fictitious liaison with the Roman Empire persisted and was so ingrained that until this century the Christian subjects were still called Rumi.

Having auspiciously survived and settled in their new land, the Christian community was beset by the onslaught of another menace, the Iconoclasts. In 729, Emperor Leo III forbade the worship of images and the Iconoclasts, having been troublesome for the previous century, went berserk destroying many beautiful mosaics and frescoes. These image breakers acted with the same ruthlessness as the Roundheads who centuries later desecrated English churches. For a few years during the reign of Emperor Constantine VI and his mother Empress Irene sanity returned, but by 802 the image shatterers were back again and were not finally condemned until the Ecumenical Council of 842.

A massive 43 metre rock pyramid dominated the village of Uchisar. Originally an impenetrable fortress, today's visitors climb to the top by way of concrete steps. The view from the summit was spectacular. We looked down on the tips of cones, each dwelling place with one or two irregularly spaced cave-like windows many decorated with red geometric patterns in the style of Iconoclasts. Quince and apricot trees interspersed with vines surrounded the village where the houses were of standard design, while the sides of a valley stretching beyond were indented with tiny holes which our guide described as pigeonniers (dovecotes). Millions of pigeons had been encouraged to nest, the tons of guano they produce affording a natural and convenient fertiliser for the orchards and vine-yards.

Our guide was well trained and half way to our next port of call he made the driver stop, allowing us to clamber out and admire the view of a new valley flowing with fairy chimneys, an appropriate nickname adopted by the local population. Nearby a chapel had been scoured out of a cone, its floor encrusted with hollowed tombstones laid bare by treasure seekers, but a Byzantine cross remained carved in the apse.

In the valley of Goreme we met, for the first time in Anatolia, mass tourism. Charabancs filled the car park and as well as hearing French and German, snippets of Russian reached our ears. Entrance fees, half price at weekends, also encouraged many Turks to have a day out, but luckily there were numerous churches to examine and the hordes spread out, thinned, straggled and became less irritating. Although there were only one hundred and fifty known churches and monastic establishments in

Cappadocia, half of which possessed wall paintings, it was rumoured that originally there were over twice as many. The majority remain undiscovered because either they are extremely well hidden or protected by rock fall; a few have been unintentionally revealed by outer walls collapsing and unkindly displaying their entrances and secret interiors.

The early churches and chapels were decorated with primitive paintings. The Iconoclasts used solely geometric designs but allowed the drawing of animals and a few symbolic representations of the human figure, while after 842 representative art flourished and continued to develop well into the thirteenth century. The actual age of the church did not necessarily correspond with the age of its frescoes, many having been hollowed out before the period of Iconoclasm. The earliest could be recognised by their flat roofs and small apses much lower than the nave. The basic plan for the majority of churches was simple, a barrel vaulted nave separated from the apse by an arch. Those of a later date were more adventurous taking the form of miniature basilicas with three aisles, or having the ground plan based on the Greek cross. The monasteries varied in size too, with dwelling chambers and store rooms hidden in a network of tunnels.

Here at Goreme we visited only churches with wall paintings. The surprise of stumbling across these interiors was made greater by their total unexpectedness, for we often had to manoeuvre our way over open graves and bend our heads in order to enter through a nondescript archway. Whether the standard of paintings was primitive or sophisticated was immaterial, they were all highly individual and fascinating in their own way.

The churches were conveniently arranged round a large amphitheatre of natural cliffs, with concrete paths leading one invitingly to their entrances and signposts revealing their names. The first church we approached happened to be the earliest, that of St. Barbara. Because of erosion the graves in the once covered burial chamber were open to the elements; fortunately the actual chapel was safe. The Iconoclasts had dictated the style of decoration. Crude geometric designs taken from triangles, squares, chequered and zig-zag motives covered the walls, and the primitive drawings were amusing to interpret: for instance those in the central dome could have been posts and banners, or they could equally have represented stiff trees and palm leaves.

Opposite the entrance the top half of an arched recess was divided into horizontal sections, the precursor of the strip cartoon. The story began with a cock about to peck at a seedling in the first stage of growth with only two leaves, its stalk, however, being the same height as the legs of the cock. One line lower the artist was unable to resist the temptation of adding small circles to the extremities of two Maltese crosses. These crosses flanked a ferocious looking beetle with two pincer-like horns protruding from its tiny head. It must have been a scarab, the religious connection coming from Egypt where the insect was revered. The rest of the story was denied to us for the lower section had been painted over by

the post-Iconoclasts, and showed St. George and Emperor Theodosius*
mounted on white horses killing a dragon. This oft repeated painting was
the reason why so many churches adopted the name 'snake church', the
scene symbolising the fight and supremacy of mankind over evil.
St. Barbara was one of the Saints drawn on the adjoining wall while the
other figurative painting in the apse showed Christ seated on a throne.
The drawing was flat, neither the principles of proprtion nor perspective
having yet been mastered, nevertheless the effect was striking and the
addition of yellow to the red added impact.

These early paintings were carried out by monks feeling the need to
embellish their places of worship. The soft rock proved a difficult surface
on which to use a brush, and they had more success with pieces of cloth
dipped in a red lime mixture and pressed on the walls; later they discovered that plaster mixed with hay provided a better base. During what
has been termed as the Archaic Period c. 850—950, local artists were
employed and painted with more freedom. In the following century
some of the most accomplished artists in the Byzantine Empire were
commissioned to demonstrate their skills.

Both the Seljuks and Ottomans were tolerant of religious minorities
recognising Christ as a great prophet and teacher. This traditional
Turkish attitude was proved by the fact that Greek Christian communities
were still living in Cappadocia and worshipping freely until 1923. The
damage to the churches since then was inflicted by the same type of
person who had destroyed the tomb outside Iznik. In the expectation of
finding treasure vandals had hacked indiscriminately at the frescoes.
Graffiti also spoiled the paintings but perhaps the worst destruction was
caused by fires which blackened and obliterated many irreplaceable works
of art. Only recently has tourism been recognised as a lucrative business,
the government taking steps to safeguard their heritage. Gates with locks
now guard the entrances to these remarkable churches.

In this so-called open air museum three churches predominated, the
Karanlik Kilise (Dark Church), the Carikli Kilise (Church of the Sandal),
and the Elmanli Kilise (Church of the Apple), and all contained eleventh
century frescoes. They were dug out in the form of the Byzantine cross
with four pillars, a central dome, side domes, an apse and semi-domes,
making them appear much larger than they actually were. The first two
churches backed onto each other and the treatment of their subject
matter was identical. The walls were plastered enabling the paintings to
flow more naturally, each scene labelled in Greek script and separated by
patterns or decorative twisted branches. In the Dark Church Christ
dominated the apse and the central dome, with the four Evangelists in a
frieze round its base, and scenes from the New Testament covered other
sections of wall space. The table in the Last Supper tilted in a naive way
so that we could see a large fish resting on a handsome bowl, two goblets,

---

* Theodosius the Great, Emperor of Byzantium (379—395) was renowned for his
Edict banning paganism.

and a few knives and forks laid on the woven cloth. The disciples looked on impassively from behind the length of the table, Judas sitting alone at one end while Christ gazed in his direction from the other. Even though their faces by modern standards showed no expression, the artist, by the tilt of the heads and the direction of the eyes, managed to convey the poignancy of the moment.

The artist tried hard to achieve a realistic figure of Christ on the cross. The anatomical details became abstract shapes, the shoulders great circles, the muscles of the arms oval lumps, and his stomach semi-circular curves. One could see how the twentieth century painters were fascinated by the implication created by a few well placed lines. A sun and a moon on either side of the picture denoted the passage of time. It was here that our guide regaled us with a long and complicated saga which necessitated several repetitions. His story told of how Judas had changed places with Christ and was crucified instead. By some extraordinary coincidence I had once heard a similar theory, but that interpretation went further: Christ had then vanished and eventually reappeared as Mohammed. The guide of the English tour in our hotel had told Andrew that he was dreading this day and having to explain the frescoes — which belonged to a strange religion — to a critical group of English men and women who were bound to ask awkward questions. Our guide had no trouble, chattering and interpreting the Bible stories quite happily and oft repeating his strange ideology.

The Church of the Sandals — whose frescoes were similar to the ones in the Dark Church — received its name after the cast of a footprint scooped out of the floor in the southern transept. This was believed to have been taken from an imprint of Christ's foot found in the sanctuary of the Ascension in Jerusalem and brought to Goreme by early Christians.

The frescoes in the Church of the Apple were lighter in tone with a background of pastel colours. Apples painted inside one cupola gave credence to the name, and graceful angels surrounded Jesus who according to ritual filled the central dome. In places where the plaster had worn away, the earlier iconoclastic motives could be seen painted in red monochrome. We had approached the interior along the original well hidden tunnel, but sadly even this had failed to keep the Church a secret. The vestibule wall which shared the cliff face had plunged into the ravine below and through a jagged hole daylight flooded the interior.

Of the remaining churches the Yilanli Kilise (Snake Church) was attractive. Simple in form it had only two chambers, that of the main nave vaulted and the inner flat roofed. The familiar fresco of St. George and Theodosius killing a dragon dominated the north wall, together with Empress Helena and her son Constantine splendidly attired and both holding a double cross. On the opposite wall St. Thomas and St. Basil stood next to a weird figure with a bearded face, women's breasts and the lower half of the body covered by a tree. She was called Onouphirius, a sinful woman, punished by the transformation of her captivating face into that of an old man.

Byzantine crosses graced the entrance of the nearby Church of the Tombs containing many excavated hollows within a single chamber, and St. Helena and Constantine appeared again joined this time by the four Evangelists. A little further on we came across the pitiful sight of what appeared to be damage caused by shell fire. In reality the outer wall had collapsed of its own accord, revealing to the world the bizarre scene of the transept of one church directly above the nave of another. We found a kitchen and store rooms next to a refectory whose long table and benches were chiselled out of the rock; niches round the walls once held water for washing and jars of wine. However we did not linger for there was one more church to be seen.

The largest and best preserved of all the Goreme churches was situated outside the turnstiles and below the car park. Named after a buckle found on the ceiling — probably a fixture from which hung an oil lamp — the Tokali Kilise was hollowed into the cliff face. It had a transverse nave purporting to be the archetype of this new innovation and the walls were completely covered with superb frescoes. Their colours, though subdued in tone, had been fortuitously conserved owing to the erosion of the facade and the blocking of the entrance by rock fall. At some stage the Church had been used as a dovecote, thereby protecting the paintings from both daylight and vandals. Eight years had been spent in their restoration and, though several periods of decoration existed, the majority dated from the beginning of the eleventh century and were painted on a plaster base. By following the cartoon strips the Life of Christ could be traced in successive scenes, and above them row upon row of Saints stood next to each other their names conveniently inscribed in ancient Greek. St. Basil (329–379) renowned in Cappadocia warranted a separate account of his life. As Bishop of Caesarea he had been instrumental in persuading hermits and their accompanying families to join together and form larger communities. He thus founded the basis of monasticism eventually to be adopted in the West.

I was delighted to find that we were heading for Avcilar. I had wanted to stop there on the way to Goreme for I had heard that in a gigantic cone one could see the facade of a Roman tomb. The guide had been sceptical when I quizzed him on the subject. A new restaurant in the central square tempted the guide to take us back the way we had come so I had not missed my opportunity after all. I enjoyed my bread and yogurt and glass of tea and, leaving the others to their pizza-like pittas, went to explore.

The cone was easy to find for it dominated the small village and half way up, looking solidly Roman, two round pillars hung as stalactites from a squared frame. Like the guide I was not altogether convinced that this was a tomb, nor indeed Roman. The structure could equally well have been Christian like so many we had already seen, the customary eroding of the rock face revealing to the outside world the once private sanctuary. The rock however looked as if it had arrived from outer space with television aerials sticking out like antennae. Walking to the far side I found a house nestling beside it, making use of the warmth and comfort of the rock and incorporating some of its rooms as an annex.

Many houses in the village were fairly new; built from blocks of local stone, the window surrounds and arches over their front doors were decorated with rosettes, triangles and circles. In a small square I took a photograph of one of those familiar lorries that tore along the main roads, handsomely painted with flowers and landscapes; but I had no luck when trying to photograph people. I approached an old man leading a donkey laden with sacks only to be waved angrily aside with a stick; a woman — her face half covered with a black shawl — bringing her cow to drink at the village well, raised her arm to shield her face when I produced my camera so I hastily lowered my evil eye; if I had known that a girl carrying an earthenware jar on her head was to appear unexpectedly from around the corner, I might have had my zoom lens ready and risked a shot. Not caring to antagonise the villagers, I returned to the confines of the Flying Coffin.

We drove to Cavusin another troglodyte village. As usual dates were vague but at sometime there had been a devastating rock slide. A large section of the plateau had split, tumbled down and disintegrated, bringing with it hundreds of cave dwellings and chapels. The present inhabitants had built their houses on top of the rubble making use of the surrounding boulders. We climbed up the cliff face to enter the impressive three aisled basilica of St. John the Baptist, thought to be the oldest known Christian sanctuary in Cappadocia, and trudged to the higher ground rising behind the village to be greeted by another sensational view of a valley decorated with cones and bordered by pink tinged cliffs.

A short distance from Cavusin I made sure the driver stopped by an imposing tower where a steep iron stairway led to a church half way up the rock face. Once more a section of the exterior had collapsed revealing the narthex and a fresco of two angels with extended wings guarding the new entrance. Frescoes covered the vaulted ceiling and walls in a similar fashion to those in the Tokali Church. They were lighter in tone with lovely shades of rose, and the four Evangelists were portrayed in medallions on a blue background. Among the portraits was one of Emperor Nicophorus II Phocas who ruled from 963—9, and his wife the faithless Empress Theophano. The Emperor, a native of Cappadocia, led a campaign against the Arabs in 964. Before he could free the Holy Land he was murdered by his wife and her Armenian lover, John Tzimisces who then usurped the throne; as a probable safeguard to his own life, Tzimisces dismissed Theophano to a monastery.

The English tour was leaving the Church as we arrived and we caught up with them again at our next halt, at the beginning of the small valley of Pasabag. They had been to Goreme in the morning, had a three course lunch in a modernised cave sitting on stone benches spread with carpets, and were now on their afternoon's itinerary. As they drifted back to their coach we trod the well worn path and gazed with curiosity at a new type of rock chimney. In this valley the rocks supported one or two, or sometimes three squat, round pillars topped by black basalt hoods.

Our guide suddenly disappeared into a narrow entrance at the base of one of these chimneys beckoning Andrew to follow him. Peeping through the cleft I saw them making their way up a vertical shaft. I could not resist the challenge but found the climb exceedingly tricky; grooves on the insides of the walls allowed me to place the palms of my hands and heels of my boots into these holes and, by pushing my way backwards, I moved slowly and in a crab-like fashion up the chimney. We emerged into a chamber with a small opening through which we waved like gleeful children to Martin and the French lady who had declined the scramble. The room had recently been used for it bore telltale evidence in the form of empty cans and the ashes of a fire, but for what purpose our guide seemed reluctant to disclose. Since there were neither rugs nor household utensils we doubted whether anyone lived here; more than likely the den provided a convenient meeting place for illegal drinking sessions.

The tour and a mass of charabancs were already at Zelve. Between the ninth and thirteenth century this well hidden valley flanked by tall cliffs rising to 500 metres on either side, had been one of the main religious centres in Cappodicia. During the Ottoman Empire, Greek and Armenian Christians migrated to Zelve from the Nevsehir area, and after their eventual repatriation Muslims occupied the abandoned cave city converting some of the churches into mosques — a carved stone minaret looked perfectly natural and not dissimilar from the open bell tower of a church. Muslims continued to live there until 1950 when New Zelve was founded in a nearby valley. Erosion had eaten away the cliff face causing the evacuation of the last of its inhabitants.

Very few chapels and frescoes remained so our guide took us on a pot holing escapade, the favourite occupation for the majority of agile visitors. We climbed a shaky ladder and plunged down a tunnel into the depths of the hillside. The guide had a torch, but since I was last in the line the light failed to help me; I clung on to Andrew's hand unable to see anything. We entered a cavern — I could tell by the echo — took right and left turns, groped our way along narrow passages and scrambled down a shaft. Although supplied with hand and foot holes, they were extremely difficult to find in the dark. I had heard horrifying tales of tourists losing themselves in the tunnels, and we had been warned of rock falls and traps laid for the unwary visitor. I knew fate would decree that I should lose Andrew's grip, slip down a gaping hole and become one of those 'oubliettes'.

My lack of faith in our guide was unjustified and we emerged high up the cliff side, but still had to negotiate a long, steep form of stairway to reach the comfort of ground level. We all decided that there should be no more exploring, and we tottered to our Flying Coffin, relieved that it was our transport in name only and not in reality.

Our driver, having performed reasonably well for the last few hours, reassumed his image of Stirling Moss with which he had begun the day. He veered away from the line of charabancs, down a farm track which frequently took to the fields and, after every bone in our bodies had been well jolted, regained the tarmac road. He hurtled on, taking blind corners on the wrong side of the road and came to a screeching halt at Urgup, all for the sake of a glass of tea. We sipped the reviving liquid in a shaded courtyard, where men of varying ages were sitting on low stools or rugs spread upon the ground. Some were playing their second — less athletic — national game, backgammon. Others watched, idly passing the time of day, the ubiquitous tea glasses littering the low tables.

Urgup was the commercial and administrative centre for the area. It made use of the numerous caves in the vicintiy for the storage of grain, fruit, vegetables and wine, and as stalls for livestock. Surrounding valleys held yet more rock treasures for those with additional time to spare. The Tourist Office had strongly advised the hiring of a guide for any expedition to remote areas — a wise precaution if only to avoid disappointment at not being able to find the elusive rock churches.

We sped on to Ortahisar, another citadel village resembling Uchisar which we had visited at the beginning of the day. We climbed to the top of the prevailing fortress-cone and realised the lateness of the hour by the changing light.   Andrew bought some apricots grown in the nearby orchards, and I chose à pair of turkish styled trousers before Martin firmly directed the guide to return to our hotel in Nevsehir.

We heard from our fellow tourists that after Zelve they had driven to Avanos. The nearby quarries produced onyx, and the tour was taken to a factory to see the stone being shaped into decorative objects.   One member of the group told me that he had visited the same place three years ago, when the incredibly hard stone had been cut with a circular saw, the teeth of which needed frequent sharpening. Now they used diamonds fixed to the cutting edge making the task far easier. The final shaping was carried out by hand and the polishing, a long and tedious job, was usually given to the children.

A woman in the party whom we nicknamed Lady C., had adopted Turkish dress. She told me of material she had bought and how she had found a dressmaker to 'run her up' a pair of trousers.   On her return to England her daughter was going to copy the pattern and make a fortune. Her well cut and amply gathered trousers rather put to shame my cheap poor quality ones, made with skimped material and sewn with rough stitching that I had purchased in record bargaining time.

Though nothing could compete with the cuisine of our hotel we went out to dinner to sample the local fare. Walking back along the deserted and badly lit streets, the sudden piercing blast of a whistle terrified us.   It came from a shadowy figure lurking in a doorway. We were about to flee when a policeman emerged. He appeared totally unconcerned at our presence. We heard an answering whistle from a distance and, as our policeman moved away, he too whistled again. They were signalling to each other.   I stirred occasionally during the night to hear their secret code, but was not altogether sure whether I appreciated knowing that it was merely 'past the hour and that all was well'.

Andrew and Christabel - a valley flowing with fairy chimneys

Avcilar

Rock Churches, Goreme

Zelve

Pasabag

Another variation of
outdoor sculpture, Uchisar

DAY XIII : THE PERISTREMA VALLEY

We were understandably dubious about the prospect of having to face many uncomfortable and nervous hours in the Flying Coffin. Because he had to attend a ceremony which entailed laying wreaths on the statue of Ataturk, the guide could not leave before 11.40 a.m.. This was really too late to start a day's excursion. We should have caught an early bus to Akseray and from there hired a taxi to take us to the Peristrema Valley. The turning to Ihlara — the village at the head of the valley — was only 11 kilometres from Aksaray, whereas from Nevsehir it was 67 kilometres. Anyhow, we had committed ourselves and could not reasonably cancel our guide nor his eccentric vehicle.

Since we had a late start I decided to accompany Andrew on his early morning walk. We wended our way up steep narrow streets and scrambled the final 100 metres through scrub to the Seljuk fortress on the acropolis, whose crenellated walls and four towers were in a good state of preservation. We tried without success to recognise our hotel amidst the growing number of tall buildings, and then made our way down to an important looking mosque. Having been open for prayer only a few hours previously, it was now, inevitably, shut. The Turks are great tree planters and some young pines surrounding the mosque were growing well. A circular sadirvan stood in a clearing with its wooden roof extended to shelter the faithful when preparing themselves for worship.

We could not resist walking through an open doorway into a court-yard scattered with pottery and stone carvings. It turned out to be a museum and, although closed, the keeper went to fetch his keys and showed us three rooms filled with relics discovered in the region. The museum had originally been a Hospice presented to the people of the town by Ibrahim Pasha. Born in 1678 the son of the mayor of Muscara — as the town was then known — Ibrahim Pasha became the son-in-law of Ahmet III and served as Grand Vizier from 1718—30. He proved one of the most enlightened men of his time, a patron of the arts encouraging cultural contacts with Europe and more especially with France. Renaming his home town Nevsehir, New Town, he carried out many improvements. He encouraged nomadic tribesmen to settle, built houses, schools and public baths, constructed a new water system and established a library. In 1730 during an unsuccessful uprising, he was murdered.

We had paid our entrance fee before entering the museum and thought that we should also give the keeper a tip since he had been so kind unlocking the doors a couple of hours before opening time. He refused Andrew's token of our thanks. Whether or not to tip presented a perpetual problem for occasionally more offence could be given by offering money than vice versa. If only we had remembered the duty free cigarettes; they would always have been welcome.

We had worked up a good appetite and, remembering the stale bread our hotel produced for breakfast, called at the bakers we had passed earlier that morning. The smell was mouth watering. There was a queue for individual orders, some customers asking for an egg to be broken on their pitta bread before they were pushed on long handled wooden platters into the earthenware oven. We bought a narrow oval-ended pitta at least half a metre long which was rolled up and wrapped in newspaper, and hurried back to breakfast while it was still warm.

We shared our purchase with the friendly English couple. They were about to visit both the underground cities that morning. Lady C. was reluctant to go, but I told her that it was an experience not to be missed, while another gentleman wanted to walk the nine kilometre tunnel connecting Kaymakli with Derinkuyu. We felt sorry for their guide. In the afternoon they were going to Hacibektas — a village 48 kilometres north of Nevsehir — the centre of the Islamic 'Bektasi' sect established in the thirteenth century by Hacibektas Veli. His morals and teachings were not dissimilar to those of Mevlana; he built a medrese for training missionaries which is now a museum and library, and the complex includes his tomb.

Our journey was not as bad as we had feared, the guide having accepted Martin's complaints, produced another friend to drive. They had both worked until midnight repairing the vehicle and certainly the contraption took on a new lease of life. It was important to start our sightseeing at Ihlara and work our way back down the valley, for I had been warned against enthusiastic guides who were keen to drag the uninformed visitor to yet another troglodyte village. I put my plan to Andrew, Martin and the French woman — who had decided to join us again — but they preferred to leave the organisation entirely to the guide since he had been so competent the previous day. Sure enough our first stop was at the rock village of Selime, where the troglodytes had abandoned their caves and now occupied stone houses. Our pattern of sightseeing resumed as we scrambled up roughly hewn steps to explore a few churches and refectories, but not much remained of this large monastic settlement.

News of our arrival had spread. As we set off across the fields children scampered after us, picking wild flowers and presenting them to us as gifts. They wanted their photograph taken, insisting on our guide writing down their names and addresses in order that I could send them a print. Our walk was to take us through a weird lunar landscape of smooth sided ashen cones sticking out of a grey gravel surface. We found one chapel in the middle of a cone the entrance two metres from the ground. With no inside shaft we had to clamber up the outside using inadequate chips in the rock surface for hand and foot holds. This time Martin followed the guide and I was pushed and pulled up through the jagged hole, but there was nothing much to see apart from a few faint red markings.

I longed to escape to Ihlara, but no such luck. We had another halt at the village of Yaprakhisar, walked alongside the river Melendiz, admired the use of irrigation and the planting of poplars, listened to nightingales, and realised that these cones housed people.   We waited patiently while the guide closed the Coffin door from the outside, the only way to keep it shut, removed the stones from the wheels which acted as a handbrake and finally, we moved on.

The previous day our guide had suggested that we brought our swimming gear, for there were some thermal baths at Ziga; but whereas yesterday had been the hottest day we were to experience in Turkey — with many members of the English tour sporting sunburnt noses — today was the opposite, so I was spared a further delay.   Hasan Dagi, which should have provided us with a spectactular background its peak covered in snow for most of the year, remained elusive in a low hanging mist.

We passed a signpost indicating the entrance to the valley.   Everyone was hungry so we drove straight on to the village of Ihlara, bought some bread, hardboiled eggs, tomatoes and a stick of turkish delight, and sat at some tables in a deserted but well situated café by a flowing river.   A woman presented us with a bunch of spring onions, and our guide and driver managed to make a substantial meal out of the few ingredients. They produced penknives and slit their portion of bread in half; they peeled their onions with meticulous care, finely sliced a tomato, and crushing the egg made a gigantic sandwich.   The tea we ordered took ages to arrive and I began to lose hope of ever reaching my valley.

The Peristrema Valley stretches for 14 kilometres running between the villages of Ihlara and Selime.   At the official entrance the visitor is confronted by vertical cliffs falling away for 60 metres, while the average width to the far side of the canyon is only 80 metres.   The Melendiz river flowing from the foothills of Hasan Dagi wends its way along the valley bed.   Over many thousands of years it had been instrumental in creating this deep fissure.   Astonishingly we had arrived, and from a bare windy plateau we looked down on a peaceful green valley with poplars and willows, a spectacular contrast.

The valley was conveniently off the beaten track, some 20 kilometres from the main Roman road which ran from Ancyra (Ankara) to Archelais (Aksaray).   There it was joined by the road from Iconium (Konya), proceeded to Soandos, a few kilometres east of present day Nevsehir and the junction of a major cross roads, and continued to Caesarea (Kayseri). A Christian community had dug themselves safely into the cliff face occupying an estimated number of 4,535 caves and 105 churches.   By the time Nicole and Michele Thierry came to investigate in the 1950s land-slides had blocked most of their entrances; covered with scree and veget-ation the churches were extremely difficult to find.   In the upper part of the valley six were signposted and we visited five of them.

We descended into the valley down concrete steps.   Sunday had been designated a day of rest by Ataturk, so large groups of Turks had gathered and were having picnics, playing games and dancing.   Hardly any of them ventured into the caves with strange paintings.   Unfortunately, before their importance was realised, intruders had been unable to resist adding graffiti to the walls and chipping out the eyes of Saints to destroy

119

any witness to their misdemeanours. Shepherds had used the caves to shelter both themselves and their sheep, and were not averse to lighting the occasional fire.

The first church, Agacalti Kilise, meaning the one by the base of a tree, was decorated between the ninth and tenth centuries. The frescoes were crude though harmonious, and the best one showed the death of the Virgin Mary — the Dormition. Christ sat near the head of the bed on which Mary lay, and beside him stood St. John holding a sceptre. The drawing of Christ wearing the same robe was repeated; this time he was standing and holding a small doll-like figure, his Mother's soul, watched over by an angel. The treatment of this scene is rare in Byzantine painting. Christ supported by angels adorned a cupola; in the Ascension his cheek bones were indicated by violent brown triangles. On a semi-circular wall in the apse the hindquarters of one lion and the neck of another, plus a possible leg of Daniel was all that sadly remained, the church sometimes being referred to by the name of the obliterated Daniel. I noticed three cocks standing in a row; either they represented 'ere the cock crows thou shalt deny me thrice', or they symbolised alertness against evil spirits. The three Kings had long hair and beards and wore Phrygian caps. They were dressed in sumptuous tunics and each one carried their gift represented by a round disc. The same determination existed to cover every inch of the walls with decoration, so where pictures ended patterns took over. The barrel vaulted ceiling had a marvellous design of petals, rosettes, diamonds and tulip shapes, while broad bands beneath were filled with flowing scrolls, chequer boarding and squares, providing yet more scope for inventiveness. The colours ranged from green to brown, red through to orange and blue to grey.

Andrew and I were fascinated by the frescoes in this small church. I was making copious notes when suddenly we realised that the others had gone. Hastily leaving the church we followed the track to the valley bed but there it divided. First Andrew went one way and returned, and then I went in the opposite direction. Having no luck we each ventured further afield. Many people strolled along the paths but none had noticed our missing friends. Eventually I sat by the junction of the tracks while Andrew set off up the valley. I felt extremely angry and at the same time close to tears — my whole day was ruined. No one had listened to the way I had suggested planning the sightseeing, and secretly I desperately wanted to see a mosque and minaret in Aksaray. Now there was no way I could contrive this visit for time was fast becoming a crucial factor. When the guide reappeared, found and sent back by Andrew to fetch me, I expressed my feelings in no uncertain terms. If he were leading a group he should make certain that we were together. Now there would be no time to go to Aksaray.

"Pas de problème, pas de problème," he kept saying, a familiar phrase used for the pacification of irate tourists. Fortunately he found two more churches upstream to conciliate me.

The Purenli seki Kilise (Church with the Terrace) was a small chapel.

120

The artist employed was not an accomplished painter and his palette was restricted. There were nevertheless certain captivating features. Mary's donkey was more like a beautiful high stepping arab horse, the saddle she used during her flight to Egypt was covered with embossed leather, while the one she sat on to ride to Bethlehem had high pommels in front and behind. A tapestry cloth covered the back of Christ's donkey as He entered Jerusalem. The flat representation of the table at the Last Supper enabled one to see clearly a wine goblet and two fish laid directly on the cloth, and also some rolls marked with crosses. I had discovered the original hot cross bun!

The most impressive aspect of the Kokar Kilise (Fragrant Church) was the western half of the ceiling. A Greek Cross covered the entire section, the gaps filled with ingenious patterns using many of the motifs I have already described. Set in a small square in the centre, the hand of God gave the sign of benediction appropriately painted on a sky blue background. Of the five shepherds grouped harmoniously in the apse, two were playing reed instruments. As well as other scenes from the life of Christ there were seated apostles and Saints holding books. Shadrach, Meshach and Abednego occupied a space by the entrance. Their inclusion was surprising, references to the Old Testament being rare. Inscribed in Greek over their heads were their Babylonian names instead of their Hebrew ones – Hananiah, Mishael and Azariah – a unique feature in Byzantine iconography.

So far each chapel had produced some gem. We retraced our footsteps and took the path downstream. Approaching the Sumbullu Monastery I was convinced that for the first time in Cappadocia we had found genuine external architecture. Pillars were joined by arches and presented a realistic facade. I was wrong. A rock fall had swept away the narthex and what was displayed to the outside world had originally been an inner wall.

The monastery was on two levels, the room above had arched recesses and an unusual ceiling pattern of diamond shaped reliefs. Below, the Sumbullu Kilise (Church with the Lilies) had paintings which have been described as artistically amongst the finest in Cappadocia. Unfortunately invading damp had faded the colours and only part of the Annunciation had survived, plus rows of Saints. Painted in the tenth to eleventh century they were immediately recognisable as being of a superior quality. Their faces had expression and they wore magnificent robes with white crosses on their shoulders. The Archangel Michael's face was superb, framed by his huge wings and his neck encircled with a jewelled collar.

We had to cross the Melendiz river by a rickety homemade suspension bridge in order to reach another Snake Church (Yilani Kilise). This time the snake was not the dragon killed by St. George and Theodosius, but a three headed serpent waiting to pounce and gobble up the damned. St. Michael was weighing the heads of the dead in the presence of a demon. No souls appeared to be going to heaven, but feet and arms

121

dangled from the open mouths of the monster and rows of men, showing only their heads and shoulders, waited apprehensively for their fate to be decided. On the right of this broad frieze four naked women were being bitten by serpents. In the centre of the ceiling Christ sat in Judgement, and around the walls were row upon row of Martyrs and Elders of the Revelation, the artist showing no concern for realistic portrayal. Helena and Constantine framed a window whose arch was decorated with flower heads in little squares. These frescoes were a century earlier than those in the previous monastery, and the same era as the three in the upper part of the valley (ninth to tenth century).

The most interesting fresco was in the vestibule and demonstrated clearly how stories from the Holy Land were brought to Cappadocia by immigrants. We were shown two scenes from the life of St. Mary of Egypt. Having lived for seventeen years as a prostitute in Alexandria, she joined a pilgrimage to the Holy Land where the Virgin Mary interceded on her behalf. Mary decided to repent and to spend the rest of her life atoning for her sins in the desert. She took three loaves of bread which lasted for a considerable time, afterwards surviving on fruit. Her clothes eventually disintegrated and her skin suffered from exposure. Zosimus, a priest, despairing of human complacency also entered the wilderness, where he came across this strange figure with grey hair. He listened to her story and arranged to meet her on the banks of the river Jordan in a year's time to administer Holy Communion, this being one of the scenes depicted in the fresco with a delightful background of stylised palm trees. (In order to reach Zosimus on the far bank Mary had walked over the water). Zosimus came back to visit her again the following year, but found the woman dead with her name — previously unknown to him — inscribed on a sarcophagus. With the aid of a lion he laid Mary in the sarcophagus, and the second scene showed the lion supporting Mary's head and shoulders with its front paws, while Zosimus lifted her feet. The portrayal of this scene has not been found anywhere else in Cappadocia. Luckily our guide had brought a torch for this church was well dug into the cliff possessing only one small window. It gave us a good idea of how dark the churches would have been originally, lit solely by candles or oil lamps, with the occasional shaft of light coming through small holes and slits in the rock face.

The guide had been nattering away to the others and now I was presented with a decision. Either we could visit the next church some distance downstream, continuing to wend our way back and forth across the Melendiz until we reached the village of Belisirma where the driver would be waiting with our transport, or we could climb back the way we had come and proceed to Aksaray. No one minded which we did and it was for me to decide. I longed to say, "both." By walking quickly I was sure that we could complete the two programmes. If only we had started the day as I had proposed everything could have been visited without any fuss, though we might have had to give one of the troglodyte settlements a miss! I dared not voice my thoughts. "Pas de problème," had been solved, so I gratefully accepted the second itinerary and we scrambled back up the cliff.

I had a nagging feeling that the driver might already have left for Belisirma, but auspiciously the Flying Coffin was in the car park. It was the driver who was missing. We searched the parked coaches and a half finished building; our guide yelled and the driver, after ten agonising minutes, was extricated from a game of backgammon.

The Melendiz river flowed through Aksaray, and the surrounding countryside owing to a dam and irrigation was green and fertile. Beyond lay the arid Lycaonian plain across which we had driven from Konya, while to the north-west the Melendiz loses itself in the great marshes which surround the salt lake, Tuz Golu. The summer days are intensely hot, with cool nights; snow covers the ground during the winter and wolves become an infernal nuisance.

From the junction with the main road it took us precisely eleven minutes to drive to Aksaray, with five more to reach the centre of the town. I made the driver stop so that I could have a closer look at the Kizil Minare, a curious leaning minaret completed by the Seljuks in 1236. Built of brick, turquoise tiles had been inserted for decoration, in the same way as in the dome of the Ince Minare Medrese in Konya.

The Ulu Cami was built by the Karamanids around 1431. Karamania, an inland province in the south-east of Asia Minor, was threatened during the Seljuk advance. The invaders were always prepared to make peace with the tribes they attacked, provided that they surrendered immediately. The Karamanids acquiesced and a daughter of the Seljuk Sultan married one of the Emir of Karamania's sons, as a result of which he was made governor of Selifka and the Karamanids retained their independence. When the Seljuk supremacy collapsed, the Karamanids took control over a large part of the country until finally annexed by the Ottomans. Only a few of their buildings have survived, and this mosque is a fine example of their type of architecture. The addition of a pediment over the square portal, pilasters each side of recesses, and a restrained form of decoration made the style more classical than the Seljuks. The interior had six aisles divided by pillars and arches which gave a sense of intimacy. The mihrab was made of marble and the mimber, beautifully carved out of walnut, came from a ruined Seljuk mosque. A balcony to the rear allowed the women to pray separately from the men.

We were soon speeding along our Roman road back to Nevsehir, but not before Martin had some trouble with the guide. First the guide wanted to visit a friend of his mother's where we could have a 'nice glass of tea'. Then, after having somehow learned that I was planning to write an account of our travels, he suddenly wanted to show us all kinds of gems, from a Hittite carving 'very close to our route', to extra special books in his house. Martin was quite firm. By now it was drizzling, time again made its presence felt and we were not quite sure whether the lights on the Flying Coffin worked. The guide wanted to exchange names and addresses and we soon gathered that there was an ulterior motive. He hoped to travel to Europe with his family later in the year. We had ghastly visions of the Flying Coffin breaking down in front of one of our houses, and streams of Turks of every age pouring out and staying with us for months.

How luxurious to be able to turn on the tap and find hot water, and how spoiling to have another delicious dinner. Lady C. had bought two carpets and her umpteenth pair of trousers, and regaled us with how she had joined in the Cossack dancing the previous evening. A party from the Ukraine was staying in the hotel and had naturally taken over the entertainment of the guests. We left her to dance away her last night, happy in the knowledge that we have five more days in which to explore this fascinating country. Tomorrow we would rejoin the Crusaders' route.

DAY XIV : NIGDE

What a relief to be sitting in a clean, comfortable bus with eau de cologne and bottled water, instead of the cramped Flying Coffin that had been our means of transport for the previous two days. Before breakfast I had walked to the main square to pay my respects to the Grand Vezir Ibrahim Pasha, whose statue portrayed an imposing man with a kindly face, full beard, turban and flowing robes. At the opposite end of the well kept garden no one could fail to miss Ataturk's statue surrounded with wreaths from yesterday's ceremony.

Andrew returning from his own walk produced fresh bread for breakfast. Having danced into the early hours of the morning with her handsome Ukranians, Lady C. failed to put in an appearance in the dining room, but the couple were down and we gave them the last of our letters and postcards which would now arrive at their destination before we ourselves returned to England. Our bus left punctually and we were soon crossing another barren steppe. Snow covered the mountains to the south-west, mere humps on the horizon to begin with but gradually regaining their majestic quality as we approached Nigde. They formed the eastern end of the Melendiz range, Hasan Dagi commanding the western edge which overlooked Aksaray.

Nigde appeared as an oasis at the end of the desert. Though well supplied with water the Romans had preferred to build their town at Tyana 19 kilometres to the south, on the site of the former Hittite settlement of Tuvana (the present day village of Kermerhisar). To the Romans, the position of the town was of prime importance; because of their engineering skills they were not dependent on the proximity of their water supply. Tuvana had hot springs and sufficient water for a small community, but the main source came from Eski Gumus (8 kilometres east of Nigde) running in underground channels and aqueducts, parts of which still remain standing. At Nigde we were to rejoin the Path of the Crusaders, but first we had some sightseeing to do.

The tour lecturer whom we had met in Konya had strongly recommended a visit to the monastery at Eski Gumus, hence one of the reasons for making this detour to the south and travelling two long sides of a triangle, instead of taking the direct road from Nevsehir to Kayseri a distance of only 80 kilometres. From the main coach stop in Nigde we found our way to the local bus station, and rattled along to the village of Eski Gumus where many hands indicated the direction of the monastery.

A keeper appeared from nowhere and unlocked a strong door at the end of a short tunnel dug into the cliff face. An inner courtyard was open to the sky and in the centre a young pine had been planted, the ancient symbol of fertility and healing. We were totally secluded, the outside world forgotten and it was easy to picture the monastic life begun here in the seventh century. On one side of the courtyard the refectory, wine store and kitchen were carved out of the hillside. On the opposite side a tunnel, now blocked by rock fall, probably led to a hidden exit some kilometres away. The fourth side held what we had come to see, the Church of St. Helena.

The outside was decorated with arches in relief, a few iconoclastic motifs and a Byzantine cross. We climbed an iron stairway to reach the dormitories and found a wall covered with faded frescoes depicting hunting scenes. The entrance chapel on the ground floor also possessed a faded fresco but the artist had reverted to serious scenes from the bible, and this one showed Mary and Jesus with the Angels Gabriel and Michael. The Iconoclasts had been to work with their customary geometric patterns, but it was the inner church that held the real treasure. On the wall above the apse was the finest of all the frescoes we had seen so far. Painted in the eleventh century and free from the restrictions imposed by the troublesome Iconoclasts, it had been expertly restored between the years 1963—68 by a French couple. The keeper could not recall their names, though he repeated with pride that the Byzantine fresco was the best in the whole of Anatolia.

The scene was the Nativity with Mary reclining in the centre and, curiously, looking away from the infant Jesus who was lying in his manger wrapped in swaddling bands, watched over by the ever faithful donkey and cow peering over a wall. Joseph as usual sat apart with his head resting in his hand looking lonely and ignored. Above centre we were shown the Visitation to the Temple, to the left three angels and the three Kings, while to the right an angel appeared to the shepherds and their flock of endearing sheep. The Circumcision took up the space to the right of centre and below St. Stephen and an unidentified Saint; on the left was the scene that began the story, the Annunciation — the angel with a face of unsurpassed beauty. We had seen many episodes from the Nativity treated in a similar fashion in other churches we had visited at Goreme and in the Peristrema Valley, but none had been so clear, nor in such perfect condition, nor grouped in such a large tableau as these. By pure chance we had reserved the choicest fresco for the last.

The remainder of the Church had a high ceiling supported by four strong pillars, and connecting arches enabled the interior to be divided into nine sections each with a dome. On none of these had any trace of painting survived, except on the pillars which were decorated with a red and white petal design on a dark background. However the south wall had some frescoes. In the niche to the left Mary held the infant Jesus; in the one to the right Christ raised his hand in blessing, while the central recess displayed a splendid mixture of characters. A bull held a scroll between his forehooves watched over by St. Luke, an angel knelt by Mary holding a napkin and Christ in his majesty gazed impassively ahead. A large area was covered with plain plaster where the frescoes had disappeared, hindering any interpretation being placed on the sequence of figures; but above in the curved semi-dome a double row of Saints were portrayed whose names, in Greek script, tested Andrew and Martin's scholastic knowledge. On the upper band only the heads and shoulders of the Saints were represented but Andrew and Martin managed to reel off from the left Philip, Simon, Jacob, John, Luke, followed by a gap caused by the plaster, and only Thomas survived on the right hand side. On the lower band the portraits were full length but more difficult to decipher. Reading again from the left, St. George presented no problem, the next was impossible, then they were delighted to identify Amphilochius, followed by Gregory, Basil, Mary, the plaster gap, Nicholas, Epiphanius and Jason.

Travelling by bus was a cheap way of reaching one's destination, providing there was no set time limit. The tour ograniser had advised us to take a taxi to Eski Gumus as the monastery was not far from Nigde, and the convenience of having transport at hand for the return journey outweighed the extra cost. I reiterated his advice earlier in the day, but Andrew and Martin had been determined to find the local bus station. I had also casually mentioned that there happened to be some interesting mosques in Nigde. "Plenty of time, pas de problème!" came the familiar retort, pronounced in the same dismissive tone that they used with the Turks when they repeated, "Cok guzel (very beautiful)," as a means of ending a conversation. My mosques and I felt duly squashed.

Our zero hour took the form of the 3.30 p.m. bus from Nigde to Kayseri. By noon we were sitting on straight backed wooden chairs in the village square sipping glasses of tea that had been offered to us. There was no question of paying for the tea; we were visitors and were treated with civility, if not with warmth. The group of men had been passing the time of day in their usual manner of doing nothing in particular, but from the room inside came the sound of clinking chips being moved on a backgammon board. Conversation was laboured, Andrew and Martin having a struggle with the dour village inmates. Their attitude was strange and I felt that something must have happened in the past to cause this frigidity; or perhaps the reason was merely that the further east we travelled the less outsiders were welcome.

I sat on the edge of the group imagining a repetition of yesterday's friction in the Peristrema Valley when I nearly missed my mosque in Aksaray. Trying to remain calm I checked and revised my itinerary — there would still be time if only a bus came soon. On the outward journey we were told that there would not be another until 2.30 p.m.. The men in the village were more encouraging, implying that there might be one in half an hour or so. After one hour a contraption rumbled into sight; the square suddenly came to life and was filled with people converging on the vehicle.

The town of Nigde nestled around the acropolis on top of which perched the familiar Seljuk fortress. This one was striking with good solid walls and a large tower. The Seljuks had captured the town in 1071, the Mongols in 1308, the Karamanids thirty years later and finally the Ottomans in the fifteenth century. The twisting narrow streets led to the acropolis and a path across the middle of a bare plateau to the Alaeddin

Cami. Built by Alaeddin Keykubad in 1223, the three simple lead domes exquisite in line and simplicity, were a triumph of design. The Islamic religion forbids the representation of the human form in mosques, but we had been told that the portal included sculptured figures. The artist no doubt felt that he could surreptitiously breach the convention since the portal was on the outside wall. We could see the usual stonework motifs and one tiny bird in the top right hand corner, but none of us could trace the elusive figures. The door was locked and the interior barred to infidels.

Martin now decided to find a bank and cash some Travellers' Cheques, and I insisted that I must take a taxi, the distances between my remaining mosques being too great for walking considering the limited time I had left. Andrew agreed to come with me and his help was invaluable for my Turkish was not up to bargaining for taxis. We had some difficulty finding one, a young boy eventually leading us to a square where they were parked. Andrew was telling a driver the names of the places I wanted to visit prior to discussing the price, when a policeman approached and acted as a mediator. A sum was quickly settled which satisfied the law and we were promptly on our way.

The Hudavent Hatun Turbe was at the top of my list. The tomb appeared more like a folly with its conical tent-inspired roof and lacy stone carvings. The sexagonal shrine decorated with birds, animals and plants also displayed a double headed eagle, the symbol of royalty. This was indeed a royal tomb built in 1312 for the daughter of Sultan Ruknettin, King of the Seljuks, and it was altogether the grandest, the best preserved and the most entrancing that I had seen so far.

Close by a smaller turbe had been erected in memory of someone called Gundogdu. He was not of royal blood for I could find no sign of an eagle, nevertheless the portal was finely carved in the form of a miniature entrance to a mosque, with the jigsaw puzzle stones set over the arch.

The next most important building to visit was the Akmedrese, an example of Karamanid architecture; unfortunately the taxi driver had never heard of it. I found this aspect of sightseeing quite frustrating. Andrew tried every form of pronunciation without success, but when we mentioned that the medrese had been converted into a museum, the driver's face lit up with understanding and he started the engine.

The modern museum was not what we were seeking. However we were guided in the right direction and soon arrived at our destination. The Akmedrese, or White Medrese, built in 1409 by a Karaman prince, Alaeddin Ali Bey, neither lived up to its name nor expectation. The surface appeared dingy and the whole building neglected. This impression was intensified by the fact that — surprise, surprise — it was shut, the contents having been removed to the modern museum! However the exterior provided some unusual features: arab styled windows revealed an inner gallery, and the Karamanids had kept the form of the Seljuk portal but incorporated their own ogee pattern within the framework. The only encouraging aspect was the sight of two spruce trees already twenty feet high either side of the entrance.

The Mongols were another race that had occupied Nigde, and the taxi driver understood our request to visit the Mosque and adjacent turbe of the Chief of the tribe, Sungur Bey, built around 1335. Again a state of decay prevailed. The original cedar door was locked, cracked, and holes rudely interrupted the ornate carving. The jigsaw stones immediately over the door were simplified and coarse, with straight lines instead of bulbous protrusions. A long plain high wall interrupted only by a solid square door on the south side of the mosque, was far more impressive in its simplicity. A large area of derelict land lay before it, and the sun blazed on the stark lonely scene.

We had some time to spare so went back to the modern museum, unaware that the day happened to be a Monday; so naturally it was closed. The custodian refused to unlock any of the doors guarding the display rooms, but we were admitted into the entrance hall and I was allowed to buy some postcards. Finding one of the entrance portal to the Alaeddin Cami, I asked the custodian about the figures. He endeavoured to point out their features but neither Andrew nor I could pick out the intricacies of this Asian art form. Pieces of Roman sculpture lay scattered outside the museum; some large amphorae were intact, and also a late sarcophagus with garlands of corn and flowers swathed over the horns of a bull with the most peculiar staring eyes.

Thanks to the taxi we had seen the most important of the Nigde monuments, so I was happy to return to the autogar in time for the 3.30 p.m. bus. Martin was already there having had an amusing and protracted conference with the Bank manager on the matter of money exchange. He also told us that he had barely been in the autogar ten minutes before a policeman had turned up and patrolled the area. Apart from Istanbul where both police and soldiers were much in evidence, and the night watchman in Nevsehir, we had hardly been aware of their presence. Their sudden reappearance in Nigde was certainly puzzling.

Back on the bus we were once more following the path of the Crusaders. From Konya they had travelled south-east to Binbir Kilise where we had reluctantly deserted them in order to make a detour through Cappadocia. They had subsequently taken the direct route to Heraclea (Eregli), a distance of roughly 60 kilometres, where they had found a Seljuk and Danismend Emir in possession of the town.

Anna Comnena, the daughter of Emperor Alexius and a historian, provides an excellent account of the Crusade in her 'Alexiad'. Though she loathed Bohemond, having met him in Constantinople and suspected him of being unscrupulous and ambitious, she admits to his charm and good looks; he was tall and, though over forty years of age, had the figure and complexion of a young man. She was kept informed of events by Taticius and mentions Bohemond's prowess as a leader. At Heraclea he had led the attack but the Turks, having no desire for a pitched battle, relinquished the town and retired to the north. Fulcher of Chartres another historian reports a comet flaring through the sky, illuminating the victory.

129

Further seeds of dissension had been sown amongst the Crusaders in Heraclea in the form of arguments over the route. There were two possible ways to Antioch (Antakya). The most direct turned south crossing the Taurus mountains and winding through the notorious Cilician Gates whose precipitous cliffs overlooked the narrow pass. These were suspected of being in Turkish hands and to march this way with a large slow moving army would be suicidal. Besides there was also the Amanus range to the east of Tarsus, which entailed tackling an equally difficult pass known as the Syrian Gates. By now it was September and, according to the Byzantine guides, sudden fierce storms could make the going treacherous. Tancred could not be dissuaded. With a band of Normans from southern Italy, together with Godrey's brother Baldwin and a collection of Flemish and Lorrainers, they both determined to try this route, aspiring to gain spoils and territories on the way.

The majority chose the second route recommended by Taticius. The recent defeat of the Turks opened the road to Casesarea Mazaka (Kayseri), where they could join the great Byzantine military road which before the years of the Turkish invasion took the traffic from Constantinople to Antioch. The country was held by Christians, Armenian princelings who, though tolerated by the Turks, were nominal vassals of the Emperor. After Caesarea they would turn south, cross the Anti-Taurus mountains to Germanicea (Maras), and march over the low broad pass of the Amanus Gates that led to the plain of Antioch.

We followed the route taken by the main army. From Heraclea they marched north-east to Tyana, a distance of about 50 kilometres. (To be precise it was here that Baldwin turned south down the old main road to Podanus (Pozanti) and the Cilician Gates, but Tancred with a smaller band of men had taken the direct route from Heraclea and was thereby three days in advance of his ally). The district to the north of Tyana had once been a great imperial estate, and as far back as the fourth century the centre for breeding race horses, while the head of the neighbouring monastery of Pasa was given the task of providing horses for the post service. The Roman road continued north-east passing through two more stations before reaching the junction at Sakasena (Suksu), where it was joined by the road from the west that had come from Soandos (Nevsehir). This was the final station before Caesarea which the Crusaders reached by the end of September.

Instead of crossing another barren Anatolian steppe between Nigde and Kayseri our coach passed through cultivated land, still flat but stretching to the snow-capped Taurus mountains to the east. Because of the direction in which we were travelling, Mt. Argaeus, renamed Erciyes Dagi (3916 metres), appeared at first straight ahead, but then the road changed direction and we drove in a wide semi-circle around its western base before reaching Kayseri on its north side. The mountain dominated the surrounding countryside. Like Uludag above Bursa, Erciyes Dagi also provided skiing, though being that much higher and grander the runs were more difficult, and only advanced skiers were allowed to the top.

Having found our hotel and immediately discarding the bug infested blankets from our beds, I quickly went to the Tourist Information to obtain a map of the city, arriving precisely at the closing time of six o'clock. Nevertheless I was shown into the large office with labels on the desk indicating whether English, French or German translations were required. Armed with information and my precious map I returned to our hotel room which by now was aired and smelled reasonable, and started to plan my sightseeing for the following day. I was interrupted for dinner, Andrew and Martin having had a preliminary stroll around the town searching for somewhere to eat. The further east we travelled, the fewer restaurants there were from which to choose. The mezes in the one we dined were dull, the kebabs tough and the dining room practically empty. I was soon reading my guide books again and scheming. Nothing was going to stop me; I had one day only in Kayseri and, besides a Caravanserai and an archaeological site, I was determined to visit all the mosques on my list.

DAY XV : KAYSERI

Kayseri, situated roughly in the centre of eastern Anatolia, holds an important position commanding the main trade routes from the four points of the compass. Archelaus I (37 B.C. — A.D.17), a puppet of the Romans, changed the city's original name of Mazaka to Caesarea in honour of his patron, Caesar Augustus; with eventual Turkish domination and slight tonal variation, Caesarea became Kayseri.

Excavations in the surrounding countryside revealed signs of habitation during the Early Bronze Age (3000 — 2000 B.C.), and we know from an inscription that the indigenous inhabitants were called Hattis. They became civilised through absorbing the culture of the Assyrians — who traded near Kayseri from 2000 — 1750 B.C. — and in due course became known as the Hittites developing into the great empire that held sway from 1700–1200 B.C.. The Phrygians took over, and there followed in rapid succession Persians, Greeks and Romans. During the Byzantine era the city developed into the principal monastic centre ruled by Basil the Great (329–79), Bishop of Caesarea. He was to be made a Saint and we had seen his portrait on numerous occasions in the Cappadocian Rock Churches.

Kayseri was overrun by Arabs during the seventh and ninth centuries, the first incursion into Anatolia by a Turcoman horde taking place in the second half of the eleventh century. On the whole the various tribes tolerated one another and even joined forces to fight the Crusaders. The Danismends reigned supreme from 1070, followed by the Seljuks in 1174. The Seljuks had to cope with invasions from the Mamelukes and the Mongols. The Eretnids claimed an independent state in Central Anatolia in 1335 and, though they only survived fifty years, managed to leave behind some remarkable buildings. They in turn were defeated by the Karamanids and finally in 1515 Selim I, the Grim, conquered the town for the Ottoman empire.

Each conqueror in turn left behind evidence of his occupation, thus Kayseri contained a wealth of architecture, from a fragment of Roman wall to the beginnings of tall office blocks and sprawling suburbs. The huge main square, the Cumhuriyet Meydani, was a nightmare to cross and only possible by a series of pedestrian lights and policemen directing the traffic, but the mosques and medreses offered peace and quiet. Turbes, or rather Kumbets as they were called here, abounded; everywhere I walked one was generally visible. The Alaca stood in the middle of a dual carriageway and was therefore rather discoloured by exhaust fumes, the only one I found open and ventured inside appeared to be inhabited by a very old man. They were in various stages of decay, but all had either conical or pyramidal roofs, except for the Sircali Kumbet built by the Eretnids, whose shallow dome topped a tall circular tower with a large entrance portal.

132

The most renowned Kumbet in Kayseri was the Doner Kumbet. This delightful mausoleum had been built in memory of another princess, Sah Cihan Hatun. The Seljuks obviously respected their princess for, like the Hudavent Hatun turbe in Nigde, it was beautifully carved. A round tower stood on a high pedestal and, by chiselling into the stone, twelve narrow arches were cunningly made to stand out in relief, thereby breaking up the surface and transforming the squat drum into an elegant and imaginative structure. As well as the usual rosettes, intricate patterns and stylised plumage, a pair of leopards added charm and the double-headed eagle denoted royalty. Moss was beginning to spread on the conical roof decorated with some unusual mouldings, and wispy strands of grass sprouted through innumerable cracks.

We had passed the Doner Kumbet by the side of the Talas Caddesi on our way to the Archaeological Museum, where we arrived five minutes after nine o'clock, the scheduled opening time. This modern building contained some excellent specimens: clay tablets from Kultepe, a Bronze Age settlement not far from Kayseri, large Hittite stone reliefs, a collection of coins, some enchanting small Roman objects in the form of bronze gods, a gold head of a woman, paper thin gold leaves that once made up a replica of the crown of olives, engraved seals, glass, silver and Byzantine mother of pearl articles; also some child mummies from the site of the Old Hittite Kingdom of Bogazkoy.

As we emerged from the museum I announced that I was off to see my mosques.

"What, all day?" Andrew and Martin asked incredulously.

"Well, I might take a taxi and. . ."

"No," came the concerted reply. There was no point having an argument at this stage, so I agreed to meet them in the hotel at one o'clock and hastened to seek the Koske Medrese. From the museum curator a vague direction had been indicated, but after ten minutes hard walking and shrugs of shoulders as answers to my enquiries, I gave up. I had too much to see to waste time on a wild goose chase at this time of day. Instead, following a railway line, I made for a Kumbet that I glimpsed in the distance. It had been built in memory of Ali Cafer who must have been a very important person because the tomb was large, sexagonal, with a pyramidal roof and a grand Seljuk type entrance.

Making my way back to the centre of Kayseri, I went into anything that looked interesting. The Koske Medrese was nòt actually marked on my map, so when I came across a building the identity of which I was in doubt, I asked the inevitable loiterers whether it was the Koske Medrese? "Cok, Cok;" but as I received exactly the same reply at my next enquiry, I took it to be a reflex response, or that they were simply trying to please me.

An important looking mosque that I visited had been built in 1237 by a Greek woman, Mahperi Huant Hatun. She was the wife of Alaeddin Keykubad I and mother of Keyhusrev II, and had been responsible for the mosque, medrese, hamam and cesme (fountain), the first complex to be built in Anatolia.   Well secluded in a tiny courtyard and standing on an ornate base, I found an octagonal turbe containing her marble sarcophagus.   The mosque itself, in the style favoured by the Seljuks, had seven aisles with arches joining the pillars, a dome over the mihrab and a painted mimber.   The medrese adjoined the mosque, the outside unmistakably Seljuk though the interior could easily have passed for a Christian cloister.   Surrounding a courtyard was a covered arcade from which doors led into rooms of varying sizes.   Formerly studies and class rooms they proved ideal for museum displays, and a good selection of items were on view in well lit show cases.

By now I was determined to visit the archaeological site at Kultepe and had worked out how this could be achieved. It entailed calling at the Information Bureau in the adjoining square and afterwards, feeling satisfied with my plan, I set off on a circuit in a different area of the town. Crossing the Cumhuriyet Meydani and walking through the park, it was noticeable that every seat was taken by a male Turk enjoying the sun.   I recalled one of Mevlana's quotations which read, "Man must earn his bread by the sweat on his brow."   I arrived at the only important Ottoman mosque in Kayseri, the Kursunlu Cami, built in 1584 for Ahmet Pasha a member of an old Seljuk family who retained power under the Ottomans.   Thought to have been designed by Sinan, it had an imposing lead dome and a porch stretching the length of the entrance side surmounted by cupolas.   Even though the mosque was shut the sadirvan was being used by an old man for his morning's wash.

The whole area behind the mosque was devastated, looking as if it had been struck by an earthquake.   In fact a demolition gang had been at work clearing the slum.   Even a mosque had not been spared, though the top of a minaret remained perched precariously on a broken wall.   I saw no signs of rebuilding; children played amongst the rubble and families still lived there making use of whatever walls, stones or wood were available for makeshift homes.   Women resting with heavy loads beside them indicated the direction I wanted, and behind a crumbling row of houses I found the oldest Seljuk medrese in Anatolia.   Built in 1205 it consisted of two buildings, a medical school and a hospital.   One guide book called it the Giyasiye Sifahiye, the other, the Cifte Medrese.   The first meant the Hospital (Sifahiye) of Giyasiye and the other, the Double (Cifte) Medrese. Both were correct, but alternative names and spellings given to many of the mosques and medreses made locating them difficult.   A tomb I had visited named on one reference as the Cifte Kumbet stood on its own with one roof and one sarcophagus, nothing 'double' about it in the least. Besides the problems of identification, dates seldom coincided, often varying by only a year or two, but sometimes by as much as a century.

I managed to locate the Haci Kilic mosque and medrese bordering the Istasyon Caddesi.   The interior had five aisles and soft carpets, and the mihrab was a miniature replica of the handsome portal.   From next door came the sound of children's voices.   The adjoining medrese had reverted to a place of learning, admittedly not to teaching such erudite pupils as in past centuries, but lessons were nevertheless taking place. I heard chanting interrupted by occasional laughter, and noticed a few scattered balls in the courtyard. The medrese had an equally fine portal; both the mosque and medrese were built in 1249 by the Vizir Abdul Gazi.

The Turks make delicious ice cream, and I chose one from a selection of familiar varieties. I felt rather mean enjoying it as I watched, for the third time that day, a parade of nursing cadets. They and their leaders looked decidedly weary; the drums were not beaten with quite such vigour, and the baton achieved fewer twirls per beat than at eight o'clock in the morning, when they had first marched by while we were having breakfast. Returning to the main square I found the Sahabiye medrese, built in 1267 as a school for learning the Koran, with distinctive geometrical ornamentation on its portal. Its founder, Sahip Ata Fahrettin Ali — who had commissioned the Ince Minare Medrese and the complex named after him in Konya — would have been astonished at its present day usage. Recently restored, the class rooms of bygone years had been converted into arts and crafts boutiques.

With the medrese behind me and facing the Cumhuriyet Meydani, I produced my camera to take what was meant to be a spectacular photograph. Part of the old Seljuk fortress with all nineteen of its black basalt towers still standing would frame the left hand side of the picture, the modern Burunguz Camii the right side and, though set back but soaring high between the two, the majestic snow capped peak of Erciyes Dagi. I had come to the end of my film so returned later in the day with a new one, but the peak was shrouded in a white cloud. I ventured through the great doors of the fortress. Andrew told me later that he had walked round the battlements, achieving more than I had! Whatever buildings remained inside the citadel had been razed to the ground, the only one left being a mosque erected by Sultan Mehmet II when he captured Kayseri in 1466.

The quickest way to reach the Great Mosque, the Ulu Cami, was to walk through the Bedestan, an Ottoman structure of the late eighteenth century. Goldsmiths occupied the hallowed central court of the market, and the souks were filled with locally woven carpets and rugs, leather, and a miscellany of household goods. I avoided replying to the annoying question, "Do you speak English?" repeated by the young men, and lost my way in the wool section, great sacks of the stuff being pulled apart and inspected. The older wizened men dealt with this important side of business, and they politely guided me to the open courtyard before the Ulu Cami. This had been built by the Danismends in 1135 and I was thrilled to find a flat wooden ceiling, the beams painted red, yellow and blue, exactly as I remembered seeing through the half open window of the Alaeddin Cami in Konya. The ceiling was supported by antique pillars, in this instance from the Byzantine period. Unable to discover enough of these old ones the numbers had been completed with columns bearing plain capitals. There were five aisles, with a dome above the mihrab and the central square section of the mosque, and three extra aisles raised at the back for the women. I was intrigued by a grandfather clock made by Edw. D. Prior of London, with flowers on the face and an inlay design of drums and flags decorating the long case, similar to the one in the Orhan Gazi Camii in Bursa.

The increasing murmurs and soft shuffles on the carpets warned me that the mosque was filling for a service, and a devout but worried looking Muslim approached pointing to his watch. I took the hint and crept outside, and soon the sound of chanting reached my ears. The founder of the mosque, Melik Mehmet Gazi, who died in 1143 was buried in a simple crypt, not in the more usual free standing and grand turbe. Steam issued from the domed hamam across the road, and a restored building nearby displayed a plaque stating that it was the Bu Medrese built by Mehmet Bey in 1432. Having gone to the trouble of carrying out considerable repairs, it seemed a pity not to be allowed inside. Anyhow, my watch reminded me to stop dawdling; I would have to hurry to be back at our hotel by one o'clock.

The quickest way amidst the tangle of streets was to return by the same route. I had to pass through courtyards which were part of the Vezir Hani (Inns of the Vezir) where the merchants would unload their caravans and stay in comfort and safety for the night. A narrow pathway with high walls on either side led to the market. A middle aged and rather large Turk approached from the opposite direction. We were about to cross when he raised his hands above his head and uttered a fearful roar. Then I knew what the authors of horror stories meant when they wrote that their heroine's 'heart froze' or 'missed a beat'. I was not, however, 'rooted to the spot'; in fact I have never moved so quickly in my life and was back out of the passage way 'like a shot'. For once I appreciated the group of men sitting on a low stone wall at the entrance, for they immediately rose to their feet and shouted curses at my assailant – who had either consumed one raki too many or was the local Bedestan idiot – and with polite bows they ushered me through to safety. I did not feel happy until I emerged from the covered market at the far end of an interminable arcade with, as far as I could see, nothing but shoes for sale.

A fizzy Maden Su relieved my dry throat as I prepared for the next obstacle of the day. Andrew and Martin were late. They were not particularly interested in my mosques, but then neither was I captivated by their tales of carpet bargaining. They had called at the Tourist Information and heard about a village called Talas on the lower slopes of Erciyes Dagi which, incidentally, had a recommended restaurant.

"We could all have lunch there," they announced, after which there would be plenty of time to complete present buying in the Bedestan. They agreed that the English speaking Turk behind the desk was polite and helpful. I told them that I too had been to see him, and had asked if he could find someone trustworthy to drive me to Sultan Hani and Kultepe, because my husband was reluctant to allow me to go on my own.

He had replied that a friend of his had worked at Kultepe on an archaeological dig during his vacation, and was now the owner of a taxi. He had
advised me as to the correct price, so everything was settled. I waited.

"Why on earth do you want to go to another Caravanserai, you have
seen two already — there is nothing to see at Kultepe except a pile of
stones." There were simple answers to these philistine statements, and
before they could continue I said that I was very sorry but I refused to
waste my last afternoon eating, drinking and bargaining. They could
come and inspect the taxi and driver if they so desired.

We were early at the Tourist Information; I had ordered my carriage
for two o'clock, but Andrew and Martin's bus was waiting so I urged them
to take it.

"I am perfectly all right," I insisted, as I waved them goodbye and
"bon appétit."

I was surprised when the driver opened the front door of the car as I
was making for the rear. Not wishing to appear rude I accepted his offer.
He seemed a pleasant young man, I suppose about thirty years of age and
well educated, so I attempted conversation as a form of politeness. We
had not driven for more than ten minutes before his hand enveloped mine.
My reflex actions were quick, and an icy retort conveyed my anger more
than adequately. I could have told him to return to the Tourist Information but I wanted to see the ruins, so from then on I read my books and
admired the scenery. I had not confessed to Andrew, afraid that if he
knew he might forbid me to go sightseeing alone, but in Konya a similar
incident had occurred when exploring one of my medreses. While I had
been studying some tiles the custodian had reached out and touched my
face. Such a situation could be dealt with easily and without drama, but
it was a pity because it meant that for a woman to travel on her own
through Turkey, life was made more complicated. Instead of being able
to concentrate fully on any specific object, one continually had to be on
one's guard. The Turks, certainly in remote areas, were simply not used
to seeing women on their own. I know that in the tourist resorts of the
Aegean coast the situation is entirely different, and even bikinis are
acceptable. I was always properly dressed with sensible boots, trousers
or jeans and my shirts had short sleeves, so I could not have looked
especially provocative!

We passed the turning to Kultepe but I wanted to go to Sultan Hani
first. (Kultepe was 19 kilometres from Kayseri and Sultan Hani, 43 kilometres). We approached a road block manned by police but were waved
through, only lorries being checked. The driver bore right continuing to
Malatya. I noticed a signpost to Sivas which pointed straight ahead. By
pure chance I had a map open and checking saw that Sultan Hani was on
the road to Sivas. I pointed out the driver's mistake; he turned the car
around and took the correct road. I remarked that I was sure the police
had interrupted his concentration. He replied that he had never been to
Sultan Hani before. I recalled Andrew's query which I thought rather
stupid at the time, "What happens if he goes the wrong way?"

We arrived at Sultan Hani built by Alaeddin Keykubad between 1232 –36, and described in a guide book as, 'one of the handsomest in the entire Middle East'. It scored third place out of those we had visited: the winner being the restored Sultan Hani west of Aksaray, and a very close second the Agzikara Han east of Aksaray. The driver now proved helpful and found the key to the door. The covered area of the Han had five aisles with seven cross sections, and the central tower with its mescit was well decorated with rosettes and calligraphy, and serpents' heads entwined over one of the arches. A little girl in a bright red skirt followed me wherever I went, and made me feel guilty that I had no sweets with which to reward her devotion.

"On to Kultepe," I said, checking the time on my watch, and the driver obligingly pointed the car in the correct direction. A range of mountains framed a lake called Tuzla Golu. Nothing could be more artistic than the sight of these snow capped peaks set behind the expanse of turquoise water.

Kultepe, ancient Kanes, was one of the most important settlements of the late Bronze Age, 2000 – 1200 B.C.. Barbed wire fencing surrounded the great mound and the gate was locked, so we went first to the Karum, the lower town, inhabited by the Assyrian traders during the same period. We crossed some fields to reach the site, and I tried to make my driver explain the excavations and to show me where he had dug. He pointed vaguely about and did not appear much interested. Visitors are only supposed to walk around the edge of the excavations and look down at the myriad of broken walls and heaps of stones, and try to work out which are houses or streets. Various areas had been trenched, and as there was no one about I could not resist scrambling into a section. I now felt part of the busy metropolis and could imagine the Assyrian traders at their work.

The Assyrians founded nine Karums (trading centres), the most important being at Kanes; their own capital was Assur on the east bank of the Tigris. Their caravans, composed of as many as two to three hundred donkeys, carried tin to be alloyed with Anatolian copper making bronze. The merchants also brought ready made clothes, scents, ornaments and other luxury goods which they exchanged with the natives for gold and silver. The Assyrians had no desire to conquer nor to exert political influence, for theirs was purely a commercial and economic relationship. They lived in a separate colony, and paid taxes to the feudal lords of the country to ensure the safety of their caravan routes and settlements. The years between 1950–1850 B.C. were the most glorious in the life of these trading colonies. Clay tablets pertinent to this phase came exclusively from Kanes and related to economic, judicial and literary matters, and also messages dealing with the private affairs of the merchants. They were written in the cuneiform script adopted from the Babylonians, who in turn had appropriated the characters from the Sumerians.

The city was devastated by a tremendous fire, but apart from wood and woven material much was preserved due to the custom of burying the dead under the floors of their houses. They were surrounded by funereal gifts, their mouths and eyes often covered with gold leaf. I was to see the choicest of the contents of these graves in the Museum of Anatolian Civilisations in Ankara. These included numerous tablets some still in their clay envelopes. Their burnished pottery in cream coloured ware decorated with designs in red, brown and black, was as brilliant as the day it had been baked. Besides elegant jugs, they made birds and animals, and even a fashionable boot with an upturned toe. Gold plates, ear rings, necklaces, figurines of the mother-goddess were also found; such a wealth of treasure that I remember, when I was looking at them in Ankara, feeling grateful that I had actually been to the site of excavation.

At the present time I was exploring the houses and streets of the Karum. In a store room I picked up some fragments of pottery, the lip of a vase and the handle of an urn. I was gently sweeping the sandy soil to one side when my guide peered over the edge and uttered a warning; the keeper had observed our car and had arrived with the key to unlock the gate to Kanes.

Kanes proved to be altogether different. This Palace of Kings was planned on a vast scale, and consisted of three excavated areas named the Large Palace, the Temple, and the Palace of Warsana. Four levels had been recorded, the Large Palace at the second level dating from 1920—1840 B.C.. Mud and bricks had been used for the walls built on a stone foundation; the central courtyard was paved with stones of varying sizes, and further along store houses flanked the main causeway.

The Temple was a square building with huge stones used as corner buttresses. This was at the level 1B and therefore dated 1800—1750 B.C.. Traces of fire damage could be seen, but it was at the Palace of Warsana that the effects of the violent conflagration were clearly visible. The ferocity of the heat had caused a remarkable change in the colour and texture of the earth and stones, turning them to yellow and reddish black, and forming curious shapes.

For four months last year excavations had taken place close to the old museum. An area roughly the size of a tennis court had been dug to a depth of two metres, revealing many treasures and buildings. There was a half-buried amphora and though broken, more rewarding to see left in situ; a short flight of stone steps indicated a house of more than one storey. The keeper showed us the old museum; apart from a few enormous amphorae the contents had been moved to Kayseri. I was offered a glass of tea but refused, explaining that my husband was expecting me back by six o'clock. Anyhow, that was my excuse, but in reality I could not face having to make forced conversation in this isolated place while waiting for the kettle to boil. I felt under no obligation to be polite. I asked my driver to tip the Kultepe guide — presuming he would rather accept money from a man — and I reimbursed him as soon as we left the site.

At the Tourist Information I duly handed over the agreed fare and went into the office to thank the Turk who had organised my afternoon.

139

I was still puzzled as to the whereabouts of the Koske medrese, hoping that I might have time to walk to it.

"Much too far," was the reply, the Turk indicating that my original driver could whisk me there immediately. I accepted his advice. It was indeed a fair distance, turning out to be a few kilometres beyond the Archaeological Museum. One of the guide books mentioned that the walls were crenellated, but they were not; they were plain and built of solid white stone. Eretna (King of the Eretnids) commissioned this medrese in 1339 in memory of his wife Suli Pasha. The door was locked, but I could peer through a hole next to the rusty padlock and observed a splendid turbe where both husband and wife were entombed. I had now seen all the mosques, medreses and kumbets that I had planned to visit, and felt well pleased. Others existed in Kayseri but they were not marked on my map; they were further afield and I would have needed another day to have traced their whereabouts.

Andrew and Martin had thoroughly enjoyed themselves. Their lunch was not perhaps as exotic as they had hoped, but the view overlooking Kayseri was worth the trip. They had driven through a smart suburb and the higher they climbed Erciyes Dagi, the more exclusive were the houses and the taller the walls that protected them; when less space became available garages had been dug into the rock face. Living at that altitude during the summer months was infinitely preferable to the hot dusty plain. They were now in the middle of bargaining for rugs. Andrew had come back to the hotel to see if I had returned safely, to revise the cash situation and to create a nonchalant air in the long drawn out process of negotiation. He left me to complete my notes and an hour later burst into the room bearing an exciting looking parcel, but as it was tied with metres of string and endless knots, I had to await our return home before being shown the prayer rug. Martin was also successful, but his carpet had to be sent to England for he had another week of travelling ahead and could not cope with the heavy bundle.

Andrew and I were returning to Istanbul via Ankara, so Andrew was determined to have a celebration dinner on our last evening with Martin. The restaurant he chose was one that we had walked past the previous evening, on the first floor of some building, but not until we climbed the stairway did we discover that they only served doner kebabs. It was too late to search for another restaurant, and anyhow I was delighted for I had not eaten this Turkish speciality since Bursa; they were served with yogurt on pitta bread. Andrew loathes yogurt and shoved it to one side, but what made him even more miserable was the drink situation, the only available ones being ayran or coca cola. He had longed for a good bottle of wine, and back at the hotel for the first time in three weeks, he accepted a glass of Martin's duty free whisky.

The whistling policemen were busy that night and kept me awake, though I no longer cared. I thought of every mosque and medrese that I had seen. If I had been a Seljuk princess, would Andrew, my prince, have built me a Kumbet? It could be decorated with garlands of my favourite flowers, though I prefer trees, so perhaps a motif of acorns from the Quercus cerris (the oaks that dotted the plain before Lake Iznik) would be more appropriate; or the serrated five lobed leaf of the Platanus orientalis (the huge hollowed plane tree in Bursa). I thought of the Judas trees that I had seen such a long time ago, in Constantinople. Would their blossom now be over . .?

Seljuk portal,
Sultan Hani

Hudavent Hatun turbe, Nigde

opposite

top left: Seljuk stone-work, Hudavent Hatun turbe, Nigde

top right: Cedar door and portal of the Mongul Sungur Bey Mosque, Nigde

bottom: Gundogdu turbe, Nigde

Karamanid portal of the Ulu Cami, Aksaray

Doner Kumbet, Kayseri

Chimneys of the Vezir Hani

DAY XVI : ANTIOCH AND ANKARA

By the time the Crusaders approached Caesarea (Kayseri) the Turks had already deserted the city, so the army continued on the main road their objective now being Antioch (Antakya). Swinging in a south-easterly direction they first relieved Comana, a prosperous Armenian town besieged by Danishmend Turks. At Coxon (Guksun) the Crusaders were again welcomed by Armenians and there, in the fertile valley below the Anti-Taurus mountains, they rested for three days.

The next part of the journey proved the worst that the Crusaders had to tackle. By now it was early October and, due to the autumn rains, the road over the Anti-Taurus — already in an appalling state of repair — had become a treacherous muddy track. Knights dared not ride their horses for they were liable to slip on the steep twisting tracks and plunge into the ravines below; instead they struggled up the mountainsides trying to sell their armour or discarding the cumbersome weight in despair. The Anti-Taurus claimed more lives than had hitherto been lost fighting the Turks. With intense relief they reached the far side and were welcomed by friendly Armenians in Maras.

Baldwin rejoined the main army, hurrying from Cilicia to be with his dying wife and sick children. Baldwin was not popular. Tancred, having taken the shorter route from Heraclea, passed through the Cilician Gates before Baldwin and arrived at Tarsus which he found occupied by Turks. Word came from the Greek and Armenian inhabitants begging Tancred to come to their rescue, so he sent a message to the main army for reinforcements and surrounded the city. The Turks held off the assault for three days, but then news of Baldwin's arrival through the pass made them realise that defeat was imminent. They fled under cover of darkness. The Christians opened the gates at dawn and Tancred raised his standard on the battlements. Baldwin was furious at being out-manoeuvred, demanding that Tancred hand over the governorship. Tancred was forced to agree owing to the superior numbers of his rival. Humiliated, he marched east to Adana. Scarcely had Tancred left than the relieving force of three hundred Normans arrived as requested. Baldwin refused to allow them into Tarsus. Whilst camping that night outside the city walls, marauding Turks massacred every single soldier.

Baldwin was soon bored by the humid, swampy and malaria stricken plain around Tarsus realising that there were better lands and cities to be gained. On his way back to join the main army he again confronted Tancred who had secured Adana and Mamistra for the Christian population. This time Tancred refused to allow Baldwin into Mamistra, and was foolishly persuaded by his fellow compatriots to take his revenge and launch a surprise attack on his antagonist. Baldwin's army was far too strong and a superficial reconciliation was forced upon the two leaders. Tancred then made for Alexandretta (Iskenderun) — founded by Alexander the Great in 333 B.C. after his victory over Darius III — event-

145

ually crossing the Amanus range through the Syrian gates and joining the main army before Antioch.

Baldwin had as an advisor on his staff an Armenian by the name of Bagrat, formerly employed by the Emperor. Bagrat, whose family connections lay to the east, urged Baldwin to continue to Edessa. Having buried his wife and children and no doubt feeling the hostility of his fellow princes, Baldwin left the main army — accompanied by the chaplain and historian, Fulcher of Chartres — and made for the Armenian principalities near the Euphrates. During the winter of 1097 he freed the land of Danishmend Turks and, by March 1098, was acclaimed head of this newly formed Frankish state and had taken the title, Count of Edessa. This was contrary to the oath of allegiance sworn to Emperor Alexius in Constantinople, for Edessa had belonged to Byzantium before the Turkish invasion and should therefore have been placed under a representative of the Emperor. Baldwin justified his move on Crusading policy, since he was well positioned to provide protection for any state eventually set up in Palestine, he also commanded the main routes to Antioch from the east.

Later in the campaign fellow knights were to join Baldwin. He rewarded them with gifts from his treasure store, and having had the foresight to marry an Armenian princess he encouraged his compatriots to do likewise. He allowed Muslims freedom of worship, an act of leniency unappreciated by the Crusaders of the main army; but Baldwin's policy worked. He started out as a penniless younger son and was already a great potentate, having broken away from the overpowering authority and also the petty squabbles of the leading nobles.

The Crusaders now approached Antioch. They were awe-struck at the sight of the city which, during the early Byzantine period, had rivalled Constantinople in size and splendour. Antioch was founded in 300 B.C. by Seleucus who as a young man of twenty-three years had accompanied Alexander into Asia, and had later sided with Ptolemy of Egypt. Seleucus became very powerful and, after the extinction of the old line of Macedonias, assumed the title of King thus establishing the Seleucid dynasty. With Lysimachus he defeated one-eyed Antigonus at Ipsus in 301 B.C. and when subsequently dividing the Empire added Syria to his kingdom. This gave him an opening to the sea, and he built his city of Antioch — named after his father Antiochus — by the banks of the Orontes (the Asi) and its port, Seleucia ad Pieria, 28 kilometres away at the mouth of the river.

Antioch is a mere shadow of its former magnificence. Only fragments of the old walls rise steeply up the craggy mountain to the citadel at the top of Mt. Silpius, but nothing can detract from the view from the summit: the city nestles at its feet and the plain beyond stretches to the hills of the Amanus rising to the north. After Rome and Alexandria, Antioch became the third largest city of the Roman Empire. The imposing bridge built by Diocletian was replaced in 1970 by a concrete structure, the strong Roman foundations finally succumbing to the fierce currents created by the construction of a dam. The sole relics surviving from this great period are some superb second and third century mosaics now on view in the archaeological museum. Most of them graced sumptuous villas scattered over an idyllic valley eight kilometres to the south of Antioch. Harbiye has now become a favourite picnic area; steeped in legend it was known in the days of antiquity as Daphne for, in these cool woods and amongst the waterfalls, the nymph Daphne was changed into a small fragrant shrub in order to escape from the amorous advances of Apollo.

Christians looked upon Antioch with special favour, for there Peter had founded his first Bishopric and decided that the followers of Jesus should be called Christians. Antioch suffered from earthquakes and declined in stature following repeated invasions from Persians and Arabs, but some of its greatness was restored when retaken by the Byzantines in the tenth century. Only by treachery had the city been entered and captured by the Turcoman Yaghi-Siyan in 1085. He found his new subjects to be mostly Greek, Armenian and Syrian, and although he could rely on the Syrians for support — for they loathed their fellow Christians — Yaghi-Siyan feared above all betrayal from the Greeks and Armenians. Hitherto he had been tolerant, but as the Crusaders approached he imprisoned many leaders and desecrated the Cathedral of St. Peter turning it into stables for his horses. He laid in stocks for a long siege and hastened to make peace with his allies.

Antioch's fortifications were originally constructed by Justinian, and had been repaired a century previously by the Byzantines using the latest techniques. The wall surrounded the city whose houses, bazaars and pasture-land covered an area of five by one and a half kilometres between the River Orontes and Mt. Silpius. Four hundred towers rose at intervals so that every inch of the walls was covered by bowshot. To the north they rose out of low marshy ground by the river, to the east and west they climbed steeply up the slopes of the mountain, and to the south they ran along the ridge with the citadel at its peak 3,000 metres above the town. There were three main gates, a fourth by Diocletian's fortified bridge, and two other smaller gates.

The task that confronted the Crusaders looked daunting indeed. Surrounding Antioch was impossible because of the steep terrain to the south and the inaccessibility of most of the east and west walls. They were not to know that Yaghi-Siyan himself was nervous for, lacking sufficient troops, neither could he guard every section of his garrison. Had the Crusaders attacked immediately, as Raymond advocated, they might well have scored a surprise victory. Jealousy and intrigue prevented a quick decision, and the siege that began on October 21st 1097, lasted until the following June 3rd 1098.

THE SIEGE OF ANTIOCH

Bohemond opposed Raymond's idea of an immediate assault

147

because, if by chance they had succeeded through a joint effort, Bohemond would not have been able to claim Antioch for himself. He had learnt tactics from the siege of Nicaea, and realised that if he could arrange for the city to surrender directly to him alone, in the same way as the citizens of Nicaea had surrendered to the Emperor Alexius, he could achieve his ultimate aim. Through gaps in the defence and the blockade both camps knew each other's plans. Bohemond soon made contact with Christians inside Antioch via refugees who had found ways of keeping in touch with their families within the walls. Similarly, Syrian Christians in villages outside the city, sensing that Turkish rule was preferable to Byzantine or Frankish domination, kept Yaghi-Siyan informed as to the Crusaders' intentions. Yaghi-Siyan learning of their reluctance to launch an attack took heart and began to organise sorties, his men harassing any small groups of Franks separated from the army. His confidence grew as he heard news that his son's peace mission to Damascus had succeeded and that a large army was being raised for his benefit.

The Crusaders made no headway, and as winter approached their living conditions grew worse. They had given no thought to conservation. At first there had been plenty of livestock and grain from the recently gathered harvest to be collected from the surrounding villages; but soon they had to search farther afield for supplies and consequently came under attack from raiders from Antioch, or bands of Turks lurking in the mountains. By Christmas stocks of food were exhausted, so Bohemond set off with Robert of Flanders and twenty thousand soldiers to find more provisions. They were ambushed by Duqaq's army from Damascus who had been joined by the Emir Janah ad-Daula of Homs. Robert's troops were ahead at the time and bore the brunt of the onslaught. Bohemond, unobserved, held his soldiers at bay and at the strategic moment charged, routing the Turks who minutes before had imagined their battle won. The survivors fled to the town of Hama but the Crusaders were too weakened either to pursue or to continue their foraging. They returned empty-handed to the camp before Antioch only to be greeted with disastrous news. On the night of December 29th the Turks had poured out of Antioch and taken Raymond by surprise. A fierce battle ensued with many casualties on either side, the Crusaders, with difficulty, forcing the Turks back into their city.

There followed a succession of ill omens: an earth tremor which was even felt by Baldwin in Edessa and the same evening the aurora borealis illuminated the sky. During the next weeks the weather grew steadily colder and torrential rain drenched the miserable Crusaders. One man in every seven was dying of starvation. Envoys were sent as far as the Taurus mountains to scavenge for food, while some supplies came from Armenian monks in the Amanus range. Communications were opened with Cyprus where the Patriarch Symeon of Jerusalem had retired and, although no friend of the Latin church, he co-operated for the sake of Christian unity. He arranged for food to be sent to

St. Symeon*, but on the way to the camping Crusaders the supplies were often raided, while the Turks within the city were still able to add to their stocks through the unbeleaguered Gate of St. George.

Soldiers began to desert, amongst them Peter the Hermit and William the Carpenter. However, they were pursued by Tancred and brought ignominiously back to camp. In February Bohemond persuaded Taticius to flee, with the warning that a plot was afoot to kill him in order to exact revenge, a rumour having been spread that the Emperor, by not sending help, was encouraging the Turks. When Taticius left for Cyprus, where incidentally he helped to organise food supplies, Bohemond's propagandists suggested that he had fled out of cowardice. Since Taticius had been the Emperor's representative, many Crusaders no longer felt any obligation towards the Empire, making the eventual decision not to restore Antioch to Alexius relatively simple.

The Crusaders were now threatened with a second relieving force. Yaghi-Siyan had settled his differences with Ridwan (ruler of Aleppo) who, with a cousin from Diabekir and his father-in-law the Emir of Hama, was fast approaching Antioch. A plan devised by Bohemond was accepted and on the night of February 8th, with only seven hundred knights fit for duty, he slipped out of camp leaving behind the infantry to cope with any sortie from the city. The Turks appeared at daylight and a detachment of knights at once charged before the archers could form their lines. Bohemond then made his cavalry withdraw luring the Turks to the position he had chosen for the confrontation — a narrow stretch of land between the Lake of Antioch and the River Orontes, both of which provided a natural safeguard for his flanks. Here the Crusaders about turned and galloped in full force, the sheer weight of the charge shattering the Turkish lines and effectively destroying the might of Ridwan's army which fled in confusion back to Aleppo. Having won this spectacular battle the knights returned to Antioch just in time to save their fellow soldiers from succumbing to Yaghi-Siyan's troops. At the sight of the approaching knights the Turks quickly withdrew to the safety of their city.

The Crusaders were still desperately short of food but their morale rose when, on March 4th, siege materials and mechanics arrived at the Port of St. Symeon. Bohemond and Raymond, neither trusting each other, set out together to meet the delivery hoping as well to find recruits amongst the sailors. Returning a couple of days later they were ambushed; they scattered leaving behind their precious goods. News was brought to the camp and Godfrey left at once with a relieving force. He too was attacked by Turks but was saved by the sudden reappearance of Bohemond and Raymond. They drove the Turks back into the city and then they also planned an ambush. The first raiding party, returning

---

* The Port of Seleucia had been renamed St. Symeon in the sixth century, after the Saint who ascended a column — two metres in diameter — upon which he spent most of his life in fasting and prayer.

laden with their booty, were overpowered and massacred as they struggled to reach Diocletian's fortified bridge. Nine Emirs and fifteen hundred Turks were slain. That night their compatriots crept out of the city to bury the dead. The Christians saw them but left the Muslims in peace; the following day they dug up the bodies in order to recover any gold or silver ornaments that might have adorned the corpses.

At last the Crusaders began to make some progress. With the materials sent by the Emperor they built the castle of Mahomerie thereby effectively preventing any sorties from the fortified bridge — it was given to Raymond to man. Tancred was delegated a tower erected by the Gate of St. George, which stopped convoys of food reaching the city and the Turks from grazing their flocks outside the city walls.

Spring approached and the fear of starvation abated. The merchants could no longer trade with the inhabitants of Antioch so instead they sold food to the opposing forces, albeit at high prices. Danger now lay with the terrible Kerbogha of Mosul, who by early May was on the march with a massive force of soldiers provided by the Sultans of Baghdad and Persia, and the princes of northern Mesopotamia. They were delayed for three vital weeks attempting to storm Edessa. Baldwin, too weak for any offensive action, was secure in his fortress and by the fact of his presence kept the Turkish army occupied, thus giving Bohemond extra time to make his final preparation.

Bohemond had established a liaison with a high government official living in Antioch. His name was Firouz, an Armenian converted to the Islamic faith, who was jealous of Yaghi-Siyan having discovered that his wife was having an affair with one of his Turkish colleagues; he was therefore willing to betray his master. By devious means Bohemond had ensured that the leaders — with the exception of the Bishop of Adhemar and Raymond — were prepared to concede Antioch to him, provided his troops entered first and those of the Emperor failed to arrive in time. The Crusaders were furious with the Emperor for his seeming lack of concern following their continual pleas for help.

As Kerbogha approached Antioch panic swept through the ranks of the Crusaders, for they realised the probability of being trapped between the two Turkish armies which would result in their certain massacre. Many soldiers deserted including, on June 2nd, Stephen of Blois and his companions. A few hours later Firouz sent his son to Bohemond announcing that he was ready. Bohemond ordered the troops to prepare for a raid and then summoned the chief princes to his tent and revealed his secret plans. None dared refute his scheme and everyone gave their loyal support.

At sunset the army set out towards the east giving the impression that they were off on a foraging party, so that those within the walls were lulled into a false sense of security. In the middle of the night orders were issued to about turn and to line the west and north-west walls of Antioch. Just before dawn Bohemond placed his ladders against the tower of the Two Sisters, and sixty knights entered through a high window into a room where Firouz was nervously waiting. The knights took two more towers and Bohemond and his troops scaled the walls. With the help of the Christian inhabitants the Gate of St. George and the great Gate of the Bridge were flung open. There was little opposition, apart from the Citadel where Bohemond was unable to dislodge Yaghi-Siyan's son. Yaghi-Siyan fled. He was thrown from his horse on a mountain path and, whilst lying half dazed, was recognised by some Armenians, killed, and his head presented as a trophy to Bohemond. By nightfall on June 3rd, not a single Turk was left alive in the city. Every man, woman and child had been slaughtered, every house looted regardless of whether it belonged to Muslim or Christian, booty seized, treasures wantonly destroyed; but Antioch was once more Christian.

THE DEFENCE OF ANTIOCH

Kerbogha's mighty army arrived two days later, and by June 7th they were firmly encamped in the Crusaders' former positions outside Antioch. The situation was reversed and the Crusaders within the city were no better off than before. Food was virtually non-existent. Adhemar tried to gather supplies to alleviate the conditions of the poor for, besides the soldiers, there were the numerous camp followers to be looked after; in desperation they ate leaves and chewed dried hides, but many died of starvation.

Kerbogha insisted on taking over the citadel, despite Shams-ad-Daula's (Yaghi-Siyan's son) plea to be allowed to remain in command. The Crusaders erected a rough secondary wall to protect the city from the citadel. Being the weakest part of the defence Kerbogha quickly launched an assault, but after fierce fighting and heavy losses he withdrew and decided to starve out the Christians. A company led by William and Aubrey of Grant-Mesnil, and Lambert, Count of Clermont, succeeded in crossing the enemy lines and reaching the port of St. Symeon. They boarded Frankish and Genoese ships and, reporting that the defeat of the Crusaders was imminent, the entire fleet set sail for Tarsus where they joined Stephen of Blois.

John Ducas, the brother-in-law of Emperor Alexius, had cleared Lydia and Phrygia of Turks and reopened the road north from Attalia (Antalya). He had made the way safe for the Emperor to march to Philomelion and now, in mid June, Alexius was preparing to continue to Antioch. Fate intervened. First by way of Stephen and William who had marched north from Tarsus to tell the Emperor that the Crusaders were surely overwhelmed, and secondly from Peter of Aulps. Peter had been left in command of the town of Comana south-east of Caesarea, and he had fled to the west to report that a Turkish army was advancing in order to intercept the Emperor's troops before they reached Antioch. Alexius held a council. The only person present to beg him to continue and fulfil his promise to help the Crusaders was Bohemond's half brother, Guy de Hauteville, a member of the Emperor's staff. No one else supported his plea. Alexius, responsible for the whole of his Empire, could not afford an irresponsible campaign, so his great Byzantine army retreated to Constantinople leaving a wide stretch of wasteland as a barrier against the Turks.   The Emperor was never forgiven for this act of desertion which naturally intensified the hatred that existed between the Greeks and Latins.

Meanwhile some curious spiritualistic phenomena were taking place amongst the besieged community in Antioch.   A pilgrim by the name of Peter Bartholomew, claimed that St. Andrew had appeared to him on numerous occasions and revealed the whereabouts of the Holy Lance that had pierced the side of Christ.   A greater part of the floor in the Cathedral of St. Peter was excavated and a piece of iron eventually discovered.   Such was the delight at finding this relic that no one dared question the miracle.   A priest from Valence called Stephen also had a vision which the Bishop of Adhemar accepted as genuine.   Christ told Stephen that if the Crusaders returned to a Christian way of life and repented their sins, he would send them protection in five days time.   It was five days later that the Lance was unearthed.   A meteor was seen to fall upon the Turkish camp on June 14th.   Expectations of a victory rose amongst the weary Crusaders.

Raymond became ill and Bohemond, with no opposition, determined to launch a full scale attack on Kerbogha's camp.   He left Raymond with two hundred men to keep guard on the Citadel, divided the remaining soliders into seven armies and gave the chaplain and historian, Raymond of Aguilers, the honour of carrying the Holy Lance into battle.   On the morning of June 28th the Crusaders marched over Diocletian's fortified bridge and out of Antioch.   Kerbogha refused to attack immediately for he wished to destroy the whole army and not just the advance guard, so he lured the Christians to the hills from where his archers could shower them with deadly arrows.   The Crusaders could not be halted.   Their lines never wavered and many swore that they had been encouraged by the vision of knights on white horses waving white banners, and whose leaders they recognised as St. George, St. Mercurius and St. Demetrius. Kerbogha sent a detachment to harass the Christian army from the rear, but Bohemond had kept his seventh army in reserve to deal with this eventuality.

The Crusaders were no doubt helped by dissension within the Turkish ranks.   Kerbogha had to deal with squabbles amongst his own leaders, each jealous in case one of the others became too powerful; the Emirs also feared that if Kerbogha were to prove victorious they would come under his domination.   Duquq of Damascus was the first to leave the field of battle and soon others panicked and followed suit.   Kerbogha set fire to the field between the enemy lines hoping to delay the Franks long enough for him to restore order, but it was a vain attempt. Deserted, he finally fled, his power and prestige lost forever.

Large numbers of Turks were massacred if not by the Crusaders then by Armenians in the countryside.   Merwan the commander of the Citadel surrendered but refused to hand over his banner to the sick Raymond, preferring to wait for Bohemond's triumphal re-entry into Antioch. Bohemond allowed the garrison to walk out unharmed and many, including Merwan, joined Bohemond's army and were converted to Christianity. After eight gruelling months victory was complete.

We said good-bye to Martin at the bus station in Kayseri. He was to continue to Antioch following the path of the Crusaders which I have described. The month was May and the sun shone; it was not October when the rains were at their worst, nor was the route over the Anti-Taurus a muddy track. The wheels of his bus held firm on the tarmac road and it reached Maras in six hours. Martin changed buses and three and a half hours later drove in to Antioch, present day Antakya. The city was easily entered and the following day, after visiting the Citadel, Harbiye and the Mosaic Museum, Martin left as quietly as he had arrived. He left the Crusaders too, for the last stage of their journey to Jerusalem took them through foreign countries which, in this modern day and age with the paraphernalia of passports and visas, and with battle fields to negotiate, would prove more complicated than the Crusaders' march nearly one thousand years ago.

Andrew and I caught a bus to Ankara. The most curious incident in an otherwise uneventful journey occurred as we approached the village. A strange sound greeted us and became increasingly loud; so loud that it was frightening. As we drew to a halt we were encircled by a swarm of black shrouded figures. The uproar came from these wailing women. Our bus remained stationary for some time; once the doors were opened the clamour became intolerable. The entire female population of the village must have congregated to bid farewell to the family that was setting out to seek its fortune in the big metropolis. The sounds of mourning receded as we moved on, but inside the wailing from our new passengers continued for a good five minutes, finally subsiding into snuffles, hiccups and long drawn out sighs.

One of the reasons for visiting Ankara, apart from its being en route for Istanbul, was in order to visit the Museum of Anatolian Civilisations. Exhibits from the Palaeolithic age onwards filled the fifteenth century Bedestan and Caravanserai restored at the instigation of Ataturk. Massive Hittite sculptures occupied the central hall, while the surrounding traders' booths and galleries displayed the best from the numerous civilisations that inhabited Asia Minor.

We climbed to the acropolis fortified since ancient times and overlooking the important east-west highway. It had witnessed the passing of many armies. In the sixth century B.C. Croesus, the last king of Lydia, extended his empire as far as the ancient river Halys (Kizilirmak). Cyrus the Great, founder of the Persian Empire marched by on his way to subdue Lydia, and in the fifth century B.C. Xerxes I, son of Darius I, brought his army across Anatolia to seek revenge for his father's defeat at Marathon. We know that Alexander reached Gordion in 334 B.C.. He undoubtedly set foot on this citadel for Ancyra was only 95 kilometres north-east of Gordion, and he welcomed the surrender of tribes to the north.   (The following year he led his army south passing through the Cilician Gates to Tarsus and confronted Darius III in the major battle at Ipsus.   He continued south, and after his Egyptian campaign turned east through Mesopotamia to Persia and on to India).

Gauls, Romans, Persians and Arabs tramped past Ancyra in their turn.   The Byzantine walls failed to keep out the Turks, and by the beginning of the fifteenth century they occupied most of Asia Minor as well as Thrace.   Sultan Bayezid I was preparing to lay siege on Constantinople when he learned of Tamerlane's approach.   He withdrew his army giving the Christians a remaining half century in which to enjoy their city, and met the mighty force of Tamerlane on the plain below Ancyra. Bayezid was deafeated, and so began his horrible humiliation which I have related in an earlier chapter.

The Ottoman Sultans ruled in Constantinople from 1453 until Ataturk took over the leadership of his country making Ankara its capital. In 1925 it was a town of scarcely seventy-five thousand; now the population has grown to over three million.   Thousands of homeless and jobless Turks answered Ataturk's call and walked across the bare plains of Anatolia to create this city, but although the new town — Yenisehir — has wide boulevards, imposing government buildings, office blocks and modern hotels, the citadel bears witness to old Turkey.   Dogs barked, women wore their carsafs (black shawls) and old houses bordered the narrow streets, the lower halves built of stone and the upper decorated with patterned brick, wood or plaster.   Frequently we would notice a broken roman capital used as a seat or a twisted column supporting a rough wall.   The most bizarre setting for Roman stonework could be seen embedded in the high wall by the South Gate.   Four bas-relief statues were laid sideways with a row of tombstones above, the centre one decorated with a rosette and a swathed garland.   Whenever I raised my camera children appeared and stood directly in front hoping to be included in the photograph, but none of them followed us up the steepest path to the summit.   Fifteen of the twenty Byzantine towers remained and the view from the highest was impressive.   Ankara has spread over a series of hills and on the nearest, to which we now made our way, stood the imposing Temple of Augustus and the Haci Bayram mosque.

The Temple had been built in the second century B.C. as a shrine to Cybele.   Subsequent fashion demanded that the name be changed to Diana and later the Galatians wishing to show their gratitude for the leniency of Roman rule, dedicated the temple to Augustus.   Augustus left a testament summing up the achievements of his reign, which was engraved on two bronze tablets and placed outside his mausoleum and also, on the orders of the Roman Senate, on every temple of Augustus throughout the Empire.   In 1555 Ghislain de Busbecq stopped in Angora, as it was then called, on his way to Amasya.   He had been sent by Ferdinand I — the youngest brother of Charles V — with a mission and in

Constantinople had discovered that Suleyman the Magnificent was away on a campaign, so he decided to follow him. Sightseeing in Angora he realised the importance of the long inscription and, though he could not translate it himself, he copied the text faithfully. Both politically and historically the document turned out to be priceless, and the only complete record of this famous 'Res Gestae Divi Augusti' (The Achievement of the Deified Augustus).

Haci Bayram Veli was the founder of the Bayrami order of dervishes, and he is buried in a turbe next to the mosque named after him. Evliya Effendi, a seventeenth century traveller and writer, recounts a delightful tale of this Muslim saint. Apparently Haci Bayram had in his youth been tempted by a woman who praised his hair, beard, eyebrows and eyelashes. The monk retired and prayed to be delivered from the temptation of lust. He returned devoid of any hair and the woman, shocked at his ugliness, turned him out of her house.

Wending our way down the hill we passed children playing football, waddling geese and women knitting. They were all noisy, either shouting, squawking or chattering, but these were inoffensive sounds compared with the hideous roar of traffic which hit us once we reached the busy highway at ground level. Here it was impossible to recreate visions of ancient armies. Our Crusaders had not passed by Ankara. We had left them in possession of Antioch, but tomorrow we would rejoin them in Constantinople at the beginning of their march, where they had set off full of hope, before friction and aggressive power politics had crept into their tactics.

DAY XVII : ISTANBUL 3

Although we had not been away for long, it seemed strange to be once more in Istanbul. We entered the old city through the familiar archway set into the thick defensive walls, felt the cobbles beneath our feet and climbed the twisting streets to the acropolis. I approached the two buildings for which the city is renowned with slight trepidation, in case the impression borne with me throughout Anatolia failed to live up to expectation. Even though St. Sophia was surrounded by minarets I thought of it as a Christian building. It was still there, as strong and as solid as I had envisaged. Beyond the transformed and weed-free gardens rose the symbol of Allah, the Blue Mosque, its forest of cupolas soaring towards the dome. Both survived the test of the return visit, their impact being even greater than I had first remembered.

We turned our backs on the Blue Mosque and walked behind St. Sophia, for we were making our way to Topkapi Palace. Since Martin's fated visit in March the entire area to the south had been newly paved, not in rounded cobbles but in flat, slightly larger pieces of grey stone, and set in a mosaic pattern. While we had been in Anatolia the section to the east had also been finished. Gone were the team of workmen, the perilous planks, piles of stones, sand and cement mixers; the wide pavement was washed and brushed, not looking glaringly new but blending into the surroundings.

The organised gangs had similarly vanished from the First Court of Topkapi. On our thwarted attempt to enter the Palace during our previous visit to Istanbul we had watched them hacking away at the unyielding stony soil, piling it into barrows and struggling to another group of men who passed the contents through a large sieve. The fine tilth was returned to the prepared ground, and already fresh young blades of grass showed through, while in the borders beneath the high wall to the right, well watered young shrubs grew in perfect conditions.

Topkapi was already open and teeming with visitors when we arrived, and we had to buy tickets and join the queue for a tour round the Harem. Originally established in the Eski Saray — the first Palace of the Sultans — Topkapi had been kept solely as the administrative centre of the Empire. A fire in 1541 destroyed the Old Seraglio (the Eski Saray), and Roxelana moved with her accompanying retinue consisting of a hundred ladies-in-waiting, a guard and eunuchs, together with servants, dressmaker and purveyor, to the Grand Seraglio (Topkapi). Roxelana, Russian by birth, had been captured by Turkish raiders in Galicia and, because of her charm and infectious wit, was presented to the Harem. Suleyman I already had a Sultana and an heir, Mustafa, but when he met Roxelana he fell passionately in love with her, remaining faithful unto death and ignoring the pleasures offered by the Harem. Roxelana produced a son, Selim, became the second Sultana, and forthwith Suleyman acceded to her demands of marriage. No Sultan had married for centuries, and the whole of Constantinople was astounded when Suleyman promised, "This woman I set free from slavery and make her a wife. All that belongs to her shall be her property." The festivities continued for a week; donations of food and gifts of money and silks were distributed amongst the citizens, and sumptuous presents arrived for the new Empress. Wrestling and archery competitions were organised, tumblers and jugglers entertained the crowds, and the highlight was a procession of strange looking animals from Asia and Africa.

From the moment Roxelana entered the Grand Seraglio, the empire of the Sultans' was doomed. For the next century and a half it was the women of the Harem who ruled Turkey. The most important woman, and the one to whom the running of the Harem was assigned, was the Sultan Validé, the Queen Mother. She presented no problem to Roxelana for she conveniently died. Mustafa, the heir, was appointed governor of the Province of Magnesia and his mother, the Rose of Spring, accompanied him leaving the monopoly of the Harem to Roxelana. Ultimately Roxelana was able to manipulate Mustafa's murder. Since the shedding of royal blood was not permitted the customary method of disposing of an adversary was by strangulation. Deaf mutes carried out the deed using a bowstring or a silken cord for those of importance. Her third rival was the Grand Vizier Ibrahim, a Greek Christian, who had been a childhood friend of Suleyman and to whom Suleyman had given his sister in marriage. Roxelana managed to persuade her husband that Ibrahim was usurping his power, so Ibrahim too suffered the fate of the bowstring. Roxelana died before Suleyman and therefore never aspired to the title of Sultan Validé, but she had the satisfaction of knowing that her son would inherit the throne.

Building began immediately Roxelana arrived and continued until Abdul Mecit moved to Dolmabahce in 1855. The guided tour, for there was no other way of visiting the Harem, fairly raced through a selection of rooms. The general impression gained was that of sumptuous splendour, the walls of the majority of the rooms covered with tiles brilliant in colour and bold in design, the best from both Iznik and Kutahya. The artists placed the tiles so as to create scenes and illusions. In one room they imitated large ogival windows framing trees and flowers, while Iznik's greatest period was shown to perfection in Murad III's salon – designed by Sinan – which included a ravishing panel of plum blossom.

We walked along the Golden Way where the Sultan chose his companion for the night. The preliminaries were exacting. First he had to approach the Queen Mother and make an obeisance. His choice made he had to wait a further two hours while the odalisque (concubine) was prepared for the bedchamber. She was washed and scrubbed, cleansed with a mudpack of oil and rice flour, perfumed and pomaded, and her nails and eyebrows painted. The date of her visit was recorded. If she produced a son she was made a Sultana, if not she might never see the Sultan again and was relegated to a life of boredom cooped up in one of a veritable warren of small rooms on an upper floor of the complex. After a Sultan's death all his odalisques were banished to a former palace nicknamed the Palace of Tears.

We were shown the Hall of the Black Eunuchs, in reality a narrow passage two stories high lined with cell-like rooms. The Eunuchs were brought as slaves from the upper reaches of the Nile. They were under the command of the Kislar Aga (the Master of the Girls) and were needed to keep order when inevitable jealousy and intrigues disrupted the peace of the Harem.

A two storeyed building called the Cage had no windows on the ground floor, while those on the upper floor looked out only to the sea. From 1603, and for the next two centuries, heirs to the throne were kept locked in the 'Kafés'. They were cared for by deaf mutes and provided with odalisques who were also imprisoned. If, despite elaborate precautions taken by the palace doctors, the girls carelessly became pregnant, they were immediately drowned. One prince remained in the cage for fifty years and when released in order to be proclaimed Sultan, he had practically lost his power of speech. It was therefore not surprising that the quality of rule declined, each successive Sultan appearing more degenerate and unequal to the task, and by the nineteenth century Turkey had indeed become 'the sick man of Europe'.

The Cage had been invented by Sultan Ahmed I (ruling from 1603 – 17) because he rebelled against the law of fratricide introduced by Mehmet the Conqueror, whereby it was legitimate for any heir to execute his brothers in order to avoid the consequences of disputed succession. Ahmed's father, Mehmet III (1595 – 1603) had been forced by his powerful mother, the Sultan Validé Baffo, to murder his nineteen half brothers all under eleven years of age. Mehmet had summoned them to the Throne room where one by one they were circumcised, taken into an adjoining chamber and dextrously strangled by deaf mutes using the silken bowstring. Mehmet was notified of his brothers' deaths in the official manner, by a document on black paper written in white ink. The bodies were laid out in nineteen small coffins and given a state funeral.

Baffo, the Queen Mother and instigator of this evil deed, came from a noble Venetian family. Some say that she was abducted by Turkish pirates, others that she was a secret agent planted by the Venetians. Either way, she was presented to Murad III (1574 – 95) at the age of thirteen. She only produced one son, Mehmet, but like Roxelana became the power behind the throne. Because of connecting passages and the curtained window above the Divan, these dominating women were able to overhear the meetings and thereby influence and interfere in the affairs of State. Baffo filled the Harem with five hundred concubines and, even though Mehmet had sworn to remain faithful to his Sultana, the temptation of the voluptuous life was too great. Over indulgence soon reduced him to a complete nonentity. The hated Baffo reigned supreme, but shortly after her son's death she was strangled in her bed.

By far the worst crime in the Harem was carried out by Sultan

158

Ibrahim (1640 –48).   His favourite, 'Sugar', passed on a rumour that one of Ibrahim's concubines was unfaithful.   To have an affair was well nigh impossible;   lesbianism was naturally rife and occasionally liaisons were formed with eunuchs, but no proof whatsoever of this particular incident was traced.   The Kislar Aga even tortured some of the girls trying to discover the identity of the wayward concubine.   Ibrahim waited for three days, prowling around the Harem like a caged tiger, until finally his anger was unleashed.   He ordered every single one of his two hundred and eighty concubines to be drowned with the exception of Sugar.   They were tied in sacks weighted with stones, rowed in batches to the Sea of Marmara and tipped out of the boats.   One managed to escape, the knot of her sack being badly tied.   She was rescued by a passing boat bound for France.   Only one excuse can be offered for this appalling deed. Ibrahim had been placed in the Cage at the age of two, and was dragged out after twenty-two years in order to be made Sultan.   Believing that those who summoned him had only arrived to put him to death, Ibrahim refused to open the door barricading it with furniture.   Only when finally convinced of his brother's death and realising that he was the sole heir, did he emerge to begin the most despotic and barbarous reign of all the Ottoman Sultans.

Ibrahim committed many other crimes before falling victim to the bowstring.   Kiusem the Queen Mother was equally loathed.   Tremendously powerful she had been the mother of the last three reigning sultans, and soon she too was brutally murdered thus ending for ever the power of the Harem.   Sugar became Constantinople's most exclusive procuress and was finally poisoned in the traditional Turkish manner: chopped hair and ground glass being mixed with her coffee, which destroyed the intestines and caused a long and painful death.

I cannot leave the Harem with nothing but tales of horror and woe, for towards the end of the eighteenth century there occurred an interlude which can only be described as a fairy story.   Aimée Dubucq de Rivery was returning from a convent in France to her Norman parents living in Martinique.   She was captured by Algerian corsairs and presented to the Harem.   There was nothing she could do, so she sensibly adapted to the life of the community.   She was respected and admired by her fellow odalisques, taught the trade of her profession by the black eunuchs and proffered to the fifty-five year old Sultan Abdul Hamid (1774 – 89). Within a year she gave birth to a son, Mahmud, and became the Sultan's favourite.   Abdul Hamid's heir, the eldest living male, was his nephew Selim, who was about the same age as Aimée.   He had been allowed complete liberty for Abdul had abolished the cruel system of the Cage. He and Aimée spent many hours together discussing literature and French politics — Aimée's cousin was Josephine Bonaparte.

Selim became Sultan on his uncle's death.   He was not interested in the Harem, his chief aim being to suppress the Janissaries who had become far too powerful.   In 1807 while the majority were away fighting on the Danube, Selim attempted to increase the size of his rival New Army, but he was not yet strong enough. The remaining Janissaries overturned their kettles in a symbolic gesture; the huge kettles cooked the food ostensibly provided by the Sultan, so by this demonstration the Janissaries indicated that they intended to overthrow the Sultan as well. Selim wisely made for the Cage for it still provided sanctuary; he abdicated and made obeisance to Mustafa (Abdul Hamid's eldest son and next in line to the throne). Selim's friends tried to reinstate him and by the following July 1808, Bairactar, Pasha of Rustchuk, encamped with forty thousand troops outside the walls of Constantinople. With a small band of trusted supporters he tried to enter the Seraglio. Mustafa realising the danger, ordered the murder of Selim and Aimée's son, Mahmud. Selim managed to send a message to Aimée and fought a delaying action, stabbing two deaf mutes before the bowstring gripped his neck.

Aimée grabbed Mahmud and flew down the Golden Road. Her faithful Georgian slave threw a brazier full of red hot coals at the assailants giving Aimée time to hide Mahmud up a chimney. Meanwhile Bairactar had hammered down the Gate of Felicity. Mustafa kicked the dead body of Selim into the courtyard in front of Bairactar who fell weeping on the corpse. Revenge now had to be taken, and at the precise moment that Mustafa·was dragged off his throne and daggers were raised, the bedraggled figure of Mahmud appeared his face covered in soot. Mahmud was made Sultan, later to be nicknamed the Reformer. Aimée was a supportive and gentle Queen Mother, and Mustafa was confined to the Cage.

Troubled times obviously followed and to avoid Civil War Mustafa had to die by the bowstring. Mahmud lost a substantial part of his Empire but he achieved the near impossible, the elimination forever of the powerful Janissaries. His greatest act of love and courage was at his mother's death bed. He sent for Father Chrysostom, the Superior of the Convent of St. Antoine in Pera, to hear Aimée's confession. Mahmud bade the Greek doctor and the slaves retire while he prayed to Allah, and Father Chrysostom gave Absolution to the dearest and most gentle Sultan Validé of the Ottoman Empire.

Andrew and I had become so involved in the beauty and the intrigues of the Harem, that to emerge into the bright sunlight and to be transported back into the twentieth century, came as quite a shock. Even more so because of a strange sound that filled the courtyard – that of a rotary mower. Albeit rather old and small it was the first we had seen in Turkey, making a quicker job of cutting the grass, though I missed the silent swish of the scythes and the clean finish they achieved, as opposed to the line of churned up green gunge left behind by the modern machine.

The Clock and Miniature rooms were still shut and so was the Archaeological Museum below Topkapi, which was a pity because it contained Alexander the Great's sarcophagus; so we decided to visit the Mosaic Museum, checking first that the day and hour were correct. The stables of the old Byzantine Imperial Palace were ideal for displaying the exhibits, having wide open-ended arched sections either side of a central alley. Set into the ground or against the back and side walls, the floor mosaics — their colours still fresh and clear — were a delight to inspect. Some came from churches, others had been discovered as recently as 1950 on the site of the Imperial Palace. A fight between an elephant and a bear was clearly depicted, the bear's neck held in a tight grip by the elephant's trunk; a leopard attacked a stag while another leapt towards a man. In a more peaceful countryside scene a shepherd carried a lamb and two children rode a camel. The most humorous episode showed a horse who had bucked off his rider but the irritating bundle of faggots was still attached to the saddle. These captivating scenes were surrounded by borders ornamented with fruit and trailing leaves. The exhibition was small, therefore easy to remember and well worth a visit.

We now decided to cross Istanbul and caught a bus to the Edirne Gate. A flight of steps led to the entrance of the Mihrimah Mosque and also to a terrace from where one gained a sensational view. Suleyman had commissioned this mosque in 1562 for his favourite daughter Princess Mihrimah — whose mother was Roxelana — and, with Sinan the architect, had chosen a perfect site on the Sixth Hill and the highest point in Istanbul. (Rome was built on seven hills; when transferring the seat of power from Rome to Byzantium, Constantine was determined to retain something of his former city and appropriately managed to name seven new hills). Sinan had adopted the basic design of St. Sophia; the dome 37 metres high and 20 metres in diameter rested on a square base, with the tympana on all four sides pierced with three rows of windows. There were also windows encircling the base of the dome, and the sunlight filtering through the stained glass helped to create a magical effect in the lofty and spacious interior — it was one of Sinan's materpieces. The four massive granite pillars supported high triple arcades to the north and south, which revealed side aisles with six slighter pillars their joining arches decorated with inlaid marble. The painted walls in soft colours imitated tiles; the mihrab and mimber were also plain and the mihrab had two enormous wax candles on either side standing on solid brass bases. The effect was spoiled by ugly electric wires hanging clumsily to the side, for no longer were these splendid candles lit but were topped instead by modern light bulbs.

Andrew acquired our lunch from barrow boys, two ringed sesame rolls and a couple of baby cucumbers which were peeled, quartered and sprinkled with salt; a bite from each in turn tasted delicious. We bought our dessert from a man struggling up the cobbled streets, his cart laden with cherries. It proved quite a performance for he produced some hanging scales and proceeded to weigh a huge amount. We showed him a 100 lire note and tried to explain that we only wanted sufficient cherries for that sum (Andrew had a 10,000 lire note in his money belt, but this was not the place to extricate it). The cherry-seller looked most unhappy and our Turkish and sign language were not achieving any result, so Andrew took handfuls of cherries off the scales himself and returned them to the cart.   Eventually the sale was concluded to the relative satisfaction of the parties concerned.

Andrew now took charge of the sightseeing and led the way to the top of the Byzantine walls; it turned out to be a scramble.   Edging around a tower was bad enough, but when he wanted to cross a narrow ledge with a drop of 14 metres to the road below, I refused to follow and begged him to return.   Andrew enjoys mountaineering so continued to a second, finer tower while I sat and contemplated the scene, seeing how far I could spit my cherry stones into the enemy lines.

These were the walls built by Emperor Theodosius II during the years 413–477, to protect Constantinople from overland invasions.   They stretched for 6.7 kilometres, from the fortress of Yedikule by the Sea of Marmara to the Imperial Palace of Blachernae, and were a triple fortification of great strength.   I was sitting on the inner wall which was on average 13 metres high and contained ninety-six towers.   A gap of between 13 to 20 metres separated the inner and outer walls, the latter being 8 metres high with eighty-two towers.   A third low wall roughly the same distance away but set deep into the ground, dammed a wide fosse filled with water.   In the twelfth century Emperor Manuel I Comnenus built a single, but higher and thicker wall to guard the Palace of Blachernae; on reaching the shores of the Golden Horn it turned east to join the existing defences.

I was near the Edirne Gate, formerly known by the name of Adrianople and in Byzantine times as the Gate of Charisius.   The lowest and most vulnerable section, the Mesoteichion, was to the south where the wall crossed the Lycus valley.   Emperor Constantine put Giustiniani — the Genoese soldier — and his army in charge of the defence of the land walls which he promptly repaired and fortified.   When the Turkish army began to march towards Constantinople, Constantine ordered his secretary, Phrantzes, to check the number of men available to defend the city.   He was horrified to be told that including monks, there were only 4,983 Greeks and 2,000 foreigners.   Lacking sufficient troops to man both walls, he and Giustiniani decided to concentrate on the defence of the outer walls only.   The Turkish army numbered 80,000, plus hordes of irregulars.   As they approached slight earth tremors were followed by torrential rains which the Christians interpreted as evil omens.

The bombardment began on April 6th, 1453.   Mehmet realised at once that his guns were wrongly placed, so for the next few days he altered their positions and began to fill in the great fosse which would hinder his troops from occupying any breach made by his artillery.   On April 11th the bombardment recommenced and continued without pause for six solid weeks.   Mehmet had difficulty keeping his cannons in position.   They had to be placed on platforms made of wood and rubble for the ground was a quagmire caused by excessive April rains; even so they kept slipping and had to be adjusted after every shot.   Fortunately Urban's great monster could only be fired seven times a day; it caused untold damage, and the sheets of leather and bales of wool hung over the walls by the defenders were no more than a pathetic attempt at protection.

Within a week the fosse had been filled and a section of the outer wall destroyed. The citizens of Constantinople rallied to the defence bringing planks, barrels and sacks of earth, enabling Giustiniani to erect a stockade. The barrels filled with soil were placed on top and acted as a bulwark, copying the former crenellation. With nightly repairs the stockade remained firm.

Meanwhile the sea battles that I have already described were taking place, and also the Turks cunning transport of their ships over the hill behind Pera to the Golden Horn. The shortage of food soon became a serious problem. The gardens of Constantinople were not producing anything for it was too early in the season; fishing boats lay idle; cattle, sheep and swine declined in numbers and likewise the stores of grain. The Venetians had promised to send help, but communications were bad and they had no conception of the gravity of the situation. They had endless arguments with the Pope as to who should pay for the ships, and the delays were interminable. Constantine also had problems within his own city, the jealousy and squabbles between the Venetians and the Genoese reaching such a pitch, that he summoned the leaders of both sides and begged them to make peace. They were after all meant to be allies, joined to save Christendom against the threat of the infidels.

The Siege continued. On May 7th, four hours after sunset, the Mesoteichion section was stormed; the Turks crossing the filled in fosse carried scaling ladders and hooks attached to their lances. Fighting continued for three hours but the attack was successfully repulsed. The Turks tried again on the 12th near the junction of the Blachernae and the Theodosian walls, this time starting at midnight; here also they were unsuccessful, the walls proving too high and strong. Mehmet, having control of the northern end of the Golden Horn, was able to move his batteries from the hills behind the Valley of Springs, across his new pontoon bridge, and consequently could pound the Blachernae walls to greater effect. The boom at the entrance to the Golden Horn remained invincible throughout the Siege, but every Venetian ship was needed for its protection; none were available to attack the pontoon in order to stop the Sultan's dreaded supplies from crossing and inflicting yet more damage to the battered walls.

New subtle methods were devised by the Turks. They had amongst their troops professional miners who dug under the walls near the Charisian Gate. I was sitting near this Gate and I looked down anxiously for signs of saboteurs; then I realised that I was on the inner wall and it was beyond the patch of wasteland in front of me that the danger lay. However the ground there had proved too difficult, so the Turks tried again near the Blachernae wall. The Christians learnt of this ruse and a counter mine was dug, the Turkish tunnel entered and the props set on fire causing a collapse of the works. After a short pause digging restarted. The Christians counteracted by flooding the tunnels or smoking out the sappers.   The climax came on May 23rd when the Greeks captured a number of miners, including a senior officer who under torture revealed the whereabouts of numerous other schemes.   The information enabled the tunnels to be demolished and effectively stopped any further attempts at this type of warfare.

Meanwhile the Christians were confronted by a yet more terrifying apparition.   On the morning of May 18th a great wooden tower on wheels, carrying scaling ladders and protected by layers of bullocks' and camels' hides, was found to be positioned opposite a Theodosian tower with its artillery destroyed.   Its first task was to provide protection for gangs of Turks who were continually needed to fill in the boggy fosse. Soon it would be pushed against the wall to make storming the ramparts a relatively simple task.   That night a group of brave soldiers crept out of the city, crawled underneath the siege-machine and placed powder against its legs.   Setting the kegs alight they beat a hasty retreat — a shattering explosion brought down the whole edifice.

One would have imagined that these courageous counter measures would have given heart to the Christians, but they were desperately tired, Constantine even fainting whilst discussing tactics.   There was no sign of relief.   The inhabitants were starving, the dwindling stocks of ammunition and powder could not last forever but even worse, fate seemed to be pitted against the proud city of Constantinople.   Prophecies were recalled.   One said that the Empire had risen with a Constantine and would therefore perish with a Constantine;   another told that the city would never fall while the moon waxed in the heavens.   On May 24th, the night of the full moon, there was a total eclipse lasting for three hours, a bad omen itself;   and now the moon would wane.   The following day the most precious icon was paraded around the city.   It slipped off its stand to the ground becoming strangely heavy, so that a great effort by many priests was needed to replace the holy picture.   There followed a torrential storm and severe flooding of the streets, and the procession had to be abandoned.   The next day a thick fog descended, a phenomenon unknown during the month of May, and that night an unexplained light played upon the dome of the great Church of the Holy Wisdom (St. Sophia), observed by both Christians and Turks alike.

Frenzied activity in the Turkish camp warned the Christians that the final assault was imminent.   The Sultan announced that May 28th was to be a day of rest and an eerie stillness settled over the land.   The Sultan rode amongst his troops giving them encouragement for the battle to come.   The Emperor ordered Mass to be said in the Church of the Holy Wisdom and, for the first time, both Greek Orthodox and Roman Catholics shared in the Service.   Positions were taken on the outer walls, and the inner gates were firmly locked.   There was to be no retreat.

At 1.30 a.m. on May 29th a screaming battle cry accompanied by drums, trumpets and fifes urged the first wave of Turkish soldiers to the walls.   These were Bashi-bazouks, a mixture of races consisting of some Turks but also Slavs, Hungarians, Greeks, Italians and even Germans.

They fought for the Sultan because he paid them well and promised unlimited booty if they entered Constantinople. Since they were apt to default, Mehmet placed a line of military police behind them armed with thongs and maces, ready to strike any who attempted to flee. The whole length of the wall was attacked, chiefly to cause a distraction, but the main force was again concentrated on the weak Mesoteichion section that crossed the Lycus valley.

After two hours the Bashi-bazouks were called back and the Anatolian Turks took over. The narrowness of the valley restricted the movement of the overwhelming number of Turks, so the Christians were able to add to their confusion by hurling back their ladders and assaulting them with stones. A shot from Urban's cannon landed squarely on the stockade bringing down a section. The Anatolians poured through the gap but the Emperor and his troops surrounded them, killing many and forcing others back across the fosse. The attack was called off but there was no respite for the exhausted Christians. Mehmet had his Janissaries ready and they marched steadily forward, the martial music that accompanied them being so loud that it was even heard above the sound of the guns from the far side of the Bosphorus. For one hour the adversaries fought hand to hand, but still the Christians held their positions and the Janissaries made no headway.

Fate now intervened. Just before sunrise a shot pierced Giustiniani's breastplate. Bleeding and in pain he begged his men to take him to safety. The Emperor was summoned and tried to persuade him to stay and support his troops, but Giustiniani's nerve had cracked. The Emperor, in a moment of pity, relented and unwisely handed him the key of a door in the inner wall. Giustiniani's bodyguard carried him back into the city and down to the harbour to a Genoese ship. The Genoese soldiers, noticing their leader being escorted from the scene of battle, imagined that all was lost and escaped through the same door before it could be relocked. Deserted, the Emperor and his Greeks faced alone the might of the Janissaries.

Fate struck a second time. The Emperor had to leave the scene of battle, an urgent message arriving which appealed for his help at the Kerkoporta. This was the name of a postern half hidden by a tower in a corner of the Blachernae wall, immediately before it joined the Theodosian wall. Blocked for many years it had been cleared just before the Siege to allow sorties against the enemy's flank. Someone returning from one such sortie forgot to shut and bar the door. A band of about fifty Turks, noticing that it was open, rushed through and found themselves in a courtyard. They could easily have been surrounded, but the Genoese soldiers defending the tower panicked hearing at this moment of the breach at Mesoteichion. Seeing their fellow compatriots making for the Golden Horn, they inferred that the battle was over and they too deserted their posts. The Turks poured through this second ill-fated door.

Constantine, realising that there was nothing he could do, galloped back with three comrades to the Lycus valley, but it was too late. The

Sultan having observed the panic had urged his troops afresh. A giant called Hasan had been the first to hack his way over the stockade. His glory was short lived for he in turn was slain, but the Janissaries forced the Greeks back into a ditch beneath the inner wall where they were duly slaughtered. When Constantine arrived the Turks were already stampeding through the inner door and their standards flew from the captured towers. Constantine discarded his royal insignia and with his companions entered the fray. None of them were ever seen again.

The Turks had broken into the city at dawn. By the code of battle they were allowed to loot for three days but Mehmet, at the end of the first evening, ordered a halt to the appalling atrocities. Mehmet entered the city in the afternoon through the Charisian Gate and rode straight to the Church of the Holy Wisdom. Kneeling on the ground before this mighty edifice, he poured a handful of earth over his turban as an act of humility before his own God and, on entering the Church, stood silently for a few minutes. Then he turned angrily on a Turk who was hacking at the marble — but this tale I have already told when I visited St. Sophia on my first day in Istanbul.

One of the reasons that we had returned to Istanbul from Ankara was in order to visit the Church of St. Saviour in Chora. After St. Sophia it was the most important Byzantine building in the city, containing a superb series of mosaics and frescoes. Chora means land, or country, for the original church was outside the Constantinian walls, though it kept its name when included within the Theodosian walls a century later. Emperor Justinian erected a church on the site of one destroyed by the earthquake in 558, but by the eleventh century it had collapsed and was rebuilt by Maria Ducas, the niece of Emperor Issac Comnenus. Desecrated by the Latins of the Fourth Crusade it was left to Theodorus Metochides, between the years 1305—1320, to restore and leave behind the work of art that we see today.

The structure of the nave belongs to the Maria Ducas period, Theodoros rebuilding the inner narthex, and adding the outer narthex and a side chapel to the south of the nave named the paraclesion. Theodoros was the most distinguished man of his time. Besides being a high court official and a diplomat, he was a noted philosopher, historian, astronomer, poet and patron of the arts. When Andronicus III usurped the throne in 1328, Theodoros and many supporters of the old regime were imprisoned. Eventually released, he spent the remaining years of his life in his beloved monastery and was buried in the paraclesion.

The Turks had converted the church into a mosque in 1511, covering the walls with customary whitewash, or plaster and paint. In 1947 restoration of the mosaics was undertaken by the Byzantine Institute of America and, on account of the remarkable works of art, the Turkish government proclaimed it a museum. Most museums shut on Mondays, the Topkapi on Tuesdays and the St. Saviour in Chora, or Kariye Camii, on Thursdays — luckily we had arrived on a Friday.

The mosaics were stunning. They covered the insides of the cupolas, surrounded the arches and the upper sections of the walls of both the inner and outer narthex. In a quandary as to where to start we bought a guide book at the ticket desk and followed the diagrams. One sequence of mosaics told the story of the life of the Virgin Mary, from her birth and her first toddling steps towards her mother — with her maid standing anxiously behind in case she fell — to the Annunciation and finally the Dormition, similar to the one in the Agacalti Kilise in the Peristrema valley. The other described the Life of Christ from the Nativity to His Entry into Jerusalem. The Massacre of the Innocents was vividly depicted and there were numerous scenes of Christ healing and performing miracles. The majority of mosaics in the nave had been destroyed. Their loss was compensated by large rectangular panels of marble covering the walls, each a different colour, their blending tones and swirling patterns creating an effect of overwhelming beauty.

The frescoes in the paraclesion were painted after the mosaics and were not discovered nor restored until 1951. They contained a superlative picture of the Resurrection and an equally fine Last Judgement. These were carried out at the same time as Giotto was producing his masterpieces in Assisi. An unknown artist captured the feeling of the Renaissance in these paintings too. They were freer and more lively than anything that had previously been painted in Byzantium, the figures beginning to bend and expressive qualities at last showing in their faces. Just above the entrance to the nave was a mosaic of the man who had inspired these magnificent works of art, Theodorus Metochides, kneeling before Christ and presenting him with a replica of his church.

In a tree-shaded café across the square, we ordered a drink and finished our cherries. We even treated ourselves to a taxi to whisk us to the Suleymaniye Mosque for we could not leave Istanbul without visiting this great building by Sinan. Born of Greek parents in the Karaman region of central Anatolia, he was one of those Christian youths taken into the service of the Sultan. By 1538 he had become chief of the Imperial architects, and during the next half century he enriched the Ottoman Empire with more than three hundred structures of every conceivable variety, from mosques to hamams, mescits to hospitals, and aqueducts to public kitchens. Eighty-four of his creations remain standing in Istanbul today.

The Suleymaniye mosque dominates Istanbul from the Third Hill. Taking from 1550—57 to complete it was the largest mosque Sinan built in the city. The basic central square topped with its vast dome — 53 metres high and 26.5 metres in diameter — was supported by four huge porphyry columns and balanced to the east and west by two semi-domes, while to the north and south the tympana were pierced as usual with windows. The extras were then added, namely side aisles with their own cupolas, galleries, and the accoutrements necessary for the worship of Allah. The mihrab and mimber were carved from white Proconnesus marble which came from an island of the same name in the Sea of Marmara; the Kuran Kursa, window shutters and doors were encrusted with mother-of-pearl and ivory; two panels of early Iznik tiles decorated the walls each side of the mihrab with sixteenth century stained glass windows above, and light from one hundred and thirty-six other windows brightened the interior. The general effect was of simple grandeur. Unfortunately the atmosphere was spoiled by a tour guide shouting explanations in German to his party. He bent down and turned back the corner of a large carpet to reveal the original beneath. From what I could see it certainly looked old, rather worn and very dusty.

The mosque stood in a vast courtyard surrounded by a complex of buildings: two medreses for the study of Islamic law — now libraries — a Medical College, hospital, hamam, caravanserai, and an imaret which had been turned into a museum of Turkish and Islamic art. Visitors in the past centuries were astonished at the generosity of the Sultan and by the efficient way the whole complex operated. Fed twice a day, sometimes with partridges and pheasants, patients in the hospital recovered from their illnesses in record time. The insane were entertained by musicians and singers employed to help cure their madness.

We wandered through the streets of Old Stamboul which sloped down to the shores of the Golden Horn. I came across a tiny mosque hidden away in the corner of a street, but it was shut. Andrew had more success buying some apricots and a splendid curved shoe cleaning brush used for the final polish by the experts of the trade. We happened to arrive at the Rustem Pasha Mosque that I had visited all too briefly before embarking on the boat trip up the Bosphorus. I persuaded Andrew to come and see the interior shimmering with light reflected from the traditional blue Iznik tiles, and I discovered another clock made by Edw. Prior of London, identical in style and design to the one I had seen in the Ulu Cami in Kayseri only two days previously! Built by Sinan in 1561 for Rustem Pasha, Suleyman's son-in-law, this small mosque was faultless.

The Spice Market provided everything we needed as presents. The goods were marked individually with two prices, one for trade and a slightly higher one for the purchaser, so there was no need to carry out long and intensive bargaining. One of the most popular items we bought was turkish delight. Besides boxes of varying sizes filled with different flavours and some with nuts, there were long sticks, rather like those sticks of rock bought at seaside resorts, but unfortunately not having Istanbul in red letters throughout the centre. We did have to bargain with some young boys outside the market for a large nylon carrier bag, for we could not have packed these extras in our small suitcases.

I had one final church to visit not far from our hotel, the Church of the Saints Sergius and Bacchus named after two Roman soldiers martyred for their Christian faith. Justinian, suspected of plotting against the Emperor Anastasius, was threatened with death when S.S. Sergius and Bacchus appeared to Anastasius in a dream interceding on his behalf. In fact Justinian became Emperor legitimately in 527 and at once commissioned this Church.   Like St. Sophia it was an innovation in design, for architecture was both flourishing and experimental in this prolific period of building.   Within square outer walls and a deep ambulatory, pillars and arches in the form of an irregular octagon rose two storeys high to support the dome.   But the main feature was a superb frieze between the two storeys consisting of four lines of decoration.   The lower took the form of an egg and dart motif, next came a protruding acanthus scroll; then a carved inscription in twelve Greek hexameters in honour of St. Sergius and praising the pious deeds of Empress Theodora, wife of Justinian.   A pediment strip of geometric tracery completed the frieze, above which slimmer marble pillars with incised Byzantine capitals reached to the base of the dome, the arches revealing a shadowy gallery.

A train shattered the peace roaring along the escarpment at gallery level barely 30 metres away.   Silence resumed and I turned my attention to the Muslim additions.   In the central section the original hexagonal flagstones had been covered with boarding and decked with rugs and carpets.   The mihrab — disarmingly off centre — and the mimber were of plain white marble which blended well with the interior.   The outside extensions took the form of a portico covered with five cupolas, a minaret, and a turbe for Huseyin Aga, Chief of the White Eunuchs during the reign of Bayezid II, who had been the patron of the mosque and responsible for its conversion.

A winding lane passed under the railway line and through the great sea-walls which I followed back to our hotel.   Constantine the Great built the first walls which were later extended to meet the Theodosian land walls, and fortified in the ninth century by Emperor Theophilus to defend the city against the Saracens.   The single walls stretched for eight kilo-metres;   they ranged from 12 to 15 metres in height, incorporated one hundred and eighty-eight towers, and thirteen sea gates provided access to the city.   They were the only walls never to have been attacked, the land walls having borne the brunt of assaults while those along the Golden Horn succumbed to the Venetians in 1202.   Deterioration occurred naturally from the elements and lapping waves gnawed at their found-ations, but in the end so called progress caused their final destruction, great lengths being pulled down to make way for a new coastal road.

I passed a section which had incorporated the magnificent sea pavilion of Bucoleon.   This had once been part of the Great Palace of Byzantium whose buildings, pavilions and gardens covered the First Hill. Erected by Constantine and added to by successive Emperors, all that remained was this outer shell with a few marble-surrounded windows; through the central frame I caught a glimpse of the dome of the Blue Mosque and a solitary minaret.   A row of modern houses backed on the old walls where once a large room would have provided its guests with a spectacular view over the Sea of Marmara; trees grew far too close to the facade and cars were rudely parked at its base, one family lighting a fire in preparation for a picnic.

In the setting sun fishermen dangled rods into the water, at peace

169

with the world and unconcerned with history and the destruction that had occurred many centuries ago.   Infidels had fought infidels, but this great Palace had been destroyed, not by peoples of opposing religions, but by those following the same faith.   The Latins of the Fourth Crusade had ransacked, pillaged and wrecked this famous building, and by the time the Emperors returned to Constantinople from Nicaea it was already in an advanced stage of decay.   They took up residence in the Palace of Blachernae on the opposite side of the city.   Even Mehmet the Conqueror was saddened when, on making a tour of his new acquisition, he came across the ruined halls and was said to have quoted from a Persian ode:

"The spider is the curtain-holder in the Palace of the Caesars,
The owl hoots its night call on the Towers of Afrasiab."*

---

* Afrasiab was a King of Turan in the sixth century.   (Turan subsequently became the State of Kalat in south-west Baluchistan).   He features in the Shahnama (Book of Kings), an epic poem by the Persian, Firdousi (c.940–1020).

Fishermen - the Sea of Marmara

The walls of the citadel incorporating Roman stonework — Ankara

171

DAY XVIII : ISTANBUL 4

Sailing up the Bosphorus Andrew and I had been struck by the majestic white marble facade of Dolmabahce, but we could not combine the Palace with any other sightseeing so alien to the concept of Istanbul was its rococo style of architecture. This was our last morning in Istanbul; or rather our last few hours as we had to be back at the hotel by 11 a.m. in order to leave for the airport. We only had time to visit one building, so now was our chance.

We thought that it would be fun to travel on the Orient Express, or at least in the path of the famous train. The railway followed the line of the coast and there was a station not far from our hotel. In reality our good idea turned out to be a disappointment. Being rush hour the trains, similar to those used by our London undergrounds, were crammed to capacity, while the milling throng of scurrying ant-like humans at Sirkeci station eliminated any feeling of glamour.

On our previous visit to Istanbul we had been told that the Palace opened at 9.00 a.m., but the hotel information proved incorrect — opening time and the first tour began at 9.30 a.m.. This was cutting our deadline rather fine but we decided to wait and, if necessary, try to escape from the tour. We bought our tickets and persuaded the guard to let us walk round the garden. What a pleasant surprise it turned out to be for it contained both rare varieties and prime specimens of trees. We were admiring a tall magnolia when the head gardener noticing our interest, approached. For once I was able to hold a reasonable conversation with a Turk — we communicated in Latin. He would say the first word "Robinia", and I would complete the name of the tree by adding "Pseudoacacia frisia" (False Acacia); or "Sequoia", followed by "sempervirens" (Californian Redwood). There was even a monkey puzzle with the glorious name of Araucaria araucana. Turks are fond of roses, and besides beds of different varieties surrounded by sweetly scented stocks, they were also trained up white painted lamp-posts. For those who liked colour a mass of bedding out plants were subtly arranged, so that the effect was neither glaring nor unpleasant. The proud keeper of the arboretum invited us to partake of a glass of tea, but we had to decline, explaining that we had to catch an aeroplane and therefore must join the first tour of the Palace. We made our way to a wide flight of steps leading to the imposing entrance up which the first straggling tourists of the day were climbing.

Dolmabahce means literally 'filled-up garden', for the land had been reclaimed from the Bosphorus by thousands of toiling slaves in the six-teenth century. In 1852 Abdul Mecit instructed his architect Nikogos Balyan to design a palace to outshine all others. Certainly Dolmabahce was enormous, the central feature being a domed throne room flanked by two wings making the whole building 284 metres long. We entered the hall at the west end of one wing and ascended a staircase with crystal

172

balustrades. A series of reception rooms on the first floor were hung with nineteenth century oil paintings, representational art finally being accepted and in keeping with the modern trend adopted by this progressive Sultan. Queen Victoria and Prince Albert were among the portraits of foreign monarchs and heads of states who had either visited or sent gifts to the country. Everything was on a grand scale and overwhelmingly ostentatious; even the bathroom was of alabaster. The throne room was the culmination of the architect's achievements, with fifty-six marble pillars many used in groups to support the 36 metre high dome. (The dome of the Mihrimah Mosque measured 37 metres, the Suleymaniye Mosque 53 metres and that of St. Sophia 56 metres). From its centre hung a Bohemian glass chandelier weighing four and a half tons presented by Queen Victoria.

Suddenly the tour was over; the heavy doors leading to the wide gravel walk by the edge of the Bosphorus were ceremoniously opened. For once I was grateful when I heard the familiar announcement that many rooms were undergoing restoration, the estimated number in the Palace ranging from two hundred to four hundred. The remainder of the day was an anticlimax necessitating numerous forms of transport: bus back to our hotel, taxi to the airport, two aeroplanes (changing in Amsterdam), coach, train and car, finally arriving home just before the clock struck midnight. I could not sleep. My thoughts kept returning to our morning's visit to Dolmabahce. We had hurried away too quickly and I was troubled by the lurid tales that were inexorably linked with the Palace.

The Crimean War was being fought at the same time that Abdul Mecit was building and moving into Dolmabahce Palace. As a pretext for needing money to modernise his army, he borrowed large sums from western financiers thus beginning the downward path to bankruptcy. In fact most of the money went to the upkeep of his grandiose folly, Dolmabahce. His brother, Abdul Aziz, who succeeded him in 1861 was no better. Aziz employed five thousand servants, increased the number of his concubines to nine hundred who in turn had to be guarded by three thousand black eunuchs. He also engaged four hundred musicians, two hundred men to look after his menagerie, three hundred in the kitchen and four hundred grooms. All this cost two million pounds sterling a year, a huge sum for the nineteenth century. After a disastrous foreign policy when an uprising in the Balkans was quelled, but was followed by disproportionate recriminations against the local inhabitants — sixty or more villages were burned and some fifteen thousand men, women and children slaughtered — Aziz was deposed. Five days later he was found dead. The veins in his arms cut with a pair of scissors.

His nephew Murad V was already a physical wreck through drink and from having been immured in the Cage — reintroduced at the whim of a Sultan. He too was deposed after three months, a specialist from Vienna and the court physician both declaring him insane. He was succeeded by his younger brother Abdul Hamid II who lived in constant fear of assassination. Hamid soon left Dolmabahce, building a palace at Yilditz two kilometres away, which took the form of a labyrinth of houses, pavilions and look-out towers. Here he took refuge. He attended the first sitting of the Turkish parliament at Dolmabahce in 1877, and managed to suspend it a couple of months later with the excuse of an impending war with Russia. He used the Palace for occasional ceremonial dinners, but soon only emerged from his fortress at Yilditz to attend Friday prayers. So in just over two decades Dolmabahce lay empty, and not until the reign of Ataturk were its doors reopened.

Ataturk was one of those rare individuals who possessed the character to lead his country from its lowest ebb to a position whereby his people could once again hold up their heads, and for that he continues to be revered. He altered Turkey's image irrevocably, severing any association with the old regime. He changed the names of towns: for instance Adrianople became Edirne, Smyrna, Izmir and Angora, Ankara, while the romantic name Constantinople became Istanbul, a corruption of the words found on old Greek signposts meaning, 'To The City'. He abolished many old established institutions. The fez was prohibited, the veil discouraged and polygamy forbidden. He cancelled the old Muslim calendar where a century consisted of ninety-seven years, and adopted instead the Gregorian calendar; and the hours of the day, which previously had been counted from dawn, now started from midnight. Latin script superseded Arabic and surnames became obligatory; Mustafa Kemal, both names of Arabic origin, became Kamal (meaning strong) and Ataturk (Father of the Turk). He gave Turkey a fresh start by making Ankara the centre of government.

Mustafa Kemal — as he was known in his early days — by his courage and brilliant military strategy, had stopped the allied troops entering the Sea of Marmara and taking Constantinople. He was the hero of Gallipoli. He refused to acknowledge the peace terms accepted by Sultan Mehmet VI and a weak government, and cleared his country of the hated Greeks who, in May 1919, had landed at Smyrna with twenty thousand troops. It took Mustafa from 1920–1922 to defeat them, for he had to train his guerilla supporters and newly enlisted recruits into a cohesive force. Every family had to contribute to the war effort producing a kit containing underwear, socks and shoes. Women trained too, driving carts to the battle front often with babies strapped to their backs. It was a tremendous achievement. No wonder every main square in every town or village displayed a statue of the 'Father of the Turks'. Of the allied armies occupying Constantinople, the French and Italians withdrew, and war with England was only narrowly avoided. Mehmet VI fled the country and Abdul Mecit II reigned as Caliph only. In 1924 the new national assembly expelled the Ottoman dynasty, abolished the caliphate, and for the first time in Turkish history religion was divorced from politics and Mustafa, son of a custom's official, became Ataturk and President of the Republic.

Although Ataturk hated and despised the Sultans and their decadent

174

way of life, he could not resist the opulence of Dolmabahce using it as his residence when visiting Istanbul. Ironically he spent the last few days of his life there in a room cluttered with French furniture, and in a huge bed made expressly for one of the Sultans. After his death on November 10th 1938, he lay in state for three days before being taken to his final resting place in Ankara, the village in central Anatolia that he had converted to the capital of a proud nation.

Dolmabahce lay empty once again until it finally became a museum, following in the footsteps of so many of Istanbul's monuments but, unlike St. Sophia and the Church of St. Saviour in Chora, and even Topkapi, all of which were exhilarating to visit, Dolmabahce felt dead and depressing. This may have been due to the fact that this great palace, upon which so much money had been lavished, was occupied for such a short space of time. Like damp that takes time to penetrate, a couple of decades of habitation were insufficient for the warmth of human emotions to seep into and become part of the surroundings. However the garden was there to enlighten the spirit. One of Ataturk's most inspiring reforms was to encourage the planting of trees for, when something grows, there is always hope. Our crusade was over, the glories of the past were only memories; but the gardener with his faith in nature gave encouragement for the future.

THE END

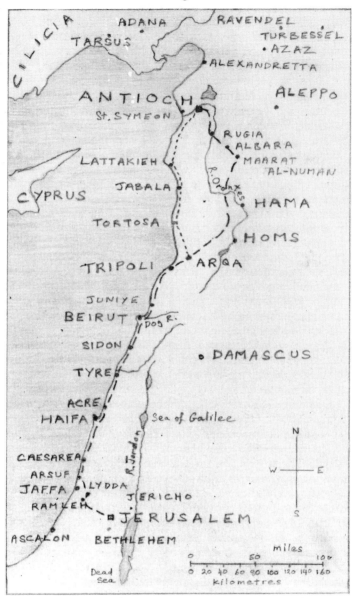

Crusaders' Route from Antioch to
Jerusalem led by Raymond — — — — — —
Route taken by Godfrey of Lorraine and
Robert of Flanders to join Raymond; and
later by Bohemond and Baldwin - - - - - - -

EPILOGUE

FROM ANTIOCH TO JERUSALEM

I could not desert the Crusaders in Antioch. Their objective was Jerusalem and by now I was captivated by their adventures; so for those readers who are similarly intrigued, I will continue with my narrative and complete the sequel of what befell those brave yet quarrelling knights.

I left them at the end of June in Antioch having annihilated Korbogha's army. Needless to say they were unable to decide which of them was to rule Antioch. The majority supported Bohemond, because by his initiative the city had been conquered. Raymond, forever jealous, refused to recognise Bohemond's claim and held firmly on to his own possessions, Yaghi-Siyan's palace and Diocletian's fortified bridge. Adhemar, Bishop of Le Puy, opposed Bohemond on religious grounds; Adhemar was trusted by the Pope and hoped to see the eastern and western churches reconciled. Loyal also to Emperor Alexius he was anxious that the knights should abide by their oaths sworn in Constantinople, namely that any land captured that had formerly belonged to Byzantium, should be returned to the Empire.

Hugh of Vermandois, the brother of King Philip of France wanted to return to his native homeland, so Adhemar entrusted him and Baldwin of Hainault with the task of explaining to Alexius the predicament of the accession of Antioch. No one in Antioch yet knew that Alexius had retreated to Constantinople and that the territory was no longer safe for only a small group of knights. Inevitably they were set upon by marauding Turks. The fate of Baldwin was never known; the survivors struggled on unable to reach Constantinople until the autumn, by which time it was too late in the year for an army to embark on a campaign through Anatolia. Meanwhile the Crusaders had decided to wait until November before continuing to Jerusalem in case the Emperor arrived; and also because they were uncertain of finding food or water throughout the hot summer months on the daunting route ahead.

In July Antioch suffered from an outbreak of typhoid, Adhemar dying of the fever on August 1st. This was one of the greatest tragedies of the entire Crusade. Adhemar was respected by everyone; he succoured the poor, he was a shrewd soldier and campaigner and, above all, he was the only stabilising influence among the leaders of the Crusade. As the epidemic spread the Crusaders sought refuge in the country. Bohemond took the opportunity to strengthen the garrisons left by Tancred in Cilicia; Godfrey of Lorraine visited his brother Baldwin in Edessa who presented him with the towns of Turbessel and Ravendel; Robert of Normandy travelled south to the coastal town of Lattakieh which was handed over to him in trust for the Emperor, while Raymond led a campaign against the town of Azaz whose loyal ruler, the Emir of Omar, was being threatened by his overlord Ridwan of Aleppo.   On their way back to Antioch they were repeatedly ambushed and many of the provisions they had collected were plundered.

The epidemic abated, but there had been no harvest that year and the new inhabitants of Antioch were still desperately short of food, so in October Raymond ventured further afield to Albara in an effort to obtain supplies.   He took the Muslim town, converted the mosque into a church and appointed one of his priests as a Bishop.   This was to be the first Latin See in Asia Minor, only possible in this instance because there was no presiding Orthodox Bishop in the area;   the irony of the situation being that a Greek Patriarch, John of Antioch, had to perform the consecration.

On November 1st the leaders once more gathered in Antioch, and on the 5th they assembled in the Cathedral of St. Peter.   With the death of Adhemar leaving no one with sufficient authority to keep peace, bitter arguments were interminable.   Neither was the question of the sovereignty of Antioch resolved nor the date on which to leave for Jerusalem.   The pilgrims and soldiers were so angry and frustrated with these endless bickerings, that they threatened to raze the walls of Antioch to the ground unless the leaders settled their differences and the Crusade continued to Jerusalem.   In order to pacify their demands the princes agreed to attack the fortress of Maarat al-Numan, south-east of Albara, which was necessary in order to prevent the army's eventual departure from being harassed on the eastern flank.

The army left Antioch on November 23rd but the task was more difficult than had been anticipated.   Two direct assaults having failed the army was obliged to build a siege-machine.   It took a fortnight to collect enough wood during which time many troops deserted in order to scavenge for food.   Raymond was in charge of the machine but his attempt to scale a tower from its platform was repelled.   Nevertheless sufficient protection was provided to enable the castle wall to be mined and by the evening a section had collapsed.   Bohemond, jealous of Raymond's success offered the citizens protection if they surrendered directly to him.   Unhappily, the next morning when the battle continued, it was Raymond's troops who entered the city and no one was spared. To Raymond went the honour of victory but Bohemond refused to evacuate the town until Raymond gave up his acquisitions in Antioch. With this ridiculous stalemate the army was near to mutiny.   A representation of soldiers approached Raymond, offering to accept his leadership of the whole Crusade if he would organise the army's departure for Jerusalem.   It was a proposal that he could not refuse, so he returned to Rugia where he tried to buy the princes' acknowledgement of his leadership.   Delays inevitably occurred and Bohemond, realising that this indecision suited his scheme admirably, suggested the following spring would be a better time of year to start the Jerusalem offensive.

Meanwhile the starving troops left behind in Maarat were reduced to cannibalism and, antagonised to such a degree by appalling vacillations amongst their leaders, they razed the walls to the ground. At last Raymond realised that he could procrastinate no longer. He returned to Maarat, and on January 13th 1099 set fire to the city so demonstrating that he would never return and, walking barefoot as a pilgrim, he led his troops forward to continue the Crusade.

Raymond's vassals reunited under his banner. Those whom he had left to guard his possessions in Antioch were unable to contend with Bohemond's might; they deserted their posts and joyfully set off for Jerusalem. Robert of Normandy and Tancred also joined him, and a month later public opinion forced Godfrey of Lorraine and Robert of Flanders to catch up with the Crusade in order to fulfil their vows. Only Bohemond and Baldwin remained in the lands they had conquered.

The direct route south favoured by Tancred was controlled by Duqaq of Damascus. Because of the depleted size of the army Raymond wanted to take the coast road, even though in places the route was narrow and susceptible to ambushes. Tancred reminded him that the coastal towns were strongly fortified and they could not indulge in siege warfare; however Raymond was now in charge, albeit precariously, and his final decision prevailed. The local Arab dynasties in northern Syria were in fact delighted with the Turkish defeat at Antioch and, even though the Emirs of Hama and Homs had supported Ridwan and Kerbogha, they readily concluded a truce with the Crusaders. The Emir of Shaizar even offered guides and provisions for the troops on condition that they passed peacefully through his lands.

Raymond's first mistake was an attempt to take the town of Arqa, 24 kilometres from Tripoli. An unnecessary campaign, it was only undertaken in order to impress the Emir of Tripoli and to gain further bounty. Arqa remained invincible. The only success the army had in the area was capturing the fortress of Tortosa. Raymond Pilet and Raymond, Viscount of Turenne, with only a small band of troops arrived at night before its walls and, by lighting numerous fires, they gave the impression of a large attacking force. By the following morning the alarmed governor of Tortosa had evacuated his garrison and sailed to Tripoli seeking refuge with his master the Emir. Now the Crusaders had communications by sea with Lattakieh, Antioch, Cyprus and Constantinople.

Peter Bartholomew never left the Crusade, but continued to make his presence conspicuous by frequent and inopportune tales of his visions. When he announced that St. Peter, St. Andrew and Christ had all three appeared to him and declared that an immediate assault must be made on Arqa, he was greeted with both derision and acclamation. Such was the dissension within the army that Peter insisted that he should justify his prophecies by the ordeal of fire. On Good Friday piles of logs were placed in a narrow passage. They were blessed by the Bishops and set alight. Peter, clutching the Holy Lance, leapt into the flames, but he staggered out the far side horribly burnt. He died of his wounds twelve days later, thereby casting doubt on his former prophecies.

179

Raymond was loath to lose face by raising the siege of Arqa but after another month he was forced to yield to his companion's pleas, and on May 13th they struck camp and moved on to Tripoli. An agreement had been arranged with the Emir who bought immunity for his capital by offering pack animals, provisions and guides. He was anxious for the Crusaders to defeat his enemy, the Fatimids of Egypt. The Fatimids invaded Palestine as soon as news reached them of the fall of Antioch and they had already captured Jerusalem. The Crusaders met with no opposition but they were always wary, knowing that the Fatimids had a strong navy which could quickly provide additional support for any of the coastal towns. They crossed the Dog river safely and were greeted by the citizens of Beirut with gifts of food, and the offer of a free passage through their land provided that none of their gardens, orchards, crops or vines were spoiled. An agreement was swiftly concluded but at Sidon, a day later, there was no such display of friendliness. Instead a sortie from the fortress attacked the Crusaders. They were easily repulsed and revenge was taken by ransacking the countryside.

The army rested for two days in the delightful lush green surroundings of Tyre waiting for a number of knights from Antioch and Edessa to join them. They were unmolested by the garrison and unopposed over a tricky pass called the Ladder of Tyre and over the heights of Naqoura, arriving at Acre on May 24th. As at Beirut, the governor of Acre secured protection for his farms by offering gifts and provisions. The Crusaders passed Haifa, Mt. Carmel, and arrived at Caesarea in time to celebrate Whitsun.

After the coastal town of Arsuf the army turned inland to Ramleh. Passing through the Judaean hills they were met by envoys from Bethlehem begging deliverance from the yoke of the Muslims. Tancred and Baldwin of Le Bourg went to their aid, and were welcomed by a procession of priests carrying the relics and crosses from the Church of the Nativity. The main army marched through the night much heartened by an eclipse of the moon, for they interpreted this as a sign representing the extinction of the Turkish crescent. At dawn the Crusaders could see the towers of Jerusalem, and by the evening of Tuesday June 7th 1099 they encamped before the walls.

THE SIEGE OF JERUSALEM

To capture Jerusalem presented new and difficult problems. The defence was formidable, the walls having originally been constructed by Hadrian and repaired and added to by the Byzantines, Ommayads and Fatimids. The east wall was shielded by the steep side of the Kedron ravine and the ground by the west wall sloped to another valley; the south-east was similarly protected by the Vale of Gehenna, so it was only the south-west and the northern walls that were accessible. The Crusaders barely numbered thirteen hundred knights and twelve thousand foot soldiers, therefore they could not anyhow cover the entire perimeter. The city was defended by the Fatimid governor, Iftikhar ad-Dawla,

180

with a strong garrison of Arab and Sudanese troops. He wisely expelled the Christian population, realising that he would have less mouths to feed in the event of a long siege and would eliminate the danger of betrayal. He poisoned or blocked any wells outside the walls, Jerusalem having sufficient water from its cisterns of Roman origin — which are still used in the twentieth century. The flocks and herds were driven to places of safety, the walls protected with sacks of hay and cotton against rocks and stones hurled by mangonels (military machines), and Iftikhar appealed to Egypt for aid.

The Crusaders suffered badly, by far their worst privation being lack of water. There was one uncontaminated pool below the south wall but it was exposed to missiles; they were forced to trek ten kilometres to find pure water, and were liable to be ambushed by companies sent out from the garrison. Food stocks dwindled, the troops and pilgrims were unaccustomed to the heat and the dust and, with the continual fear of a relieving force from Egypt, the Crusaders knew that they could not sustain a long siege.

On June 12th the princes made a pilgrimage to the Mount of Olives where a hermit persuaded them to attack immediately. However the army was ill-equipped; they had too few ladders with which to scale the walls and after several hours of bitter and useless fighting, they retired. Their disappointment was intense. As at Antioch when everything seemed lost, fortune came to their aid. Two Genoese galleys and four ships from an English fleet arrived at Jaffa bringing food and armaments, and also ropes, nails and bolts necessary for making siege machines. An Egyptian fleet promptly blockaded the port; but the cargo was safely borne to Jerusalem.

The hills around Jerusalem were bare, and timber had to be searched for and dragged many kilometres to the secret place of construction. To add to the Crusaders' troubles the sirocco blew hindering their preparations but, yet again, hope was kindled in the hearts of the pilgrims by a vision. On July 6th a priest, Peter Desiderius, testified that the Bishop of Adhemar had appeared to him and ordered the Crusaders to give up their selfish intrigues. They were to fast, and then to walk barefoot in a procession around the walls of Jerusalem. If they were truly repentant the city would be theirs within nine days. The Christians willingly carried out these instructions, jeered and mocked at by the Muslims from the ramparts. They proceeded to the Mount of Olives where they listened to sermons from Peter the Hermit, Raymond of Aguilers (Raymond's chaplain) and Arnulf of Rohes (Robert of Normandy's chaplain) considered to be the finest preacher amongst the Crusaders. Such was their eloquence that the whole army forgot their differences and vowed to fight together to enter the Holy City.

Under the skilful direction of the Genoese two large siege machines were rapidly finished, one for Raymond and the other for Godfrey and a third, slightly smaller, to provide a feint attack. The women and old men helped by stitching together ox and camel hides to be used as protection against the destructive Greek fire. A ditch had to be filled in before the great monsters were pushed into position. This occupied most of the day, the soldiers bombarded unremittingly by stones and liquid Greek fire, but they retaliated by hurling rocks from their own mangonels. By the evening of July 14th Raymond's tower was in position. The section he attacked was strongly defended by Iftikhar himself and Raymond was unable to cross to the city walls; but by midday on the 15th a bridge was successfully secured from the upper storey of Godfrey's tower. Once a foothold was established on the wall scaling ladders could be used; a gate was quickly opened and the soldiers poured into Jerusalem. Tancred penetrated deep into the city. The Muslims fled to the Temple area, many taking refuge in the Mosque of al-Aqsa where they surrendered to Tancred promising to pay huge ransoms for their safety. Tancred hoisted his banner, but it gave no protection for in the end another gang of Crusaders burst in and showed no mercy.

By now Iftikhar, realising that all was lost, withdrew to the citadel — the Tower of David — which held a commanding position on the western wall dominating the Jaffa Gate. He offered it to Raymond with treasure as an added incentive, in return for his life and the lives of his bodyguard. Raymond kept his word and they were the only Muslims to escape the holocaust that followed. Every remaining man, woman and child was slaughtered. Jews, who had taken refuge in their synagogue, were burnt alive. The massacre horrified the world and was never forgotten, leaving a deep distrust of Christians amongst the Muslims and making any future reconciliation well nigh impossible.

THE AFTERMATH

The same problem arose after the victory celebrations had abated — who was to rule the Holy City? Adhemar would have been the obvious choice, but he was dead; so also was the former Patriarch of Jerusalem, Symeon, who had retired to Cyprus. A fortnight later Pope Urban II died in Rome without knowing of the Crusaders' victory. The princes met on July 17th and after much debate the crown was offered to Raymond. He refused, remarking that he did not wish to be a king in Christ's Holy City. Possibly he realised that he would have insufficient support from his colleagues and hoped to make it difficult for anyone else to accept. The crown was then offered to Godfrey of Lorraine, who took it, albeit reluctantly, assuming the title, "Advocatus Sancti Sepulchri" (the Defender of the Holy Sepulchre). Raymond was forced to give up the Tower of David and left in a rage to set up camp in Jericho. The appointment of Patriarch went to Arnulf of Rohes. Whereas previously the Muslims had allowed the Orthodox Greeks, Georgians, Armenians, Jacobites and Copts freedom of worship, now the Latin hierarchy had to be obeyed. Orthodox priests were tortured to make them reveal the hiding places of the holy relics.

The expected counter attack materialised as the Egyptian army under the Vizier al-Afdul crossed into Palestine and approached Ascalon. The Crusaders rallied and temporarily forgot their differences, leaving only a small garrison to defend Jerusalem and Peter the Hermit to hold services and to pray for victory. The battle was won by a brilliant surprise attack. The Egyptian army was taken unawares by a monumental charge at dawn on the twelfth of August. They could offer no resistance, al-Afdul and a few officers managing to escape by ship from Ascalon. The booty acquired by the Crusaders was immense.

By the end of August the two Roberts of Normandy and Flanders, bored by Godfrey's pettiness, decided to return to their homeland. They were accompanied by Raymond frustrated beyond endurance by Godfrey, who would not allow him to accept the direct surrender of any of the fortress towns he conquered. Raymond settled in Lattakieh which had good communications with Cyprus and the Empire; he accepted an invitation from Alexius sailing to Constantinople in June 1100.

Meanwhile Daimbert, the Archbishop of Pisa, appointed by Pope Urban shortly before his death to take over from Adhemar, sailed towards the Asian shore. Daimbert was an enthusiastic Crusader, though extremely unpopular and corrupt. Alexius tried unsuccessfully to waylay the Pisan fleet which eventually moored at St. Symeon (the port serving Antioch). Bohemond decided to accompany Daimbert to Jerusalem, and invited Baldwin of Edessa to join them and observe their vows to worship at the Holy Sepulchre. According to Fulcher of Chartres, a company of twenty-five thousand set off in early November 1099 — the number including many women — leaving behind only those required to protect their territories.

Daimbert accompanied the pilgrims while the Pisan fleet guarded their flank. At Lattakieh the old jealousy between the rivals was aroused and Raymond refused to help Bohemond's army in any way; the fortress of Tortosa had been recaptured by the Muslims who massacred the stragglers, and many of the aged died due to the appalling weather conditions. December was unexpectedly cold; it rained without ceasing and there was the usual shortage of food. The pilgrims arrived at Jerusalem on December 21st in time to celebrate Christmas at the Holy Sepulchre.

Godfrey was delighted at the arrival of the army for, with the departure of the Roberts and Raymond, he only had three hundred knights and two thousand infantry, and could not have defended Jerusalem against any future counter attack. Fortunately the Egyptians were unable to reorganise themselves, and Duqaq of Damascus was involved in family quarrels. With the offer of estates Godfrey managed to persuade several knights to remain in Palestine.

As soon as the season of goodwill was over the inevitable round of scheming began. Arnulf was deposed and Daimbert elected Patriarch in his place. He, in return for Godfrey and Bohemond's support, confirmed their suzerainty over the territories of Jerusalem and Antioch.

Bohemond took the title of Prince of Antioch and his nephew Tancred — having subdued the whole of Galilee with some brilliant raids — also adopted the privilege, calling himself Prince of Galilee.

On New Year's Day 1100, Bohemond and Baldwin returned to their territories. Godfrey with his reinforcements gradually took possession of the coastal towns, the port of Jaffa was enlarged and trade flourished with the arrival of ships from Europe. The Venetians quickly took advantage of the opening and came to a satisfactory agreement with Godfrey. They were allowed free trade in Palestine with a church and a market in every town; they paid Godfrey a tribute for Tripoli and offered the aid of troops until August 15th. Taking advantage of this extra man power Godfrey decided to attack Acre, but as he became ill Daimbert headed the expedition instead in order to show himself as the leader and governor of the country. Godfrey died on July 18th while they were away and was buried in the Church of the Holy Sepulchre. His cousin Warner of Gray, a Burgundian count, was the only person of note left in Jerusalem having also been forced to leave the venturing army through illness; rousing himself from his sick bed he put Godfrey's troops in charge of the Tower of David. News of Godfrey's death was not conveyed to the army; instead Gray sent for Godfrey's brother Baldwin from Edessa. Gray died five days later.

Daimbert heard later of Godfrey's death, but he and Tancred thought it unnecessary to return immediately. Their first priority was to make use of the loan of the Venetian army, but rather than attack Acre they decided to capture Haifa instead. When Daimbert eventually learnt that Baldwin had been summoned, he entrusted his secretary Morellus to deliver a letter to Bohemond, in which he asked Bohemond to come and help him secure Jerusalem. He also instructed Bohemond to forbid Baldwin to approach Jerusalem and, if Baldwin disobeyed, to use force to curb his advance.

Morellus was detained in Lattakieh in July and his documents discovered and read. Raymond had left for Constantinople the previous month, but his stewards were naturally shocked by the contents and neither the letter nor Morellus proceeded any further. Had Bohemond received Daimbert's letter the remainder of his life might have been very different. As it was he left Antioch in August with only three hundred knights and some infantry. Full of confidence he marched to the Euphrates in order to help the Armenians of Melitene who were being harassed by Danishmend Turks. He was ambushed on the way and taken prisoner. Cutting a lock from his golden hair he gave it to a fellow soldier – who managed to escape – with instructions to take it to Baldwin. Baldwin at once set out to the rescue but the Danishmend Emir, Malik Gazi Gumushtekin, took to the hills where Baldwin dared not follow for fear of being ambushed as well.

Returning to Edessa Baldwin learnt of his brother Godfrey's death. He organised his cousin Baldwin of Le Bourg, who happened to be in Antioch, to oversee his principalities and set off with two hundred knights, seven hundred infantry and his household for Jerusalem. Fulcher of Chartres who accompanied him relates that Baldwin left Edessa, ". . . grieving a little for his brother, but rejoicing more at his inheritance." He was welcomed in Antioch and Lattakieh, where he sent his wife and ladies to Jaffa by sea. At Jabala he heard that his old rival Duqaq of Damascus with the Emir of Homs was determined to stop him reaching Jerusalem.

The Emir of Tripoli was delighted to receive Baldwin for he disliked the overbearing power of Duqaq, and he gave Baldwin food and supplies as well as useful information as to the whereabouts of the Turks. The army marched cautiously and met the Turkish force by the Dog river north of Beirut. Baldwin failed to cross the river and retired gratefully when darkness fell, ignominiously suffering a continuous bombardment of arrows throughout the night. However he had sufficient time to form his plan of campaign. At dawn he feigned a withdrawal along the narrow coastal pass placing his best soldiers to the rear. At the narrowest part of the road just north of Juniye, Baldwin suddenly switched to the attack. He launched the full weight of his charging knights into the surprised Turks who were totally at a loss and unable to cope with this miraculous change of circumstance. Confusion and panic spread amongst the Muslim army, and by the evening they had dispersed and fled into the mountains. Baldwin encountered no more opposition, even the Egyptian governor at Tyre offering him supplies.

Meanwhile Daimbert and Tancred had returned to Jerusalem and were trying, without success, to gain possession of the Tower of David from Godfrey's loyal supporters. When Tancred heard of Baldwin's approach he hurried to Jaffa to try to fortify the garrison against him, but the citizens turned Tancred away welcoming instead their hero, Baldwin. Humiliated, Tancred withdrew to his lands in Galilee, and Daimbert retired to a monastery on Mount Sion. The Greeks, Syrians and Armenians, as well as the Franks were overjoyed at Baldwin's arrival, running out of the city to greet and escort him in great style to the Holy Sepulchre. On St. Martin's day, November 11th, Baldwin assumed the title of King of Jerusalem.

Unlike his fellow Crusaders Baldwin proved a wise ruler. He declined to seek revenge and, on the contrary, showed unaccustomed leniency. Daimbert soon realised that it was better to make peace, and in return Baldwin confirmed Daimbert his See. Tancred, truculent as ever, took longer to accept Baldwin's leadership but when, owing to Bohemond languishing in captivity, he was offered the regency of Antioch, he gladly accepted handing Galilee to Baldwin. Fulcher of Chartres, a reliable and useful source of information, describes that on Christmas Day 1100 in the Church of The Nativity in Bethlehem, Baldwin paid homage to the Patriarch Daimbert who in turn crowned Baldwin, King of Jerusalem. The kingdom was founded four years after the beginning of the First Crusade.

GLOSSARY

Autogar	Bus station
Ayran	A drink made from beaten yogurt.
Bedestan	Bazaar, market place
Cami (i)	Mosque
Caravanserai	Resting place for caravans
Cesme	Fountain
Cifte	Double
Dag(i)	Mountain
Dervish	Mohammedan friar
Divan	Council chamber
Dolmuss	Shared car, taxi
Eski	Old
Eyran	Domed area of a mosque, recessed from the central court
Gulu	Lake
Hamam	Public bath
Han (i)	Inn
Hisar	Castle, fortress
Imam	Muslim priest
Imaret	Soup kitchen for the poor
Kale	Fortress
Kilise	Church
Koran kurser	Where the imam sits when reading the Koran to the congregation
Kosku	Kiosk
Koy	Village
Kumbet	Seljuk tomb, mausoleum
Locanta	Restaurant
Medrese	College linked to a mosque complex
Mescit	Small mosque, chapel
Meydan(i)	Square
Meze	Hors d'oeuvres
Mihrab	Niche indicating the direction of Mecca
Mimber	Pulpit of a mosque
Muezzin	A public crier who summons the people to prayer
Ramadan	Ninth month of the Mohammedan calendar observed as a fast during the hours of daylight
Sadirvan	Fountain for ritual washing
Saray	Palace
Sircale	Glazed (tiles)

Steppe	Vast treeless plain
Tekke	Dervish monastery
Turbe	Tomb, mausoleum
Ulu	Great
Yeni	New
Yesil	Green
Yuruk	Nomad

TURKISH EQUIVALENTS OF HISTORICAL PLACE NAMES

Akroenus	Afyon
Alexandretta	Iskenderun
Ancyra	Ankara (Angora)
Antioch	Antakya
Antioch in Pisidia	Yalvac
Archelais	Aksaray
Attalia	Antalya
Augustopolis	Nigde
Azanoi	Aesani
Barata	Maden Sehir (Binbir Kilise)
Caesarea Mazaka	Kayseri
Chrysopolis	Uskudar (Scutari)
Constantinople	Istanbul (Byzantium)
Cotyaeum	Kutahya
Coxon	Guksun
Daphne	Harbiye
Dorylaeum	Eskisehir
Dyrrhachium	Durazzo
Edessa	Urea
Germanicae	Maras
Gordion	Yassi Huyuk
Gordoserba	Sogut
Heraclea	Eregli
Iconium	Konya
Karallia	Beysehir
Kios	Gemlik
Linoe	Bilecik
Nakoleia	Seyitgazi
Nicaea	Iznik
Nicomedia	Izmit

187

Philomelion	Aksehir	
Podanus	Pozanti	
Polybotus	Bolvadin	
Prusa	Bursa	
Pylai	Yalova	
Sakasena	Suksu	
Seleucia	Samandag (St. Symeon)	
Smyrna	Izmir	
Soandos	Nevsehir	
Tyana	Kermerhisar	
Province	Bithynia	Kocaeli
Mountains	Argaeus	Erciyes Dagi
	Olympus	Uludag
Rivers	Halys	Kizilirmak
	Orontes	Asi
	Rhyndacus	Kocasu
	Sangarius	Sakarya
	Tembris	Porsuk
Sea	Euxine	Black Sea

ANCIENT ANATOLIAN CIVILISATIONS

Palaeolithic (Old Stone Age)	c.50,000 B.C.
Mesolithic	- - - 7,000 B.C.
Neolithic (New Stone Age)	c.7000—5500 B.C. (Catal Hoyuk, Hacilar)
Chalcolithic (Copper)	c.5500—3000 B.C. (Canhasan)
Bronze Age	c.3000—1950 B.C. (Kultepe)
Assyrian Trading Colony	c.1950—1750 B.C. (Kanes)
Hittite Empire	c.1750—1200 B.C. (Bogazkoy, Alacahoyuk, Yazilikaya)
Late Hittite Period	c.1200—700 B.C.
Urartian Period	c.1200—700 B.C.
Phrygian Period	c.1200—700 B.C. (Gordion, Midas)
Invasion by Cimmerians	700 B.C.
Founding of Lydia, Caria, Lycia and the Greek Colonies	c.700—546 B.C.
Persian Domination	546—334 B.C.
Hellenistic Period	334—133 B.C.
Roman Domination	133 B.C.—330 A.D.

Founding of Constantinople and the Byzantine Empire, 330 A.D.

BYZANTINE EMPERORS

324–337	Constantine I, the Great	920–944	Romanus I (co-emperor)
337–361	Constantius	959–963	Romanus II
361–363	Julian the Apostate	963–969	Nicephorus II Phocas
363–364	Jovian	969–976	John I Tzimisces
364–378	Valens	976–1025	Basil II
379–395	Theodosius I, the Great	1025–1028	Constantine VIII
395–408	Arcadius	1028–1034	Romanus III Argyrus
408–450	Theodosius II	1034–1041	Michael IV
450–457	Marcian	1041–1042	Michael V
457–474	Leo I	1042	Theodora and Zoe
474	Leo II	1042–1055	Constantine IX
474–491	Zeno	1055–1056	Theodora (second reign)
491–518	Anastasius	1056–1057	Michael VI
518–527	Justin I	1057–1059	Isaac Comnenus
527–565	Justinian I, the Great	1059–1067	Constantine X Ducas
565–578	Justin II	1067–1071	Romanus IV Diogenes
578–582	Tiberius II	1071–1078	Michael VII Ducas
582–602	Maurice	1078–1081	Nicephorus III
602–610	Phocas	1081–1118	Alexius I Comnenus
610–641	Heraclius	1118–1143	John II Comnenus
641	Constantine III	1143–1180	Manuel I Comnenus
641	Heraclonas	1180–1183	Alexius II Comnenus
641–668	Constans II	1183–1185	Andronicus I Comnenus
668–685	Constantine IV	1185–1195	Isaac II Angelus
685–695	Justinian II	1195–1203	Alexius III Angelus
695–698	Leontius	1203–1204	Isaac Angelus (second reign)
698–705	Tiberius III	1203–1204	Alexius IV Angelus (co-emperor)
705–711	Justinian II (second reign)	1204	Alexius V Ducas
711–713	Philippicus Bardanes	1204–1205	*Constantine Lascaris
713–716	Anastasius II	1205–1222	*Theodore I Lascaris
716–717	Theodosius III	1222–1254	*John III
717–741	Leo III	1254–1258	*Theodore II Lascaris
741–775	Constantine V	1258–1261	*John IV
775–780	Leo IV	1261–1282	Michael VIII Palaeologus
780–797	Constantine VI	1282–1328	Andronicus II Palaeologus
797–802	Irene	1328–1341	Andronicus III Palaeologus
802–811	Nicephorus I	1341–1376	John V Palaeologus
811	Stauracius	1341–1347	(Civil War)
811–813	Michael I	1347–1354	John VI Cantacuzenus (co-emperor)
813–820	Leo V	1376–1379	Adronicus IV Palaeologus
820–829	Michael II	1379–1390	John V Palaeologus (second reign)
829–842	Theophilus	1390	John VI Palaeologus
842–867	Michael III	1390–1391	John V Palaeologus (third reign)
867–886	Basil I	1381–1423	Manuel II Palaeologus
886–912	Leo VI	1423–1448	John VIII Palaeologus
912–913	Alexander	1448–1453	Constantine XI Palaeologus
913–959	Constantine VII		

* Ruled in Nicaea during the Latin occupation of Constantinople

OTTOMAN SULTANS

1281–1324	Osman Gazi
1324–1360	Orhan Gazi
1360–1389	Murad I
1389–1402	Bayezid I
(1402–1413	Interregnum)
1413–1421	Mehmet I
1421–1451	Murad II
1451–1481	Mehmet II, the Conqueror
1481–1512	Bayezid II
1512–1520	Selim I, the Grim
1520–1566	Suleyman I, the Magnificent
1566–1574	Selim II
1574–1595	Murad III
1595–1603	Mehmet III
1603–1617	Ahmet I
1617–1618	Mustafa I
1618–1622	Osman II
1622–1623	Mustafa I (second reign)
1623–1640	Murad IV
1640–1648	Ibrahim
1648–1687	Mehmet IV
1687–1691	Suleyman II
1691–1695	Ahmet II
1695–1703	Mustafa II
1703–1730	Ahmet III
1730–1754	Mahmud I
1754–1757	Osman III
1757–1774	Mustafa III
1774–1789	Abdul Hamid I
1789–1807	Selim III
1807–1808	Mustafa IV
1808–1839	Mahmud II
1839–1861	Abdul Mecit I
1861–1876	Abdul Aziz
1876	Murad V
1876–1909	Abdul Hamid II
1909–1918	Mehmet V
1918–1922	Mehmet VI
1922–1924	Abdul Mecit (II) (Caliph only)

TURKEY

INDEX